Focused Issues in Family Therapy

Series editor

D. Russell Crane, Brigham Young University, Provo, UT, USA

More information about this series at http://www.springer.com/series/13372

Clarissa Sammut Scerri · Arlene Vetere
Angela Abela · Jan Cooper

Intervening After Violence

Therapy for Couples and Families

Springer

Clarissa Sammut Scerri
Department of Family Studies
University of Malta
Msida
Malta

Angela Abela
Department of Family Studies
University of Malta
Msida
Malta

Arlene Vetere
VID Specialized University
Oslo
Norway

Jan Cooper
Reading Safer Families
Reading, Berkshire
UK

ISSN 2520-1190 ISSN 2520-1204 (electronic)
Focused Issues in Family Therapy
ISBN 978-3-319-57788-3 ISBN 978-3-319-57789-0 (eBook)
DOI 10.1007/978-3-319-57789-0

Library of Congress Control Number: 2017938312

Printed on acid-free paper

This Springer imprint is published by Springer Nature
The registered company is Springer International Publishing AG
The registered company address is: Gewerbestrasse 11, 6330 Cham, Switzerland

The original version of the book was revised. For detailed information please see Erratum. The erratum to the book is available at 10.1007/978-3-319-57789-0_10

Contents

About the Authors

Dr. Clarissa Sammut Scerri is Head of the Department of Family Studies at the University of Malta. She is a registered Counselling psychologist, Family therapist, and a Systemic supervisor. Her Ph.D. research entitled "Living with contradictions of love and abuse: a grounded theory of women's understanding of their experiences of domestic violence" sought to illuminate and further the understanding of the complexity of living in a family where there is violence. She has presented her research at various local and international conferences. One of her papers: "Ethical dilemmas of a clinician/researcher interviewing women about their childhood experiences of witnessing domestic violence", has been shortlisted for the Corinna Seith Award by the WAVE Network, Women Against Violence. Dr. Sammut Scerri complements her teaching and research with clinical practice and supervision in the field, including to a team of social care professionals who work with men who are violent in their intimate relationships. Dr. Sammut Scerri wrote Chaps. 1 and 2 in this book.

Arlene Vetere, FBPsS, FAcSS is professor of family therapy and systemic practice at VID Specialized University, Oslo, Norway; visiting professor of clinical psychology at Universita degli Studi, Bergamo, Italy; and affiliate professor of family studies at Malta University. Arlene lives in the UK, where she is registered as a clinical psychologist, systemic psychotherapist and systemic supervisor. Twenty years ago she established 'Reading Safer Families', a family violence intervention service, with Jan Cooper. They have published extensively on their approach to safety and safe therapeutic practice with individuals, couples and families. Arlene has also developed a narrative attachment approach to systemic practice, with Rudi Dallos, which has been widely published. Arlene co-authored Chaps. 3 and 4 with Jan Cooper, in this book; and wrote Chaps. 5 and 7.

Angela Abela is a professor and founding head of the Department of Family Studies at the University of Malta. As a clinical psychologist, family therapist and systemic supervisor, she works with couples, children and their families and supervises teams of practitioners working with vulnerable families. She chairs the National Centre for Family Research of the President of Malta's Foundation for the Wellbeing of Society and is a consultant for the Maltese government and the Standing Committees for Social and Family Affairs in Parliament. As an expert for the Council of Europe, she worked on the *Policy to Support Positive Parenting* and is lead author of the Strategic Policy on Positive Parenting for Malta launched in 2016. She has published widely and is an associate editor of *Clinical Child Psychology and Psychiatry*, an international advisory editor of *Contemporary Family Therapy* and is on the editorial board of *Children Australia.* Angela wrote Chaps. 6, 8 and 9 in this book.

Jan Cooper is a former psychiatric social worker and a systemic psychotherapist, currently holding a non-clinical registration with the United Kingdom Council for Psychotherapy in the UK. Twenty years ago she established 'Reading Safer Families', a dedicated family violence intervention service, with Arlene Vetere. They have published extensively on their approach to safety and safe therapeutic practice where violence is of concern. Currently Jan is focused on writing and training on their safety methodology. Jan co-authored Chaps. 3 and 4 with Arlene Vetere in this book.

Chapter 1
When the Violence Stops: Different Relationships and Different Forms of Violence in the Family

Physical and emotional violence is prevalent in couple and family relationships (Office for National Statistics UK 2014). There are many well-established books on how to assess for the risk of future violence in families, and on how to intervene therapeutically to help family members stop the violence, including the book by one of the present authors (Hamel and Nicholls 2006; Hamel 2005; Cooper and Vetere 2005). However, less is written on how to help couples and families once the violence has stopped.

Many couples and families wish to stay together following the cessation of violent behaviour. Facing the legacy of violence, and often intergenerational violence and trauma, is both challenging and complex—for family members and for therapists.

Healing and relationship repair is the focus of this book. In our experience, this aspect of the work takes as much, if not more, therapeutic time than helping family members to stop the violence. Consolidating change, establishing interpersonal trust, supporting more satisfying bonding and effective problem-solving begins with the assessment and intervention work, but this book is dedicated to working therapeutically with the aftermath—and dealing with unresolved loss, disappointment and hurt, masked trauma responses, developmental trauma, problems of relational esteem, affect regulation and supporting sustainable coping and the giving and receiving of compassionate comfort and care. This aspect of therapeutic work is the focus of this book. Invariably this involves extensive collaboration with the professional network of concern involved with the couple and/or family and their extended family members.

The four authors each bring a particular perspective to this book. Clarissa Sammut Scerri has completed a grounded theory Ph.D. study of Maltese women's recall of the impact of living with domestic violence during their childhoods, and the continuing developmental and relational impact in their adult lives (Sammut Scerri 2015). Angela Abela has made extensive research studies of couple relationships on

---

The original version of this chapter was revised: See the "Chapter Note" section at the end of this chapter for details. The erratum to this chapter is available at 10.1007/978-3-319-57789-0_10

C. Sammut Scerri et al., *Intervening After Violence*,
Focused Issues in Family Therapy, DOI 10.1007/978-3-319-57789-0_1

parenting and support in a changing world (Abela and Walker 2013). Arlene Vetere has co-directed, with Jan Cooper, a specialist family and couple violence intervention project in the UK (Cooper and Vetere 2005). The four authors share a commitment to safe therapeutic work with couples and families where violence is of concern and to supporting the development of trust and emotional safety in family relationships. Three authors are applied psychologists, while the other author is a social worker. All the four authors are also systemic psychotherapists.

The overarching theoretical framework of this book is systemic and integrative, drawing on family systems and attachment theory (Dallos and Vetere 2009), trauma theory and complex PTSD (Ford et al. 2005; Van der Kolk 2014), narrative theory (Bruner 1990), feminist theory (Goldner 1998, 1999), resilience and post-traumatic growth framework Morris et al. (2005), and a life span perspective (Band-Winterstein and Eisikovits 2009)—and drawing on theories of reflective functioning and their application in work with couples and families (Asen and Fonagy 2012). This reflects the authors' integrative stance in relation to theory–practice linking in their therapeutic working with couples and families. Each chapter will review the relevant and available research evidence for therapeutic practice.

In this chapter we look at different forms of family relationships and different forms of violence in these relationships. We bring together current theory and literature not only on intimate partner violence but also on violence between siblings, and violence by children on their parents. We use clinical anecdotes and research in the area to illustrate some of the complex family dynamics that family members live with and that health and social care professionals have to contend with, when working with families after the violence has stopped (DeVoe and Smith 2002; Mullender et al. 2002; Perel and Peled 2008; Sammut Scerri 2015).

The definition of domestic violence that we adopt in this book is the one used by the Council of Europe (2011) also known as the Istanbul Convention: 'All acts of physical, sexual, psychological or economic violence that occur within the family or domestic unit or between former or current spouses or partners, whether or not the perpetrator shares or has shared the same residence with the victim'.

We chose this definition because: (a) it recognises all forms of violence including psychological violence and also child to parent violence; (b) it is gender-inclusive; (c) acknowledges relationships in a family context, both in the past and present; and (d) it explicitly recognises issues of power and control in the acts of violence.

We also would like to highlight the definition of domestic violence by the Council of Europe (1986):

> Any act or omission committed within the framework of the family, by one of its members that undermines the life, the bodily or psychological integrity or the liberty of another member of the same family or that seriously harms the development of his or her personality (Recommendation No. R (85) 4).

This definition is in line with the complexity of domestic violence in families in that it addresses the notion of omissions—such as child neglect including physical, emotional, medical, educational and inadequate supervision (Child Welfare Information Gateway 2012). Neglect and acts of omission can also apply in the case of adults particularly when the person lacks the mental capacity to assess risks for themselves including vulnerable elderly family members (Oxfordshire Safeguarding Adults Board 2016).

This definition also helps us pay attention to instances when we omit to reflect about our own safety and about the family members' safety. When helping family members to predict and prevent violent escalations in their relationships, we need to help them think about what safety means to them, what it looks like, what has happened to them that they do not pay attention to it. We also find it helpful to think with them about what, in their current circumstances, helps and hinders them to prioritise their safety (See Chaps. 3 and 4 for further discussion).

Looking at Intimate Partner Violence

A novice to the field of domestic violence might be hard-pressed to find a common agreed-upon definition of intimate partner violence. Indeed different terms are used in the literature: 'intimate partner violence', 'partner abuse', 'domestic abuse', 'family violence', 'interpersonal violence' and 'interparental violence'. These different terms and the consequent different definitions as to what constitutes intimate partner violence are reflective of the different ideological positions in relation to explanations of this phenomenon and how best to intervene and respond it.

One of these prominent ideological positions is that of gender scholars who study the status of women in a male-dominated society and see violence against women as one of the ways in which social gender inequality is expressed in society (DeKeseredy 2011a). They look at the varieties of patriarchy in society for example —social patriarchy and familial patriarchy as an important explanation for violence and coercive control of women (Hunnicutt 2009). They also take a multi-dimensional approach and look into issues such as poverty, substance abuse, male peer support and other factors to understand gender and violence (DeKeseredy 2011b). One of the most important contributions of feminist scholars, activists and battered women is the recognition that violence against women including intimate partner violence exists, that it is a major social issue and a human rights issue (Osthoff 2002; Saunders 2002; Stanko 2006).

Another prominent ideological position through which researchers and scholars have attempted to understand violence in intimate relationships is through focusing on psychological perspectives such as individual men's personality disorders (Dutton and Bodnarchuk 2005), by looking at attachment strategies between men and women in abusive relationships (Godbout et al. 2009), women's experiences of love within abusive relationships (Shah and Vetere 2012) and the co-occurrence of psychiatric disorders and substance abuse (Stith et al. 2011).

These different philosophical, sociopolitical positions have created huge controversies in the domestic violence field which have led to academics and practitioners to engage in what often are hostile exchanges, accusing others in the other camp of conducting scientifically flawed research, as being anti-feminists, as being positioned as exonerating men from their responsibility for their violent and abusive behaviour, as being the 'enemy' and as gaining from women abuse (Dutton 2010; Dutton and Corvo 2006; Nicolson 2010; DeKeseredy 2011c). At the same time, there is agreement amongst scholars of different paradigms that the phenomenon of intimate partner violence is complex, that there is no one feminist approach (DeKeseredy and Dragiewicz 2007) and that there are different sides and not just two sides to the controversy (see Winstok 2013, for an in depth analysis over the role of gender in intimate partner violence).

In this book, our position is one of a both/and perspective (Goldner et al. 1990; Goldner 1998, 1999), where we acknowledge the vast scholarship of all researchers and practitioners who are keen on sharing their understanding, albeit from different points of view, about this complex and grave social problem that is violence in families. Like others in the field, we subscribe to an anti-oppressive, non-violent, socially just feminist position (Cooper and Vetere 2005; George and Stith 2014).

As systemic practitioners, we also think that it is important to have an in-depth understanding of context in which a specific act of violence occurs, to know the history of the violence in the context of the intimate relationships and to know the motivation, the meaning and the impact of the act of violence in the relationship (Kimmel 2002). We also concur with the view that not everyone who uses violence against his or her partner is a batterer (Osthoff 2002; Johnson and Ferraro 2000) including men and women who use violence in their relationship but that on the other hand, the use of violence in relationships is detrimental and leads to frozen relationships (George and Stith 2014). As scholars and clinicians we also acknowledge the difficulty of navigating the dilemma of upholding the ethical dilemmas around safety and agency when working with women who wish to remain with their partners who are abusive and wish to be assisted to cope in doing so.

We are also cognizant of the recent research that has looked at intimate partner violence in same-sex relationships, where prevalence rates have been found to be comparable (or higher than) intimate partner violence within heterosexual couples (McClennen 2005; Messinger 2011; Straus 2008). For us, this continues to underline the fact that intimate partner violence is best not only understood through a heterosexist paradigm that looks at male violence, control and sexist beliefs as a way of perpetuating the oppression of women (Russell 2015), but as a social problem that needs multiple perspectives to address the complexity of the phenomenon.

Intimate Partner Violence in Older Couples and Families

Although one may think that intimate partner violence decreases with old age, research studies seem to indicate that what changes is the form of violence, not the violence itself (Finfgeld-Connett 2014). Studies show that whilst physical violence may decrease, the rate of psychological abuse may in fact increase (Roberto et al. 2014). This is also similar to what we find in our clinical practice and our work with male perpetrators of intimate partner violence—that even when the physical violence stops, very often the psychological abuse which is less visible, more subtle and hence easier to conceal and minimise, lingers on. As practitioners, we are reminded of the importance to ask questions about this form of abuse and not to under estimate its consequences. Various studies show that it is one of the most harmful forms of abuse (O'Leary and Maiuro 2001). The following victim's experience illustrates the sense of terror, hopelessness and powerlessness associated with psychological abuse:

> The verbal hatred is worse for me. Bruises heal in time but words last forever. When you are told over and over how stupid, ugly and insane you are, you really believe it. I have panic attacks and take tablets to calm my nerve…, life is dreadful and I see nowhere to go and I am not financially nor physically capable of going anywhere (Frances, cited in Lazenbatt et al. 2013, p. 16).

Even in cases when the physical and psychological violence has stopped, older adults may have to cope with the cumulative physical and psychological sequealae of violence: for example, struggling with mobility issues resulting from fractures (Finfgeld-Connett 2014); other severe physical trauma such as broken jaws and teeth (Lazenblatt et al. 2013); psychological problems such as anxiety, depression and substance abuse and symptoms of Post-traumatic stress disorder (PTSD) and significantly more emotional distress, suicidal thoughts and suicidal attempts than non-abused women (McGarry et al. 2011; Lazenblatt et al. 2010; Stöckl and Penhale 2015). All these effects may be further exacerbated by the physiological changes and decline associated with old age (Zink et al. 2003).

Practitioners working with middle-aged and older women who have experienced abusive intimate relationships may find that with the increased frailty of the abusive partner, the power dynamics have changed and it is now the woman who 'threatens to have him removed from home, insult him, and emotionally abuse him and attempt to disrupt his quality of life as much as she can' (Band-Winterstein and Eisikovits 2009, p. 173). Paradoxically as these authors point out, this need for revenge might still keep her emotionally and psychologically engaged with her partner. Confronted by such situations, as practitioners, we might be hard-pressed to hold her accountable for her abusive and violent behaviour in the context of a history of suffering for many years, especially when her stories of pain and torment echo some of the professional's personal experiences of suffering and the need to put right perceived injustices (Lawrence 2014). But the commitment to zero tolerance to violence in its many forms remains paramount, together with an emphasis on the humanity of the persons involved, without the need for shame and humiliation when exploring the perpetrated violence (Goldner 2004). This of course is relevant for both men and women caught in a cycle of intimate partner violence.

Co-occurrence of Child Abuse and Intimate Partner Violence

It has long been recognised that working in the context of intimate partner violence also brings with it the need to look at other forms of violence in the family, such as child abuse. We know that studies have shown a significant overlap between child abuse and intimate partner violence (Appel and Holden 1998; Edleson 1999; Herrenkohl et al. 2008; Jouriles et al. 2008;). In the Appel and Holden study, rates of co-occurrence for abuse and domestic violence exposure were in the range of 6–18% for community samples and about 40% for clinical samples. In the Edleson's review of research, the rates of co-occurrence were much higher: there was an overlap of abuse and domestic violence exposure in 30–60% of all identified cases.

All this raises the complexity of working with families where there is violence and brings forth a number of practice challenges. Although there has been increasing recognition of intimate partner violence as a child protection issue, certainly in the UK (Featherstone and Fraser 2012) and even in Malta (D. Camilleri, personal communication, October, 31, 2014), workers might be caught between supporting the victimised parent, very often the mother and the need to protect the child (Fusco 2013). Workers might also fear for their safety too (Hughes and Chau 2013). The end result might be that the onus of responsibility is put on the mother, who would be already hugely struggling with her own experiences of being chronically abused. Rather than obtaining help, she would now have to deal with the fear of her children being taken away from her or worse, being indicted for not protecting the children from their father (Moles 2008).

From a domestic violence service context, work with the abusive partner, very often the father, within the services might focus on his taking responsibility for the abuse of his partner but not necessarily his responsibility for his children as father. From a child protection point of view, the father might be left in the periphery, which unfortunately seems to be still the current practice in parenting interventions across the globe (Panter-Brick et al. 2014). This might suit the fathers who may not want to be blamed or held accountable (Cooper and Vetere 2005). It might suit the workers as highlighted above and might suit the mothers who might be afraid of 'rocking the boat' and who might see parenting as their responsibility (Cooper and Vetere 2005). However, fathers who are abusive to their partners and children do not 'disappear' from their families. Children may still be emotionally attached to them and struggle to make sense of their parent's abusive behaviour. Fathers too might also 'disappear' from one family to build another one, often repeating the same abusive behaviour.

Thus for us this continues to highlight the need for systemic services for families with intimate partner violence that combine safety and therapeutic interventions (Cooper and Vetere 2005) (see also Chap. 3 of this book), that prioritise the safety of women and children, that hold accountable men and women for their abusive behaviour but also services that acknowledge the attachment bonds that the family members have with each other.

Adolescent to Parent Violence

We would like now to throw a spotlight on a different form of violence taking place in families—parent abuse—where an older child uses aggressive, controlling and intimidating behaviour towards their parents. Parent abuse or adolescent to parent violence has been defined as 'any harmful act of a teenage child intended to gain power and control over a parent. The abuse can be physical, psychological or financial' (Cottrell 2001, p. 3). Examples of physical abuse include hitting, punching, slapping and pushing. Psychological abuse includes persistent name calling, criticising, creating fear and threatening to hurt or kill a parent or themselves and financial abuse includes stealing, damaging the home and demanding things that the parents cannot afford (Cottrell 2001).

There seems to consensus in the field that this is the most under-researched form of violence that happens in the context of family relationships (Holt 2011). Prevalence rates so far suggest that 9–12% of parents are physically assaulted by their adolescent children (Calvete et al. 2014; Cottrell and Monk 2004; Nock and Kazdin 2002). It is a phenomenon that has increasingly been getting the attention of practitioners working with families and youth in the area of domestic violence, child protection and probation juvenile services (Coogan 2011; Holt 2016). A review of the literature shows inconsistent findings as to whether it is more likely that adolescent males than females are violent to their parents. Many studies have found no difference in gender (e.g. Pagani et al. 2004). Other studies have suggested that more females than males are involved in adolescent-parent violence (Day and Bazemore 2011), whilst others suggest that more male youth perpetrate violence against their parents (Ibabe et al. 2014).

It is clear to us that both in a research and a clinical context, parents find it very difficult to talk about their experiences of being abused by their children. Holt (2011) refers to the 'double stigma' surrounding experiences of violence in general and parenting challenging children and young people. They may have to contend with culture of parent blame that has intensified over the past decade (Holt 2011), coupled with the feeling that their rights as parents, have in some contexts, been subsumed to the discourse of children's rights (Holt 2016). They may also find that their experiences are minimised and/or devalued by their families and communities, further silencing their suffering and abuse (Edenborough et al. 2008). All of this may leave the parents stuck in a fear—dominated cycle, trying to accommodate unreasonable demands of the adolescent and being fearful of what the adolescent might do next (Moulds et al. 2016).

Adding further to the complexity of parent abuse, recent research suggests that parent abuse might take place in the context of a wider context of family violence—that indeed it is recursive—that is mutually influencing rather than linear or cause–effect (Daly and Wade 2016). A teenage son might assault his mother but might concurrently be victimised by his father or the mother's partner or his grandmother (Orland 2016). He might also be abusive to his siblings too (Sibling violence will be discussed below). Research also seems to suggest that witnessing interparental violence might increase the likelihood of adolescent to parent violence (McCloskey and Lichter 2003) and that parent to youth abuse might also co-occur with adolescent to parent abuse (Boxer et al. 2009). Other consistent findings in the literature indicate that it is most likely that youth–parent abuse is directed towards mothers, and is more like to happen in lone parent families and in families where parents facing significant stressors (Kennair and Mellor 2007). It is also likely that such youth also lack engagement with the school system and also associate with other deviant peers where the use of aggression is the order of the day (Capaldi et al. 2012; Orland 2016).

Thus professionals may face a number of dilemmas when dealing with families where there is parent abuse. Whilst we believe that young persons must be held responsible for their abusive behaviour, the boundaries between who is the victim and the perpetrator can be unclear, especially in the context of multiple forms of violence in the same family (UK Home Office 2015). Some youth who have grown in families where there was intimate partner violence might use aggression against their mother's partner in order to protect their mother (Cottrell and Monk 2004) or a young woman might use aggression to defy her abusive parent and put a stop to the violence herself (Sammut Scerri 2015). Other teens might use coercive tactics to get want they want (Routt and Anderson 2015). Still another hypothesis is that in the case of daughters' violence on their mother, aggression may paradoxically be used to create distance between them and their image of female vulnerability as manifested by their mother who is seen as powerless and weak (Cottrell and Monk 2004; Sammut Scerri 2015). Other scenarios could also include parents and youth engaging in mutual violence as a way of resolving conflict (Daly and Wade 2016; Sammut Scerri 2015).

At the same time, from a legal perspective, parents are seen as responsible for their adolescents even in this context when the power dynamics seem to be over turned and they are being victimised by their children. The introduction of Parenting orders in the UK in 1998 are testament to how parents are deemed responsible for their children's troublesome behaviour and if they are issued such an order, parents need to comply with the set conditions or be taken to court and prosecuted (Crime and Disorder Act 1998). If, on the other hand, parents request police assistance, they might be reluctant to take their children to court because they may still want a relationship with their children and may in any case want to avoid incurring further shame and embarrassment.

However, it is interesting to note that police intervention can also send a message to the whole system that indeed the adolescent' s violent behaviour does deserve serious attention, that it cannot be minimised any longer and that the family needed to seek help (Orland 2016). Police intervention may play a major role in calling violence by its name, which may motivate the different family members to change. In Orland (2016)'s study, the youth started working on changing his behaviour towards his mother. The workers also believed that this motivated the estranged father to be more involved in co-parenting the adolescent and attend the family therapy sessions with the mother

> 'As soon as the police got involved, he realised that something (serious) had happened… so, it was true…it's like… before when the wife used to call him, he used to think that it was some kind of excuse for him to take over the parenting and give her respite' (Line 72, social worker as cited in Orland, 2016, p. 73).

Both parents felt strongly that they did not want their son to have problems with law enforcement forces and this prompted them to take a united front against their son's violence.

It is noteworthy that upon first referral of this family, the professionals also took the view that the adolescent-parent violence was of secondary importance. Initially, the mother constructed the child's behaviour as challenging because the parents had separated years ago. The social worker thought that therapy could help the son understand better what happened and why the parents had separated. As the therapy progressed, the professionals continued to struggle to reconcile the how the youth presented himself—as an educated, sometimes, childish teenager and his violent behaviour. This is how the adolescent's psychologist described him:

> If the grandmother starts shouting and loses control, maybe he feels that he has to do the same. Again I cannot picture it. I am not saying that it does not happen but I would be shocked, because I see such a different person in front of me that I cannot imagine him violent and aggressive (Line 62, psychologist, as cited in Orland, 2016, p. 83).

For us this continues to underscore the importance of taking a systemic perspective to working with adolescent - parent violence, where liaising with different systems and keeping a both/and perspective is prioritised, including holding the adolescent accountable for his violent behaviour and offering a safe space, when and where appropriate for the youth and the parent to reflect about their different positions in their family. It is also helpful that similar reflections take place at the level of the professionals too including professionals in the wider systems such as the school.

Finally, we also find it helpful to not only look at the violent behaviour but also to look at relationships which the adolescents find supportive and ones where there is no violence despite the presence of disagreements, what in narrative therapy are called 'exceptions' (White and Epston 1990). Such relationships provide great opportunities for change and are sources of hope.

Sibling Relationships in the Context of Intimate Partner Violence: Protection, Support and Aggression

As already highlighted above, another form of family violence may take place amongst the siblings. Surprisingly, there have been only a small number of studies that have looked at the sibling relationships when they live in families where there is domestic violence, (Piotrowski et al. 2014), despite the fact that sibling relationships have been shown to have significant impact on each other's development (Howe and Recchia 2014) and likely to be the longest-lasting in our lives (Sanders 2004).

One of the themes that strike us when we work with siblings where there was violence in their family is their different experience in the same family, highlighting the need for professionals to give voice to each child's experience of the violence in their family. Whilst there may be children who take a more predominantly active role in protecting their non-violent parent and their siblings, other children might be more often seen as withdrawing from the conflict, whilst others might position themselves somewhere in between.

As illustrated in the study by Sammut Scerri (2015),[1] one of the siblings, Claire[2] talked about feeling misunderstood by other siblings who were not exposed to the kind of violence that she had lived through and she marvelled at how her sister was more able to challenge her father. At the same time, she acknowledged that when her sister was born, her father had been older and mellower. He was also no longer working shift work and she remembers him as being less irritable and less violent at home:

> Yes, yes. First of all, I was the eldest and I have witnessed a lot of things that, till this very day, my siblings did not see and if the one after me saw them, she did not see the same things or she has not realised what she saw but – she either tried to forget them or in her own way, she's trying to work it out in another way- all of us are doing it - the girls - three girls and a boy – (p. 6).
>
> So then one thing after another you start being careful about what you say - for example, I am the only one out of the siblings that I don't answer back - I am afraid… instead my siblings no- they are not afraid (p. 9).

Thus clinicians need to be sensitive to these different experiences and offer to see siblings conjointly only when it is clinically relevant and congruent with the clients' needs. This is especially pertinent when siblings disclose experiences of having been physically and/or emotionally abused by their siblings in the past or when they disclose that they themselves have been aggressors of their siblings.

---

[1]See Chap. 2 for futher details about the sample and methodology used in the Sammut Scerri (2015)'s study.

[2]All names have been changed and identifying details have been removed.

Violence Amongst Siblings

There is consensus in the literature that sibling violence is often a pervasive part of family life and yet it is the least studied form of family violence, perhaps because it is minimised or considered a less harmful form of aggression between family members or normalised as part of childhood experiences (Eriksen and Jensen 2009; Jenkins Tucker and Finkelhor 2015; Khan and Rogers 2015). Clinicians who might be more familiar with adult—adult violence or parent–child violence might similarly find themselves in a dilemma as to how best to intervene.

The few qualitative studies that have looked at the experiences of sibling abuse such as that by Meyers (2015), throw light on the harrowing incidents of physical and emotional abuse that have devastating and long-term consequences on the well-being of the victims. The participants in the Meyers' study talked about chronic despair, a perpetual state of helplessness and powerlessness brought up by 'unpredictable and relentless acts of intimidation' (p. 1). The participants also had difficulty remembering the details of specific episodes but could remember very much the emotional impact of the experiences. This is in support of memory research in contexts of trauma where experiences are thought to be stored as sensory fragments that often lack a coherent narrative (Van der Kolk 2007).

Clinicians working with families where the violence has stopped may also find themselves working with siblings who may disclose about having been aggressive with each other. In the Sammut Scerri (2015)'s study, one of the participants spoke about rage that she and her brothers directed at each other:

> What I remember most, was that in our house, there was a lot, a lot of anger, even between us siblings, between me and my brothers .., ferocious anger .., for example .., .I don't know .., we fight about something and then we used to go to each other's rooms turn everything upside down and create havoc to each other's things .., and that is the rage that we used to feel. (Mary, p. 17).

Another participant, Marika nervously described how she had ended up physically abusing her younger sister for about a year or so, until she came to the realisation that she was behaving exactly as her father did towards her and then she stopped:

> Because there was a time when I was a bit like him .., I used to beat my youngest sister (nervous giggle). She was not doing well at school and I helped her with her homework .., . but she did not obey and she didn't do well and I hit her .., (nervous snort). This went on for about a year or so, until I realised what I was doing (Marika 2, p. 13).

Whilst in Mary's narrative, the rage is described in general terms, it is clear that in Marika's words, there is clearly 'intentional physical violence inflicted by one child in a family unit on another' (DeKeseredy and Ellis 1997, p. 399). We believe that it is important that professionals clearly ask for more details about incidents of sibling violence, to identify the abusive/abused dynamics. Professionals also need to be prepared to work with issues of shame, blame and stigma (Cooper and Vetere 2005; Kennedy and Prock 2016) both from the abused and abusive sibling in revealing behaviour that violate social norms about what is appropriate and acceptable more so from members in the same family (See Chap. 6 for more discussion on how professionals can intervene with parents, in the context of sibling violence).

Workers need also to be understanding of their clients' possible fear of repeating their parents' mistakes when working with family members who were violent with their siblings and who had all grew up in family where there was violence. The fear around replicating their family of origin script (Byng-Hall 1998) was foremost in the mind of many of the participants in the Sammut Scerri (2015)'s study. Many subscribed to the dominant psychological discourse that once they themselves were abused, they were at risk of being either abused or abusive themselves and feared anything that might confirm this belief. Marika spoke about 'beating (their children) as being in the family genes- it is hereditary… I wonder whether I will be the same' (Marika 1, p. 29). Marika felt that one way of dealing with her fear was to through the strategy of avoidance—of avoiding spending time with her father so that she is less in a position to be 'contaminated' by him and more able to regulate her emotions (Fonagy et al. 1991):

> I: so it is helpful for you that you have cut all communication with your father ..,P: yes, yes a lot .., because daddy and I – we are both hard-headed, so when we fight, if we don't get our way .., And then I started becoming afraid .., in fact, when I fight with my father (nervous giggle), I start getting agitated .., I start becoming afraid that we will get into trouble .., that we will end up being physical with each other… because this part in me scares me .., because how do you say this .., it is like when I lose it .., I am afraid that I have my father's character .., so the less time that I spend with him, the better. (Marika 2, p. 12–13).

Sibling Protection and Support

Within the same family, the same family member who may have used violence may also have paradoxically taken on a protective role in the family. The same participant above, Marika, at the same time, was the one who continually worried about her siblings' emotional well-being and who took it upon herself to fight her father so that her mother is protected from his punches. The siblings also found themselves persisting in these early family of origin roles in adulthood. For example Donna found it very difficult not to take responsibility for emotionally supporting her mother with the parenting of her younger sisters, and re-experiencing this role in an intense way when she temporarily moved back to the family home for a few weeks. As professionals, we note that these siblings' parental role come with emotional losses and gains (Byng-Hall 2008). Donna reflected that having responsibility for her siblings meant that she felt it difficult to relate to her siblings from a sister point of view; as a child she remembered not wanting to play with her sisters and as an adult, she was not comfortable with her sisters in a social setting as she feels that she still finds herself watching over them, like a parent:

> I feel it is a big loss…. There's my middle sister…. I don't feel… sometimes, I tell my boyfriend… we would have friends… and we take them out to dinner… I know tht my sister would like to come with us but I don't feel comfortable with her because … I feel like I always have to take that responsibility and I won't be able to relax when I am with her… I feel like I am the aunt, if not the mother and that annoys me …. I see this as a loss because on the other hand, we understand each other a lot… the things we went through… (Donna, 2 p.66, as cited in Sammut Scerri 2015)

On the other hand, Donna was aware that as part of her role, she also developed a sense of agency and competence and that her family looked up to her. Both Donna, Marika and other participants remarked that they felt unable to talk about their relationships with their siblings, as they were afraid of becoming distressed. The need for safety hence is again underscored for professionals engaging in work with siblings. As in other forms of family violence, the different levels of complexity and the experiences of abuse need to be kept in mind with the contexts of love and attachment bonds that may characterise these family relationships.

Conclusion

When abuse happens in the context of family relationships, the person suffering the violence might minimise, accommodate and perhaps forgive the abuser in the context of the love that they have for them. This contradiction of love and abuse makes it difficult to reconcile for both the family members and also for the professionals working with them, as will be discussed further in Chap. 2. At the same time, as practitioners, it is important that we are cognizant of the different forms of violence that can be present in a family and that we keep giving space to the different voices and to the unique experiences of violence and love of the different family members. In addition, as we have seen earlier in this chapter, the dichotomy of abuser/abused may become blurred and embracing an integrative theoretical framework as practitioners becomes important to navigate the complexity of violence in families.

References

Abela, A., & Walker, J. (2013). *Contemporary issues in family studies: Global perspectives on partnerships, parenting and support in a changing world*. London: Wiley.

Appel, A. E., & Holden, G. W. (1998). The co-occurrence of spouse and physical child abuse: A review and appraisal. *Journal of Family Psychology, 12*(4), 578–599. doi:10.1037/0893-3200.12.4.578.

Asen, E., & Fonagy, P. (2012). Mentalization—based therapeutic interventions for families. *Journal of Family Therapy, 34*(4), 347–370. doi:10.1111/j.1467-6427.2011.00552.x.

Band-Winterstein, T., & Eisikovits, Z. (2009). "Aging out" of violence: The multiple faces of intimate violence over the life span. *Qualitative Health Research, 19*(2), 164–180. doi:10.1177/1049732308329305.

Boxer, P., Gullan, R. L., & Mahoney, A. (2009). Adolescents physical aggression towards parents in a clinically referred sample. *Journal of Clinical Child and Adolescent Psychology, 38*(1), 106–116. doi:10.1080/15374410802575396.

Bruner, J. S. (1990). *Acts of meaning*. London, UK: Harvard University Press.

Byng-Hall, J. (1998). *Rewriting family scripts: Improvisation and systems change*. London, UK: The Guilford Press.

Byng-Hall, J. (2008). The significance of children fulfilling parental roles: Implications for family therapy. *Journal of Family Therapy, 30*(2), 147–162. doi:10.1111/j.1467-6427.2008.00423.x.

Calvete, E., Orue, I., Bertino, L., Gonzalez-Díez, Z., Montes, Y., Padilla, P., et al. (2014). Child-to-parent violence in adolescents: The perspectives of the parents, children, and professionals in a sample of Spanish focus group participants. *Journal of Family Violence, 29* (3), 343–352. doi:10.1007/s10896-014-9578-5.

Capaldi, D. M., Knoble, N. B., Shortt, J. W., & Kim, H. K. (2012). A systematic review of risk factors for intimate partner violence. *Partner Abuse, 3*(2), 231–280. doi:10.1891/1946-6560.3.2.231.

Child Welfare Information Gateway. (2012). *Acts of omission: An overview of child neglect.* Washington, DC: U.S. Department of Health and Human Services, Children's Bureau. Retrieved from: https://www.childwelfare.gov/pubpdf/acts.pdf.

Coogan, D. (2011). Child to parent violence. Challenging perspectives on family violence. *Child Care in Practice, 17*(4), 347–358. doi:10.1080/13575279.2011.596815.

Cooper, J., & Vetere, A. (2005). *Domestic violence and family safety: A systemic approach to working with violence in families*. London, UK: Whurr Publishers.

Cottrell, B. (2001). *Parent abuse: The abuse of parents by their teenage children.* Ottawa, Canada: Health Canada, Population and Public Health Branch, National Clearinghouse on Family Violence.

Cottrell, B., & Monk, P. (2004). Adolescent-to-parent abuse: A qualitative overview of common themes. *Journal of Family Issues, 25*(8), 1072–1095. doi:10.1177/0192513X03261330.

Council of Europe. (1986). *Violence in the family: Recommendation no. R (85) 4 adopted by the Committee of Ministers of the Council of Europe on 26 March 1985 and Explanatory Memorandum.* Strasbourg: Council of Europe. Retrieved from http://trove.nla.gov.au/work/18751928?selectedversion=NBD5968784.

Council of Europe. (2011). *Council of Europe convention on preventing and combating violence against women and domestic violence: Istanbul, 11 V.* 2011. Council of Europe. Retrieved from https://rm.coe.int/CoERMPublicCommonSearchServices/DisplayDCTMContent?documentId=090000168008482e.

Crime and Disorder Act of 1998. *Part 1, Chapter 1, Youth crime and disorder, Section 9.* Retrieved from: http://www.legislation.gov.uk/ukpga/1998/37/section/9.

Dallos, R., & Vetere, A. (2009). *Systemic therapy and attachment narratives: Applications in a range of clinical settings*. London, UK: Routledge.

Daly, K., & Wade, D. (2016). Gender and adolescent-to parent violence: A systematic analysis of typical and atypical cases. In A. Holt (Ed.), *Working with adolescent violence and abuse towards parents: Approaches and contexts* (pp. 148–168). UK: Taylor & Francis.

Day, S. E., & Bazemore, G. (2011). Two generations at risk: Child welfare, institutional boundaries and family violence in grandparent homes. *Child Welfare, 90*(4), 99–116.

DeKeseredy, W. S. (2011a). Feminist contributions to understanding woman abuse: Myths, controversies and realities. *Aggression and violent behaviour, 16*(4), 297–303. doi:10.1016/j.avb.2011.04.002.

DeKeseredy, W. S. (2011b). *Violence against women: Myths, facts, controversies*. Toronto, Canada: University of Toronto Press.

DeKeseredy, W. S. (2011c). *Contemporary critical criminology*. London, UK: Routledge.

DeKeseredy, W. S., & Dragiewicz, M. (2007). Understanding the complexities of feminist perspectives on woman abuse: A commentary on Donald. G. Dutton's rethinking domestic violence. *Violence against Women, 13*(8), 874–884. doi:10.1177/1077801207304806.

DeKeseredy, W. S., & Ellis, D. (1997). Sibling violence: A review of Canadian social research and suggestions for further empirical work. *Humanity and Society, 21*(4), 397–411.

DeVoe, E. R., & Smith, E. L. (2002). The impact of domestic violence on urban preschool children: Battered mothers' perspectives. *Journal of Interpersonal Violence, 17*(10), 1075–1101. doi:10.1177/088626002236661.

Dutton, D. G. (2010). The gender paradigm and the architecture of antiscience. *Partner Abuse, 1* (1), 5–25. doi:10.1891/1946-6560.1.1.5.

Dutton, D. G., & Bodnarchuk, M. (2005). Through a psychological lens: Personality disorder and spouse assault. In D. R. Loseke, R. J. Gelles, & M. M. Cavanaugh (Eds.), *Current controversies on family violence* (2nd ed., pp. 5–18). London, UK: SAGE Publications.

Dutton, D. G., & Corvo, K. (2006). Transforming a flawed policy: A call to revive psychology and science in domestic violence research. *Aggression and Violent Behaviour, 11*(5), 457–483. doi:10.1016/j.avb.2006.01.007.

Edenborough, M., Jackson, D., Mannix, J., & Wilkes, L. M. (2008). Living in the red zone. The experience of child-to-mother violence. *Child and Family Social Work, 13*(4), 464–473. doi:10.1111/j.1365-2206.2008.00576.x.

Edleson, J. L. (1999). Children's witnessing of adult domestic violence. *Journal of Interpersonal Violence, 14*(8), 839–870. doi:10.1177/088626099014008004.

Eriksen, S., & Jensen, V. (2009). A push or a punch: Distinguishing the severity of sibling violence. *Journal of Interpersonal Violence, 24*(1), 183–208. doi:10.1177/08866260508316298.

Fonagy, P., Steele, M., Steele, H., Moran, G. S., & Higgitt, A. C. (1991). The capacity for understanding mental states: The reflective self in parent and child and its significance for security of attachment. *Infant Mental Health Journal, 12*(3), 201–218. doi:10.1002/1097-0355(199123)12:3<201:AID-IMHJ2280120307>3.0.CO;2-7.

Featherstone, B., & Fraser, C. (2012). Working with fathers around domestic violence: Contemporary debates. *Child Abuse Review, 21*(4), 255–263. doi:10.1002/car.2221.

Finfgeld-Connett, D. (2014). Intimate partner abuse among older women: Qualitative systematic review. *Clinical Nursing Research, 23*(6), 664–683. doi:10.1177/105477813500301.

Ford, J. D., Courtois, C. A., Steele, K., van der Hart, O., & Nijenhuis, E. R. S. (2005). Treatment of complex posttraumatic self-dysregulation. *Journal of Traumatic Stress, 18*(5), 437–447. doi:10.1002/jts.20051.

Fusco, R. A. (2013). 'It's hard enough to deal with all the abuse issues': Child welfare workers' experiences with intimate partner violence on their caseloads. *Children and Youth Services Review, 35*(12), 1946–1953. doi:10.1016/j.childyouth.2013.09.020.

George, J., & Stith, S. M. (2014). An updated feminist view of intimate partner violence. *Family Process, 53*(2), 179–193. doi:10.1111/famp.1.

Godbout, N., Dutton, D. G., Lussier, Y., & Sabourin, S. (2009). Early exposure to violence, domestic violence, attachment representations, and marital adjustment. *Personal Relationships, 16*(3), 365–384. doi:10.1111/j.1475-6811.2009.01228.x.

Goldner, V. (1998). The treatment of violence and victimization in intimate relationships. *Family Process, 37*(3), 263–286. doi:10.1111/j/1545-5300.1998.00263.x.

Goldner, V. (1999). Morality and multiplicity: Perspectives on the treatment of violence in intimate life. *Journal of Marital & Family Therapy, 25*(3), 325–336. doi:10.1111/j.1752-0606.1999.tb00251.x.

Goldner, V. (2004). When love hurts: Treating abusive relationships. *Psychoanalytic Inquiry, 24* (3), 346–372. doi:10.1080/07351692409349088.

Goldner, V., Penn, P., Sheinberg, M., & Walker, G. (1990). Love and violence: Gender paradoxes in volatile attachments. *Family Process, 29*(4), 343–364. doi:10.1111/j.1752-0606.1999.tb00251.x.

Hamel, J. (2005). *Gender inclusive treatment of intimate partner abuse: A comprehensive approach*. New York, NY: Springer.

Hamel, J., & Nicholls, T. L. (Eds.). (2006). *Family interventions in domestic violence: A handbook of gender-inclusive theory and treatment*. New York: Springer.

Herrenkohl, T. I., Sousa, C., Tajima, E. A., Herrenkohl, R. C., & Moylan, C. A. (2008). Intersection of child abuse and children's exposure to domestic violence. *Trauma, Violence, & Abuse, 9*(2), 84–99. doi:10.1177/152483.8008314797.

Holt, A. (2011). Responding to the problem of 'parent abuse'. *The Psychologist, 24*(3), 186–188.

Holt, A. (2016). Adolescent to-parent abuse as a form of 'Domestic Violence': A conceptual review. *Trauma, Violence and Abuse, 17*(5), 490–499. doi:10.1177/1524838015584372.

Howe, N., & Recchia, H. (2014). Sibling relationship as a context for learning and development. *Early Education and Development, 25*(2), 155–159. doi:10.1080/10409289.2014.857562.

Hughes, J., & Chau, S. (2013). Making complex decisions: Child protection workers' practices and interventions with families experiencing intimate partner violence. *Children and Youth Services Review, 35*(4), 611–617. doi:10.1016/j.childyouth.2013.01.003.

Hunnicutt, G. (2009). Varieties of patriarchy and violence against women. Resurrecting "patriarchy" as a theoretical tool. *Violence against women, 15*(5), 553–573. doi:10.1177/1077801208331246.

Ibabe, I., Arnoso, S., & Elgorriaga, E. (2014). Behavioural problems and depressive symptomatology as predictors of child-to-parent violence. *European Journal of Psychology Applied to Legal Context, 6*(2), 53–61. doi:10.1016/j.ejpal.2014.06.004.

Jenkins Tucker, C., & Finkelhor, D. (2015). The stage of interventions for sibling conflict and aggression: A systematic review. *Trauma, Violence and Abuse*, 1–11. doi:10.1177/1524838015622438.

Johnson, M. P., & Ferraro, K. J. (2000). Research on domestic violence in the 1990's: Making distinctions. *Journal of Marriage and Family, 62*(4), 948–963. doi:10.1111/j.1741-3737.2000.00948.x.

Jouriles, E. N., McDonald, R., Smith Slep, A. M., Heyman, R. E., & Garrido, E. (2008). Child abuse in the context of domestic violence: Prevalence, explanations, and practice implications. *Violence and Victims, 23*(2), 221–235. doi:10.1891/0086-6708.23.2.221.

Kennair, N., & Mellor, D. (2007). Parent abuse: A review. *Child Psychiatry Human Development, 38*(3), 203–219. doi:10.1007/s10578-007-0061-x.

Kennedy, A. C., & Prock, K. A. (2016). "I still feel like I am not normal": A review of the role of stigma and stigmatization among female survivors of child sexual abuse, sexual assault and intimate partner violence. *Trauma, Violence and Abuse*, 1–16. doi:10.1177/1524838016673601.

Khan, R., & Rogers, P. (2015). The normalization of sibling violence: Does gender and personal experience of violence influence perceptions of physical assault against siblings? *Journal of Interpersonal Violence, 30*(3), 437–458. doi:10.1177/0886260514535095.

Kimmel, S. K. (2002). "Gender symmetry" in domestic violence: A substantive and methodological research review. *Violence Against Women, 8*(11), 1332–1363. doi:10.1177/107780102237407.

Lawrence, J. A. (2014). Managing dissonance: Implications for therapeutic practice with partner violence. *Partner Abuse, 5*(2), 119–151. doi:10.1891/1946-6560.5.2.119.

Lazenbatt, A., Devaney, J., & Gildea, A. (2013). Older women living and coping with domestic violence. *Community Practitioner, 86*(2), 28–32.

Lazenbatt, A., Devaney, J., & Gildea, A. (2010). Older women's life-long experience of domestic violence in Northern Ireland. A CAP-funded research project report. Belfast: Queen's University of Belfast.

McClennen, J. C. (2005). Domestic violence between same-gender partners. Recent findings and future research. *Journal of Interpersonal Violence, 20*(2), 149–154. doi:10.1177/0886260504268762.

McCloskey, L. A., & Lichter, E. L. (2003). The contribution of marital violence to adolescent aggression across different relationships. *Journal of Interpersonal Violence, 18*(4), 390–412. doi:10.1177/0886260503251179.

McGarry, J., Simpson, C., & Hinchcliff-Smith, K. (2011). The impact of domestic violence for older women: A review of the literature. *Health and Social Care in the Community, 19*(1), 3–14. doi:10.1111/j.1365-2524.2010.00964.x.

Messinger, A. M. (2011). Invisible victims: same-sex IPV in the national violence against women survey. *Journal of Interpersonal Violence, 26*(11), 2228–2243. doi:10.1177/0886260510383023.

Meyers, A. (2015). Lifting the veil: The lived experience of sibling abuse. Qualitative Social Work, 1–18. doi:10.1177/1473325015612143.

Moles, K. (2008). Bridging the divide between child welfare and domestic violence services: Deconstructing the change process. *Children and Youth Services Review, 30*(6), 674–688. doi:10.1016/j.childyouth.2008.01.007.

Morris, B. A., Shakespeare-Finch, J., Rieck, M., & Newbery, J. (2005). Multidimensional nature of posttraumatic growth in an Australian population. *Journal of Traumatic Stress, 18*(5), 575–585. doi:10.1002/jts.20067.

Moulds, L., Day, A., Mildred, H., Miller, P., & Casey, S. (2016). Adolescent violence towards parents—the known and unknowns. *Australian & New Zealand Journal of Family Therapy, 37* (4), 547–557. doi:10.1002/anzf.1189.

Mullender, A., Hague, G., Imam, U., Kelly, L., Malos, E., & Regan, L. (2002). *Children's perspectives on domestic violence*. London, UK: SAGE Publications.

Nicolson, P. (2010). *Domestic violence and psychology: A critical perspective*. London, UK: Taylor and Francis.

Nock, M. K., & Kazdin, A. E. (2002). Parent-directed physical aggression by clinic-referred youths. *Journal of Clinical Child Psychology, 31*(2), 193–205. doi:10.1207/153744202753604476.

Office for National Statistics. (2014). *Chapter 4—Intimate personal violence and partner abuse*. UK: Office for National Statistics. Retrieved from: http://webarchive.nationalarchives.gov.uk/20160105160709/http://www.ons.gov.uk/ons/dcp171776_352362.pdf.

O'Leary, K. D., & Maiuro, R. D. (Eds.). (2001). *Psychological abuse in violent domestic relations*. New York, NY: Springer Publishing Company.

Orland, M. (2016). *Child-to-parent violence: A case study* (Master thesis). Malta: University of Malta.

Osthoff, S. (2002). But, Gertrude, I beg to differ, a hit is not a hit is not a hit. When battered women are arrested for assaulting their partners. *Violence against women, 8*(12), 1521–1544. doi:10.1177/107780102237968.

Oxfordshire Safeguarding Adults Board. (2016). *Neglect and acts of omission.* Retrieved from: www.osab.co.uk/themes/neglect-and-acts-of-omission/.

Pagani, L. S., Tremblay, R. E., Nagin, D., Zoccolillo, M., Vitaro, F., & McDuff, P. (2004). Risk factor models for adolescent verbal and physical aggression towards mothers. *International Journal of Behavioral Development, 28*(6), 528–537. doi:10.1080/01650250444000243.

Panter-Brick, C., Burgess, A., Eggerman, M., McAllister, F., Pruett, K., & Leckman, J. F. (2014). Practitioner review: Engaging fathers–recommendations for a game change in parenting interventions based on a systematic review of the global evidence. *Journal of Child Psychology and Psychiatry, 55*(11), 1187–1212. doi:10.1111/jcpp.12280.

Perel, G., & Peled, E. (2008). The fathering of violent men: Constriction and yearning. *Violence Against Women, 14*(4), 457–482. doi:10.1177/1077801208314846.

Piotrowski, C. C., Tailor, K., & Cormier, D. C. (2014). Siblings exposed to intimate partner violence: Linking siblings relationship quality and child adjustment problems. *Child Abuse and Neglect, 38*(1), 123–134. doi:10.1016/j.chiabu.2013.08.005.

Roberto, K. A., McPherson, M. C., & Brossoie, N. (2014). Intimate partner violence in late life: A review of the empirical literature. *Violence against women, 19*(12), 1538–1558. doi:10.1177/1077801213517564.

Routt, G., & Anderson, L. (2015). *Adolescent violence in the home: Restorative approaches to building healthy, respectful family relationships*. New York: Routledge.

Russell, B. (2015). Bridging the gap in knowledge about partner abuse in LGBTQ populations. *Partner Abuse, 6*(1), 3–7. doi:10.1891/1946-6560.6.1.3.

Sammut Scerri, C. (2015). *Living with contradictions of love and violence: A grounded theory study of women's understanding of their childhood experiences of domestic violence* (Doctoral dissertation). University of Surrey, Guildford, United Kingdom.

Sanders, R. (2004). *Sibling relationships: Theory and issues for practice*. New York, NY: Palgrave Macmillan.

Saunders, D. G. (2002). Are physical assaults by wives and girlfriends a major social problem? A review of the literature. *Violence Against Women, 8*(12), 1424–1448. doi:10.1177/107780102237964.

Shah, G., & Vetere, A. (2012). *Narratives of love: How do women who have left abusive relationships narrate the story of that relationship?* (Unpublished manuscript). Department of Psychology, University of Surrey, Guildford, United Kingdom.

Stanko, E. A. (2006). Theorizing about violence: Observations from the economic and social research council's violence research program. *Violence Against Women, 12*(6), 543–555. doi:10.1177/1077801206289137.

Stith, S. M., McCollum, E. E., & Rosen, K. H. (2011). *Couples therapy for domestic violence: Finding safe solutions*. Washington, DC, US: American Psychological Association.

Stöckl, H., & Penhale, B. (2015). Intimate partner violence and its association with physical and mental health symptoms among older women in Germany. *Journal of Interpersonal Violence, 30*(17), 3089–3111. doi:10.1177/088626051454427.

Straus, M. A. (2008). Dominance and symmetry in partner violence by male and female university students in 32 nations. *Children and Youth Services Review, 30*(3), 252–275. doi:10.1016/j.childyouth.2007.10.004.

UK Home Office. (2015). *Information guide: adolescent to parent violence and abuse (APVA)*. Retrieved from: https://www.gov.uk/government/uploads/system/uploads/attachment_data/file/420963/APVA.pdf.

Van der Kolk, B. A. (2007). Trauma and memory. In B. A. van der Kolk, A. C. McFarlane, & L. Weisaeth (Eds.), *Traumatic stress: The effects of overwhelming experience on mind, body, and society* (pp. 279–302). London, UK: The Guilford Press.

Van der Kolk, B. (2014). *The body keeps the score: Brain, mind, and body in the healing of trauma*. New York, NY: Viking Penguin.

White, M., & Epston, D. (1990). *Narrative means to therapeutic ends*. London, UK: W.W. Norton & Company.

Winstok, Z. (2013). What can we learn from the controversy over the role of gender in partner violence. *Partner Abuse, 4*(3), 399–412. doi:10.1891/1946-6560.4.3.399.

Zink, T., Regan, S., Jacobson, C. J., & Pabst, S. (2003). Cohort, period and ageing effects: A qualitative study of older women's reasons for remaining in abusive relationships. *Violence Against Women, 9*(12), 1429–1441. doi:10.1177/1077801203259231.

Chapter 2
Living with Violence in the Family: Retrospective Recall of Women's Childhood Experiences

This chapter looks at some key clinical themes that may arise when working with families where intimate partner violence has stopped or when working with clients who have grown up in families where there was domestic violence. Clinicians may also find these themes relevant during the course of therapy with other clients, who might initially be present to therapy with difficulties other than experiences of domestic violence.

In writing out this chapter, we draw from our clinical experiences, from the current literature and from a grounded theory study by one of the authors (Sammut Scerri 2015) which has focused on Maltese adult women's recall of their experiences of childhood domestic violence and their understanding of its continuing developmental and relational impact on their adult life. The use of the participants' quotes from the grounded theory study will hopefully illuminate both the intensity of the experience and its complex impact on the relationships in the women's family of origin and on the women's intimate and parenting relationships. Emphasis will be made on drawing out clear links between the research findings presented and the implications for practice for social and healthcare professionals working in the field.

Key Clinical Themes

Paying Attention to Dissonance, Double Binds and Dilemmas of Love and Abuse

The women interviewed in the Sammut Scerri (2015)'s study lived the coexistence of two intense, paradoxical and unresolved experiences, which manifested in their lives in different ways. They were of an average age of 28.5 years, were well-functioning women, in paid employment, and had significant relationships in

---

The original version of this chapter was revised: See the "Chapter Note" section at the end of this chapter for details. The erratum to this chapter is available at 10.1007/978-3-319-57789-0_10

C. Sammut Scerri et al., *Intervening After Violence*,
Focused Issues in Family Therapy, DOI 10.1007/978-3-319-57789-0_2

their lives but had lived in families where they witnessed physical assault by their father-only on their mother, which in some cases was callous and sadistic in nature. They also witnessed mutual emotional violence between their parents and experienced physical and emotional abuse by both their parents. In some instances this was perpetrated by the father, whilst in other cases, it was perpetrated by both their parents.

Some of these women were also physically and emotionally maltreated by their siblings. One or two women also had been physically and emotionally violent towards their younger siblings. However, these were not the same participants who reported being abused by their siblings.

The theme of dissonance was an ever-present core category in the women's narratives. At times, it was articulated by the participants; at other times, it was apparent in the participants' narratives. The core contradiction seemed to be organised around love and fear: My father loves me but he beats me till he almost kills me! How can mother love my father and be so afraid of him? How can my mother protect me from my violent father and then insist that I love him and respect him? The following subcategories and related quotes illustrate in more detail these contradictory experiences which might be helpful for clinicians working with similar intense double binds and dilemmas in therapy.

Being Terrified of Father and Admiring Him a Lot

One of the participants, Geraldine[1] a 34-year-old woman, shared her very vivid childhood memories of witnessing horrible, physical and psychological abuse by her father on her mother. She also spoke about the abuse that she directly suffered at the hand of her father—of being sadistically, physically and psychologically assaulted by her father. Yet, during the same interview, she also talked about how much she admired her father as a child and imitated him in everything, including how he sat down, and how he spoke. The following quote brings forth her feelings of absolute terror of her father and the callousness of the abuse she suffered:

> This was the time when my father had an accident with the ploughing machine and he had made this sacred promise to God that if his leg would not be amputated then he would carry heavy chains during the Good Friday procession, and once he got better and he could walk well, he did carry these chains .., Yes, the Good Friday procession. And he used to beat us with the same chains he carried in this procession. Of course you would think he was going to kill you, man!!
>
> Because I knew .., that the same chains he used on the Good Friday during the procession were the same chains he used to beat us with. I mean think about it .., damn it! (blasphemes against God) … he goes to walk behind the statue of Jesus and then .., But he was a real great hypocrite! I used to get really angry that during the procession, Jesus, Good Friday,

[1]To protect the anonymity of the participants, all names have been changed. All identifying details have been removed.

> something so sacred and serious and so solemn and are you not fucking ashamed of God? Because God is supposed to know what you are dragging .., then you beat us with them .., do you understand? .., (Geraldine I, p. 51-52).

In this same interview, Geraldine also said

> My father had two things which I admired a lot- He was very good with his hands, a very practical man and he was very strong and very powerful… when I was growing up, I wanted to be like him – powerful and not take any shit from people (Geraldine 2, p. 72)

Thus, together with the dynamics of violence, fear and terror, the participants also spoke about instances of wanting to reconnect with father, highlighting the strength of the attachment bonds (Bowlby 1988). In the same manner, in her interview, Jessica told me

> "Because at the end of the day, he is still your father… you cannot break the bond between you and him, even if he were a monster, you cannot" (Jessica, p. 19).

Even though Jessica's father murdered her mother, she did not want to break her bond with him because she felt that having lost her mother, she did not want to lose her other parent and she did not want to deprive her children of having a grandparent.

Seana's interview also illustrated how caught up participants were struggling with being abused and trying to maintain a connection with their father. The following quote from Seana, brings to light this dilemma:

> He phoned me at home and he spent an hour on the phone and it is like he makes you cower and hide into your shell. So you start saying to yourself, I did something wrong. Let me see what I did wrong. But then when you start reflecting .., you start saying but what did I do wrong? It's not like I never did anything wrong, I did do wrong things for sure because I am human like everyone else but he did more wrong things especially in his role as a father .., he did more wrong than I did. Because logic tells you or better it's like a lot like how many Maltese people think, "He is your father so you must be submissive".
>
> Now the last telephone conversation .., I went for the medical certificate and he told me now I will get it for you .., because I spent the whole Christmas holidays in hospital because of a slipped disc and he told me that he will get me the certificate himself and so that he doesn't say that his daughter wants to exclude him completely from his life or so that he does not feel .., so I let him take the role of father .., I went all out for him .., I told him okay and he took very long to get it for me and when he got it for me, it had a mistake and I phoned him and I was almost in tears because he took 2 months to get it for me and at that time I told him 'Can you tell me .. where I can go' .., and he started: 'I am not your servant and leave me in peace'.. I told him, I .., and I remember him telling me, but I don't want to use his words .., he told me I .., ..of you .., and at that time, it is like the world closed down and I cried so much ..,
>
> … Yes, I was like a bouncing ball .., bashed against the wall and re-bounding .., . This is how I used to see myself .., like a bouncing ball .., I used to say but am I a puppet? But let me let it go so that I leave the family in peace as much as possible .., but I was the one who suffered ultimately because I did not stand up to him (p. 46–48).

This struggle, where children are caught between two opposing emotions concerning their father, has been researched by Peled (2000) and also supported by Mullender et al. (2002). These children lived and continued living this dilemma in adulthood. Donna, a 23-year-old woman talked about going back and forth, in a cycle of cutting-off and connecting with her father:

> You really would like to build a relationship with him… because you wish that things, one day will be different, but then you rationalise… it is like you do recognise the need inside you but you know it is not helpful,… I believe that it is the feeling that every girl feels about her father… that he should be in her life but then reality kicks in and you realise that it cannot be possible.. (Donna 1, p. 61).

One can hypothesise about the different explanations of why women/daughters like Seana, and Donna were caught in the cut-off/connection cycle. Perhaps they yearned for their father's love; perhaps besides the horrible memories of abuse, they also had other memories which they associated with love from their father; perhaps they also wanted to please their mother who wanted them to keep their connection to their father and because they also felt pressured by cultural beliefs around daughters' submission to their father's authority and by the beliefs around the need to keep the family together. Thus the relationship with the father was not only intrinsically complicated by way of the intense opposing emotions but also because it was embedded within the child–mother relationship and the cultural discourses around fathering, around being a daughter and about the importance of family in the Maltese context (Sammut Scerri 2015).

Seeing Mother so Full of Love and Fear Towards the Father

The need to make sense and manage contradictions was not only in relation to the daughters' relationship to the father, but also in relation to how their mother related to their father. Seana was one of the women who found it very hard to understand her perception of her mother's very clear feelings of terror of her father and also her love for him

> Because I used to see mum so frightened, so full of bitterness and yet so full love towards him… that I used to try and draw some conclusion—is it because my mum really loves him or because she is afraid of him? She was very frightened of him but she loved him a lot" (Seana, p. 8).

Other women also could not understand how their mother tried to protect her children from her husband's violence and at the same time minimised his violence and/or expected her daughter to respect him and pressured her to maintain contact with him. Donna explains it in this way

> Mum did her best to protect us from him but it was not enough as she was terrified of him and he had a lot of influence on her…..
>
> She never gives up on trying to convince me to keep contact with him… she had been saying how much he had changed and how calm he has become, so I started wondering whether I was being too harsh; and finally I went with her for a visit. As soon as we went in, he started blaspheming and threatening that he would kill her. I was shocked and so angry

and devastated that she had put her life and that of my sisters and mine in danger again… I vowed to listen to my innermost feelings and not go there again" (Donna 2, p. 53).

Marika, a 20-year old, spoke of her great disappointment of her mother's minimization and justification of the father's violence (Bogat et al. 2013; Cooper and Vetere 2005). She also recalled an incident when Marika had filed a police report and after about a week or so, she had to withdraw it because her mother pressured her not to press charges against her father

> And once he had punched me, here and in my stomach. Of course, he hit me with the table and pushed me on the floor. When I regained consciousness, I left the house and mummy came with me and we filed a police report. When they summoned us to court, my mother told me, 'Why don't you withdraw your charges?' You know what happens to my mum? Time goes by, things calm down, for example, a week goes by, and she then tells me, 'Drop the case. We only filed the report because we were angry.' So I could never take action against my father. I was under age, I had to live with them and obey them, and I didn't want them to hate and blame me if my father went to prison (Marika 2, p. 26).

Thus again these two opposing intense emotions in relation to their parents' relationships made it hard for them to process how they make sense of such experiences. The fact that they were involved in an intense, significant relationship with their parents, the contradictory nature of the experiences and perhaps their inability to comment about it are characteristically how double binds are defined in communication theory (Watzlawick et al. 1967; Gibney 2006). Bateson (1972) also highlights that when such situations are repeated, an individual caught in these double binds is unable to decipher this communication and to respond to it.

Further Reflections on Working with Dissonance, Double Binds and Dilemmas in Clinical Practice

In our experience, we find that both in therapy and in supervision, practitioners need to manage these contradictions and dilemmas brought up by the family members. We find it that it is important to acknowledge the existence of these contradictions and to bring them out in the open to be talked about (See also chapter eight on supervision and consultation). Unless this happens there is a danger that in listening to the horrific experiences of these family members, we can only make sense of them by constructing the perpetrator as "all-bad", and we may find ourselves minimising or pathologising the attachment experiences of these adult children with their parents who were abusive towards them (Kaufmann 2002). But if we recognise, contain and attempt to integrate incongruent information—that someone can both love and hate another person—we remain consistent and enduring objects and help the family members in their turn, integrate some of their distressing and fragmented experiences (Lawrence 2014).

Paying Therapeutic Attention to Interpersonal Processes Such as Family Systems Triangulation and Parentification

In working with families where there was violence, processes such as triangulation and parentification are helpful theoretical concepts with which to understand some of the persistent and intense family dynamics. All the women in the Sammut Scerri (2015)'s study described ways in which they were drawn, or drew themselves into the conflict with their parents—what early family therapists such as Minuchin (1974) described as triangulation. This finding supports and is supported by studies from the divorce and marital conflict literature (Amato and Afifi 2006; Buehler and Welsh 2009; DeBoard-Lucas et al. 2010; Fosco and Grych 2010) and by the work of Pat Crittenden (2008) on triangulation from dynamic-maturational attachment perspective.

As Dallos and Vetere (2012) clearly explain, Minuchin stated that the utilisation of one child in the spouses' conflict could take many forms. He distinguished three forms of rigid triadic processes: (a) The first form involves each parent actively recruiting the child to side with him or her, with the other parent interpreting the child's action as an attack; (b) In another form, which Minuchin called detouring, the parents, rather than focusing on their unsatisfactory relationship focus on the misbehaviour of the child, by diverting all their attention towards him or her, with the child becoming the family problem; (c) The third form—the stable coalition can take the form of one of the parents forming an alliance with the child against the other parent.

It is interesting to note that all three forms, in one form or another were present in the participants' families. Some of the participants were actively recruited to take sides by one parent whilst others felt that it was their duty to get involved (Fosco and Grych 2010), either because they wanted to protect their mother at all costs or because they saw themselves as being the most courageous person in the family.

Geraldine recalled a step-by-step routine in the way that she was explicitly triangulated in—that once her parents would start fighting, her father would invariably ask her to act as a judge and decide who should win the argument—him or her mother

> First they used to mention Abraham Galea (name of first Maltese psychiatrist), then I would be judge. Always like that. Because in those days, I only remember Abraham Galea's voice on the radio. Then he used to accuse her of needing Abraham Galea .., then she would tell him something back .., not that she used to tell him a lot. The only time she would tell him .., Then after Abraham Galea would be mentioned then I would end up being .., on hearing Abraham Galea's name then I would say here it comes .., Here we go again, do you understand? But the one who was mentioned a lot .., not that the mental asylum was not mentioned but the name most mentioned was that of Abraham Galea. So it meant now it is time for the verdict. Do you understand? You have to give judgement. Do you understand? You have to pass judgement. Because the fighting used to have a pattern in those days (Geraldine 1, p. 40–41).

Geraldine recalled that when she had to give her verdict it was like court sentence with people taking turns to speak. But at the same time, the whole scene seemed very fast and she had to pass judgement very quickly. Geraldine recalled that it was very hard for her to decide that her mother was right. She said that her father was a very good orator, like an extremely good lawyer and he always won the arguments. As a child, the only thing that she made sense of was that: "my father was right, he was intelligent, and my mother was ignorant… (Geraldine 1, p. 39)". Moreover, whilst she admired his competence, she was terrified of him and his beatings, and consistently took his side against the mother, with whom she said that she had a rocky relationship. Being in this double-bind situation (Bateson et al. 1956), Geraldine's focused her energy on surviving and not getting beaten by her father.

Marika, Donna, Rose, Mary, Sandra and Sara on the other hand, could not stand their mother getting hurt and got involved in their parents' fight to protect her. A quote from Marika's interview illustrates her process of triangulation

> I: what did you (as children) do?
>
> P: my sisters didn't do anything. But I was the one who always got involved between them. It's because these things bother me. It bothers me to see my mother getting hurt and beaten. So I used to go between them.
>
> I used to get the punches, even though I knew I would be punched. As long as I managed to separate my mother away from him. That's what I always used to do.
>
> I: you got his punches?
>
> P: yes, yes I get the punches
>
> I: So you protected her?
>
> P: Yes
>
> (Marika 1, p. 20).

Donna, too felt that her mother tried to be the perfect wife and mother and there usually were not many arguments going on but once her father lost his temper, he would then become violent, without any provocation whatsoever. Donna felt that it was an injustice that her mother suffered so much (Jory et al. 1997) and as she grew older, she used to be the one to challenge him to protect her mother and her siblings. Donna remembered that as young as a 7-year old, she started putting pressure on her mother to leave their father and trying to convince her that they would be so much better off without him. Marika remembered doing the same thing.

When Marika and Donna were asked why they felt that they had to get involved rather than their siblings, they were not sure of the reasons. Marika said that she felt that it was her duty, being the eldest and having the reputation of being the courageous one in the family. Donna said that she felt her mother and siblings knew that she was competent and was able to stand up to their father and she felt that implicitly it was expected of her. This perhaps implies that the process of triangulation incorporated both precipitating and maintaining factors, which were reinforced by the family dynamics including between the mother and the siblings and the relationships between the other family members.

The women also talked about the great distress that they experienced as their contradictions and dilemmas intensified and described how the more severe the violence, the more they felt the need to intervene. They did remark about how sometimes the violence between their parents and themselves got worse with their involvement. The process also was present across the life span of the clients: that is in childhood, adolescence and adulthood, although it was during adolescence, that these women felt a great need to stop the perpetrator from continuing to spread fear and terror in the family. Perhaps this was these young women's way of getting a sense of their power back and feeling less frightened and less out of control (Gorell Barnes and Henessy 1995).

For some participants, the process of triangulation was closely tied to a process of taking responsibility for their parents and their siblings as if they were the parents themselves—a process referred to as "Parentification" (Boszormenyi-Nagy and Spark 1973; Chase 1999; Jurkovic et al. 1991; Minuchin 1974) as mentioned earlier in this chapter.

Marika described how she felt that it was her responsibility to emotionally take care of her mother and her siblings instead of her father who had abdicated his role and instead of her mother who she saw as weak (Mullender et al. 2002). Again, Marika was not sure why she took on this role but she gave the same reasons that she gave for being involved in her parents' conflicts:

> … because I am the oldest, I feel responsible, you see? In fact I always feel the responsibility to help my mother, my sister and my youngest sister. I took that responsibility. I don't know from where it came and how it came about but I took the responsibility because there isn't father and I think that in my case, I did it because my dad failed to take it as a father and my mother was too weak to take care of all of us. I took the responsibility as the oldest, not financially because I didn't earn any money but example if my mother is sad today, or if she is irritable, I try to find out what happened to her; I try to make her happy. I tell her "come mum, let us go out …
>
> Example, if my siblings need something, I have always bought it for them. When I started to work, I used to buy something for everyone so that I see a smile on everyone's face. They are small things but for you they mean a lot. Example, up to the present day, I still say that before I leave home, whether I get married or not, I would like to have my own house. Before I leave home, I would like to see everyone settled. Example, I would like to see my middle sister settled with her boyfriend. I would like to see my other sister [settled] at school. I want my mother … mother will remain the same… I don't know (Marika 1, p. 21–22).

Donna recalled doing similar things-taking care of both her middle and youngest sister, including taking her baby sister with her to religion lessons as the father wanted the mother for him

> He was abusive too .., he was addicted to sex .., it's like sometimes my mother would be asleep next to us, he used to watch a lot of pornographic movies, then he would tell her come on next to me .., you understand .., when we started growing up, then he would tell me go grab your sister and take her away from there .., I never saw them during sex .., but I knew what was going on .., my younger sister, sometimes, out of curiosity would peep

> through the keyhole .., I would get angry at her, my mother really felt like an object .., and that was it, I was always worried about protecting them .., then when I started growing older I began to stand up to him and he disliked that (Donna 1, p. 6–7).

> My sister .., she is now 12 years old .., she was the fruit of jealousy, my father wanted my mother completely to himself .., it's like he did not want her to take care of my baby sister. So I had to feed her, change her, wake up during the night to look after her, and he would tell me take her with you, even if I went to religion lessons, and it's like if I took her with me to religion lessons there would be lots of things… (Donna,1, p. 9).

Donna, too, was not sure how she got to take on this role but she said that it was something that she grew into, since she was three years old. She also recalled making sure that the house was safe and every door was locked when her father had left the house. As highlighted earlier, Donna was not only a reference point for her mother when it came to issues of discipline and raising her youngest sibling but Donna felt that she was her mother's only joy in her life and that she owed it to her to do well at school so that her mother would be comforted

> And I remember, I used to do well at school and I remember that I wanted to be her champion. And even during Parents' Day, they would tell her, you have such a bright and polite daughter and they used to praise me and so on and I knew what these words meant a lot for her, especially when in her family, there were a lot of delinquent children. She would say, 'So I must be doing something right?' I used to feel this a lot (Donna 2, p. 30).

In a similar way, Sandra was also sensitive to her mother's difficulty with making ends meet and she remembered that as a young girl, she would choose the least expensive packet of sweets so that her mother would not spend a lot of money. Sandra also recalled the many times she took care of her mother when she was depressed. Sara too as highlighted earlier took over the caring role of her siblings like a parent. However, Sara seemed less burdened than other participants, like Donna and Marika, for example, with her role and was more in touch with the fact that she had a lot of support from her family. Donna continued struggling not to take a parental role with her mother and her sisters well into her adulthood, and although she and her mother and sisters were working on interacting differently, their positions shifted back and forth across time. However, in situations of danger, Donna felt herself cementing herself and being cemented in that role again.

The Impact of Triangulation and Parentification on the Women's Development: A Sense of Loss, Feelings of Distress and of Competence

Both triangulation and parentification led to a loss of relationships with their parents and their siblings. Although Mary said, "taking sides is almost automatic when father is terrifying and feeling safe and secure only with mother" (Mary, p. 11); she also expressed how painful it was to lose her relationship with her father (Amato and Afifi 2006). Perhaps it is also this sense of loss that continues to propel the daughters to remain open to some connection with the father. Seana expressed the same sense of loss at the cut-off between her father and her siblings as a result of divided loyalties and alliances between the siblings and a parent against the other parent and the other sibling. As mentioned earlier, with being parentified, Donna felt that she missed being cuddled and mothered by her mother. She also lost her sibling relationship with both her sisters. She was unable to relax with her family and, in some ways, this led her to feel different from them, and feeling isolated.

Getting involved through the processes of triangulation and parentification also meant that the daughters felt very distressed and angry (Gerard et al. 2005; Earley and Cushway 2002). Rose observed that whilst it was very difficult for her not to get involved and not protect her mother, her involvement sometimes made the fighting worse (Fosco and Grych 2010). Marika too felt distressed with taking on her mother's fight and sometimes her sister's fight with the father. She acknowledged that it was an extra burden, which did not end when the fighting stopped. She would then be left with worrying about the effect on her sister and also sometimes worrying about herself and wondering whether she was becoming aggressive like her father, as mentioned earlier

> It's a lot of stress (said with emphasis). Because you would want to take control of everything that happens. Some time ago, my sister (the one after me) had a fight with my father and I went down and I tried to explain things to him and tried to make him understand. I ended up fighting with him because he is hard-headed. He does not accept that he makes a mistake. This kind of thing. So I continued fighting with him myself and then it's like you end up with your head hurting because this is all a hassle, it's stressful. This is an extra burden for me – because it is like you take in everything yourself. Then when they fight, you end up worrying for her (Marika 1, p. 23).

The women acknowledged developing a sense of competence and a sense of agency with being in the middle of things (Byng-Hall 2002, 2008). In some instances, when they got involved in their parents' violence, they did manage to protect their mother and they did manage to stand up to their father. In this way, they got in touch with their sense of power and as Donna recalled, although she was afraid of her father, she was adamant that she would not show it. They also got validated by the sometimes implicit and other times explicit approval of their family and extended family—Marika was known as the courageous one

In summary, the process of triangulation seemed ubiquitous in all the participants' narratives and it does seem strange that so far, the process has not been much more empirically studied in systemic literature (Dallos and Vetere 2012). In some of these participants' narrative, triangulation was closely related to parentification, with the relationship seemingly being proportional—that is the more a person was triangulated, the more, she felt that she needed to provide for her mother and siblings' needs.

In exploring such patterns, therapists can ask about gains and losses that their clients experienced such as feeling a sense of competence at having a pivotal role in the family dynamics and/or a sense of loss around losing their childhood or their relationships with their siblings when they related to them more from a parental role rather than as siblings.

The participants also described how processes like triangulation and parentification were long-standing challenges, which they regularly had to revisit especially in their relationships with their family of origin. Two of the participants, Geraldine and Donna also spoke about how they were able to find pockets of respite space from being triangulated in their parents' conflicts through a lot of psychological work in therapy and also through other alternative therapies like meditation, yoga and mindfulness.

This implies that therapists can help create a reflective space for clients to think about how best to position themselves and manoeuvre the sticky and difficult contexts of marital conflict, even when the parents have separated and the children are adults. Therapists can also keep themselves informed of research and clinical studies that have looked into how meditation, and mindfulness have been helpful methods for trauma-related distress (Briere and Scott 2015).

Drawing from Trauma Theory and Looking at the Traumatogenic Effect of Violence on the Child and Adult Development

One can argue that the terrifying component and the impact of the violence in the family also exerted an important influence on hindering the reflective capacity of the children and all the family members involved. Drawing from trauma research and how the brain functions in conditions of high arousal and danger, we know that the prefrontal cortex which is normally associated with this function, is "bypassed" by the amygdala in the limbic system, so that persons operate more in a flight-flight-freeze mode and lose their capacity to think about the mental state of others (Asen and Fonagy 2012).

All the women narrated overwhelmingly horrifying experiences of abuse that led them to try and survive in different ways. Both Anita and Carmen described their childhood as "living in hell". Anita was terrorised by the frightening scenes between her mother and father and also remembered herself praying to God and pleading that He delivers her from the physical abuse, neglect and psychological abuse that she suffered at the hands of her mother and father. Anita described her father has an alcoholic and her mother as a person, who every so often, just stood up and left the house, when she could not cope anymore with what was going on in the family

> When my mother used to leave home .., she used to wake up one fine day and it's like, 'I can't take this anymore' and she leaves - my father was an alcoholic .., when she used to leave home, he would drink more .., but it almost was better when she left home because she was disorganised .., the house was always topsy-turvy; she used to begin washing the clothes at 8am and it would come to midnight and she would still be at it .., it was like that .., today I know that she had some personality disorder ..,

> I remember when I was about 4 or 5 years old, I remember it very clearly .., my sister and I spoke about it a few days ago .., my eldest sister and I .., my mother was pregnant with one of my siblings, he put a flick knife against her legs. Thank God someone knocked at the door because he told her I will slash you to pieces .., that is what it was like at our house (Anita, p. 3).

Geraldine realised that she was raised not to feel anything and to shut out her emotions, what Kolk (2007) refers to as "emotional numbing" (p. 188), a process, which according to Geraldine led her to shut down her emotions in both trauma-related and everyday experiences in daily life.

On the other hand, Jessica remembered being constantly alert and preoccupied with her mother's safety as a child: "I used to wake up, and go near mummy, checking that she is still alive. I could not sleep unless I made sure that she is okay [eyes welling up with tears]" (p. 6). Geraldine also remembered waking up at night and rushing to the top of the stairs, staying there, keeping very still, without moving one finger, to listen to what her parents would be saying to make sure that her mother was alright (Rivett et al. 2006) and then rushing back to the bedroom when her parents seemed to have stopped talking. Geraldine remembered not being able to understand all their words and straining very hard to listen. In such cases, both Geraldine and Jessica's behaviour can be understood as forms of hyperactivating strategies (Mikulincer et al. 2003) as they tried to reassure themselves repeatedly that their mother, as their attachment figure, was safe despite the dangerous environment.

After her mother's death, Jessica recalled needing medication to sleep, having panic attacks, and being constantly on the go. Sara recalled too that she was constantly on the go as a child. All the participants, as adults, understood their behaviours as being consequences of what they were going through, highlighting the overlap in the literature between hyperactive behaviour, post-traumatic stress disorders and the effects of children of witnessing domestic violence (Dallos and Vetere 2009):

> Nowadays, I say that that I was feisty because of the things that were happening; that nothing used to scare me, do you understand? My brother says that I drew people's attention because I used to know what to say to people if they told me something. I used to feel like I was a big (older) girl. I did not feel like I was a young child" (Jessica, p. 8).

Remembering and Forgetting

The theme or category of "remembering and forgetting" came up very often in the interviews and may have direct relevance on how family members tell their story in therapy. As the participants were trying to recall their experiences, some participants commented that they were able to remember only bits and pieces and that, sometimes, it was difficult for them to remember a coherent whole

> I cannot remember what role my brother played, I cannot remember. In my mind, in the way that I remember things, perhaps he had a passive role .., I cannot recall him .., I think that he used to cry a lot but I don't think that this happened all the time. I think that he used to be in a daze .., It is like I cannot see the whole piece .., it is not coming to me (Geraldine 2, p. 84).

and Mary too

> … yes, of pieces of episodes .., and sometimes, you wouldn't understand what is happening so it's easier to see pieces .., and there would not be that glue between them .., (Mary, p. 20).

Rose was one of the participants who had difficulties to remember large aspects of her childhood experiences. Whilst she said that her relationship with her mother was good, she could not recall any specific instances, which illustrated such a close relationship. Her memories at times were not only fragmented but they also seemed incoherent, that is they lacked a sequence of events or other vital detail (Kolk 2014). I (Clarissa Sammut Scerri) also observed that she used a lot of minimisation, and distance from affect in her language (Crittenden and Kulbotten, 2007). When she was asked to describe what the atmosphere at home was like when she was young, she replied

> What I don't remember is .., the atmosphere at that time .., obviously I was still young .., what I remember is that there used to be .., even when we came to live at (name of village), there was shouting, a little fighting in the family and the like (Rose, p. 3). I also remember that there was a bit of beating .., and ehm .., things flying (p. 5).

At the same time, in line with Kolk (2014) research on traumatic memory, Rose's memories for one particularly violent episode which involved her, were very clear and vivid

> I remember one episode very clearly .., I was eating .., we have a combined kitchen and dining room just separated by an arch. He grabbed an ornament .., mummy's, that her father had given her before he died; he grabbed this doll and broke it and threw it at me the .., and I saw that it was coming in my direction .., and so episodes like these .., of this kind (Rose, p. 8).

Other participants recalled similar episodes very vividly too. Thus in similar ways, family members talking about their experiences, may remember things very vividly or have gaps in their memories or may narrate their stories in a fragmented manner.

Other participants also talked their experiences of intrusive reliving of traumatic events—which is the first PTSD criterion—re-experiencing of the traumatic event (American Psychiatric Association 2013). One particular striking example was that of Geraldine locking herself up at home for three days for fear that her boyfriend was going to come and beat her after he told her in the course of a conversation "You are right!":

> No…no….no….in front of people he would just tell you one word "You are right". And that word for me it took me a long time to learn what it meant, even up to the moment when I was a grownup woman. It was very difficult when someone told me I was right. Because I used to say (haqq ghal Madonna- blasphemy against the Holy Mother) now a beating will follow.

> Once I had a boyfriend. I do not remember what we were talking about but it was something trivial .., But I remember distinctly in the car, while he was driving and I was in the passenger's seat ok? He said you are right. Now you must keep in mind that he had the keys to my house. He used to use the key only when he was going to come over in the evenings and I would know he would be coming. Emm…and he said, we were talking and he said you are right.
>
> I froze and I was focusing only on the fact that as soon as I arrive, I will scoot out of the car and gas down run into my house. I fell silent so he would leave as soon as possible… And then much later he phoned me at work
>
> He phoned me at home and I ignored him. Then about three days after, I called him because I felt ridiculous. Then he said, 'you suddenly left without warning just like that for no reason .., my mother and aunt got worried too'.
>
> Then I found the courage from somewhere and told him 'Please do me a favour, come over and we will talk..' I told him don't tell me 'You are right'. Do not ever tell me that word again. I told him because for me, you are right means .., he had never raised his hand to me .., it's true he had never done anything to me physically .., but at that instant I had thought he is going inside the house with me and then he would .., because for me you are right means a beating from hell is coming next. It means 'I will not beat you in front of people but when we are at home you will get .(Geraldine 1, p. 30–32).

Geraldine's memory triggers and subsequent flashbacks (Kolk et al. 2007) were distressing and had a disturbing impact on her quality of life and relationships. Geraldine also recalled being overwhelmed with pain in her head whilst travelling to work and what kept her sane was the tremendous support of her psychologist who had discussed with her the nature of flashbacks (Briere and Scott 2015). Geraldine associated the pain with the beatings that she got on her head whilst being dragged down the stairs by her hair by her father. The psychologist's explanation was vital to her mental health.

Trauma theory can also be a helpful lens to understand some of the experiences that the women went through as individual adults as part of legacies of trauma as well as how they understood the impact of these legacies on their intimate relationships.

In the interviews, the participants described their psychological pain emphasising that it was worse than physical pain. Rose talked about her father's insults which continuously played in her head as an adult making her feel incapacitated and finding it difficult to pluck up courage to go out alone to meet new people. Claire felt that part of the legacy of the immense fear that experienced in her childhood was her fear of being bullied, which remained very much with her in her adult life (Band-Winterstein 2014). She still feels very afraid in situations of conflict and chooses to withdraw rather than fight back.

> He put a fist next to my face and I tried to hold off his hands but my father was really strong because he was into construction work at that time – so he was really strong and I remember that he had started telling me – almost in a jesting manner- come on, now tell me the opposite that I am telling you – and I now know that he was looking at me and "enjoying" the fact that he was seeing fear in my eyes- so that I will tell him – no, I will not do it because he knew that I would not oppose him because I was too afraid .., and I am still afraid, not only of him but of everyone because I am afraid of being bullied – so I will not answer back at anyone (Claire, p. 13).

The participants in the Sammut Scerri (2015)'s study also shared about their feelings of shame around the belief that they did not come from "a good, stable family", which came into the way of their sharing of their childhood experiences (Cooper and Vetere 2005). When such experiences were kept secret from their significant others, this in turn deprived their intimate partners from an important context from which to understand their partners' behaviour.

Carmen, Claire and Marika specifically talked about feeling very reluctant to talk about their family's background of violence to their boyfriends and prospective partners. Carmen was very afraid that although her boyfriend might accept her, his family would not

> But then when I met my husband, all the anxiety that I had, was not whether I would get married to him or not, but my greatest fear was how I was going to go about telling him about my background. Because ok-he might accept you but then there is also his family, and sometimes it is the family that does not accept you, and many families do this, they stigmatise you and say that I would be like my mother (Carmen, p. 28).

Such fears need to be understood in the context of honour and shame that continue to be concerns in Mediterranean culture (Cassar 2003), where the role of the woman, especially in the older generations, is to avoid shame, "by keeping pure, by remaining loyal to their husbands and by guaranteeing the continuity of the family lineage" (p. 12). In this sense, then it was important for Carmen not to be seen as one that would bring shame to her future husband's family. These fears need also to be understood in the wider context of shame and humiliation surrounding domestic violence in families (Cooper and Vetere 2005)

One can thus argue that the ripple effects from family violence are far-reaching and very often go beyond the confines of the one's nuclear family, even when the violence stops. Fearing other people's judgement and of becoming socially bankrupt (Abela 1997), together with loyalty to one's family are very strong inhibitors of talking about what is happening in one's home. The social isolation and the accompanying suffering are usually enormous to the extent that one can understand why some family members do not look for support from their intimate partners.

Other Trauma Legacies and Challenges in Relationships-"It Feels like You Are Trying to Make a Mountain Move"

One of the participants, Mary, echoed some of the other women's sentiments when she stated that very often she did not have the awareness of what she was bringing into the relationship but she only realised it when she found herself with the same problems again (Herman 1997). Mary succinctly described how as a result of her childhood experiences, she missed very important relational foundations, both in herself and how to deal with others (Briere and Scott 2015):

> For example .., I don't know .., I missed the sense of security, the sense of belonging, the sense of being seen for who you are and you have to get these from somewhere. And

> someone has to give them to you .., yes, you need to work on yourself but there needs to be someone to give them to you and if you do not find them, then, these experiences .., you keep living with a lot of symptoms .., symptoms of wrong beliefs, for example, where men and women are concerned, where relationships are concerned .., beliefs about yourself .., it's like there are a lot of things .., it is very complex .., for example even the way you behave, for example by being angry and leaving .., it's like nobody would have taught that you stay and talk .., and sometimes, it could be that you would know this as well, you would have learnt it but to actually do it, feels like you are moving the trauma mountain that you went through, it feels like you are trying to make a mountain move (Mary, p. 25–26).

Mary's words conveyed some of the great struggles that some of these participants had to continually contend with, in the relationship. She shared how upset she was when she found herself in circumstances similar to her parents, even though she had been determined not to replicate her parents' story. Jessica too found herself in a joy-less marriage, as described earlier. She felt un-validated and unloved by her husband. With hindsight, she reflected on how difficult it must have been for her ex-husband to understand and cope with the rage that she had, that came out of a sense of injustice and unfairness of having been abused and downtrodden for 20 years (Johnson 2004). Jessica believed that her husband had tried to get along with her but perhaps he saw her as too quarrelsome, and too determined to make her point at all costs. All this might have been too much for him. She also tried to speak to him about her dreams and wishes but felt that she was not taken seriously and he dismissed her words as adolescent fantasies.

Marika and Rose spoke about the difficulty that they had with managing their anger and coping with difference and conflict in the context of an intimate relationship (Briere and Lanktree 2012). Marika felt unable to deal with her frustration and she coped by leaving the conflictual situation, a behaviour that invariably had negative consequences on her relationship with her boyfriend. Rose echoed the same feelings, including her inability to talk about what was bothering in the relationship

> And how do you say it .., even the fact that I am afraid .., I have very low self esteem, very, very low .., even the fact that I am afraid to state my opinion or that I keep myself back .., I have been affected a lot by this .., so I am either aggressive or .., .So in relationship with other people, it is a bit difficult for me not to become aggressive .., .once I reach that point up there, I up and leave .., It does create a little (difficulty) because it does create .., .the other person, that is next to you would not know that you are going to take something negatively .., so that this turns out against you.. (Rose, p. 26–27).

During her first interview, Marika spoke about how she thought that her bad temper was stronger than her and that hard as she tried, it always got the better of her. Interestingly, in the second interview, whilst Marika was dating another boyfriend, she felt more secure in the relationship and this helped her deal better with her anger (Mikulincer and Goodman 2006). Although she was still vigilant over her boyfriend's behaviour as to whether he would turn out to be aggressive like her father, she felt that he was more committed to their relationship and this helped cope better with her temper. Although Marika did not specifically state this, her anger perhaps hid fears around being unhappy, like her mother, and around being alone and unloved in the future. This statement resonated with what Jessica also stated in her interview, "behind all the anger, the hurts are still there" (p. 76).

Geraldine too spoke about how she had to be mindful of her need to be always right in her relationships. She saw her aggressive behaviour as an echo of how her father was in control over her and everything, in her family of origin. She needed to continuously keep herself in check so that she would not engage in such power struggles—with her need to win and be always in the right, which she saw connected with her need to be in control.

How the Relationship with My Father Affected My Relationship with Men

Some participants made a connection between their relationship with their father and their relationships with men, in general. This connection is supportive of research that highlights the significant impact that the father has on his daughter's romantic relationships (Nielsen 2014). Rose explained that thanks to her father, she ended up hating men. Some boys also rejected her and this fact did not help her relationships with men in general: "Re: relationships.., thanks to my father.., I ended up hating men/not being able to stand men.., and also I sometimes got rejected by some boys" (Rose, p. 29).

Sandra spoke about looking at men as inferior to women and seeing herself as trying to manipulate them to get what she wanted. Sandra made a connection to how she used to have to manage her father so that he would not be in a position to blackmail her and also linked her behaviour and attitude to her having been sexually abused as a teenager by a family friend

> And I think that something that affected me too and I think that it affected me a lot is that I used to look at a man as inferior to a woman .., this is something that I struggle with, today, not in a sexist way or feminist way but this is something that I need to learn more about myself .., But I always used to try and manipulate a man .., so I used to say .., so it was difficult for me to find a person that is a man to go out with .., I also was sexually abused so this affects me too…
>
> I : so how did this belief come about, that you can manipulate a man as you please? P: because I used to see myself as more intelligent than a man… even in the way that I communicate with my father and my brother… I was good enough to manipulate (them)…I had to learn how to get what I want from my father so that he does not keep blackmailing me for example, or even from the other experience that I went through, so that the abuse stopped (Sandra, p. 25).

Both Rose and Sandra explained how their beliefs and attitudes hindered their intimate relationships with men. On the other hand, both had loving intimate relationships with women. Both, however, did not label themselves as gay. Although Rose had come out to her family as gay, she was at a point in her life where if the opportunity for a relationship with a boy came along, she would consider it because she was "discovering that not all boys and men are the same .., I am not saying the word .., not all are cruel sadists" (Rose, p. 30). Similarly, Sandra did not want to label herself as gay as this was not something that she felt as describing her completely. She said that being in a gay relationship with someone was part of her present but that anything could happen in the future. These findings are consistent with those of Hlazo-Tawodzera (2006) and others like Diamond (1995) who suggest that sexual identity and behaviour are not fixed for life but can fluctuate and change over a woman's life span.

Seana on the other hand, found it difficult to trust her boyfriend completely—that he will not be violent, just because he was a man, like her father. Despite the fact that he was supportive of her throughout their eight years of courtship and has never been aggressive, she was still afraid that one day, out of the blues, he would betray her trust and turn violent

> This is after 8 years, almost, so there are still things that I don't tell him because I am afraid that that devil that is in my father, will one day will appear in him, do you understand, I start saying to myself, after all he is a man. And I know that a man is totally different from a woman (Seana, p. 40).

Seana's gendered beliefs about men and violence are theoretically supported by writings about hegonomic masculinity (Connell 2005), which associates manhood with power achieved through sexual domination of women, and the exclusion of women through various means including violence. In Seana's case, the experiences that she lived through and was still living through at the hands of her father were a living testament of these beliefs. Thus one can understand Seana's fears around trusting that her boyfriend will not be violent. At the same time, one can also understand, that these gendered beliefs about men and violence and men in relationships exert a lot of pressure on both partners, in an intimate relationship. In fact, Seana found herself wondering whether she was a relationship-material.

It seemed as if the spectre of the violence always hovered over the relationship of this participant and her boyfriend "like a shadowy third in the couple's milieu" (Johnson 2004, p. 513).

In a similar way, Donna saw herself as putting a lot of restrictions and conditions in the relationship with her boyfriend, so that she made sure that her boyfriend was not like her father. However, this created a lot of distress in her, in her boyfriend and their relationship, and they ultimately decided to go for couple therapy

> They were things of the past, for example, I was being too rigid with him, I laid down rules and regulations for him, don't you dare get jealous about every single person I talk to and things like that, don't you dare do this or that and for him these were things he would not even dream of doing but I had to tell them to him .., don't you dare raise your hand to me, don't dream of becoming jealous and .., let me give you an example, I am free to speak to anyone that I want to, I want to go to Junior College, and no one is going to stop me, I want to work not like my mother .., at first she was not working because he was jealous, then he forced her to go to work even to the extent of sending the youngest daughter to a residential home because he wanted her to earn money. You totally cannot understand his thinking this man .., so I had stood up to him (her boyfriend) to the extent that even when he said he loved me, I did not attach any particular value to it .., how can I put it, there would be things, for example .., there were certain things like the truth and he used to tell me it's my principles and my word as man that are the core of my living .., if it's black it's black .., and although he used to tell me that and he appeared to be genuine, I still .., I don't know, for

> example, I send him a message and he tells me something that was not exactly as he had said it the day before or as I thought he would say it .., my goodness I would create a whole scene .., and he would tell me so you're telling me that I am lying to you? And I would tell him, no you're not outright lying to me, you're just bending the truth .., I would have then created so much fuss about something that nowadays I cannot even believe I would have created so much stress about it. Then I came to a point where the relationship was going to end. I told him, listen let's do something about our situation because I am tired, I was not even concentrating at Junior College and we went to counselling … (Donna 1, p. 40–42).

Both she and her boyfriend found it helpful for him to witness her individual work but also to work together on how he can support her and they both can support their relationship (Whiffen and Oliver 2004). She learnt that it was important for her to trust a bit more and to let go some of her control. This related not only to her relationship with her boyfriend but also to her way of managing her relationships in general. Having her father tell her so many times that people's betrayal was the order of the day, she found it very difficult to trust and also very difficult not to be ever-vigilant for when the next catastrophic event was going to happen, indicating her insecure-attachment style of relating and her strategies to protect herself from danger (Crittenden 2008; Dallos and Vetere 2009).

It was also helpful for Donna to have her boyfriend's support over what she went through in her childhood. Had not she talked about what she went through in the context of therapy and he had not been there, Donna was convinced that it would have been too difficult for him to understand her experiences

> You cannot control anything .., I had to work very hard .., I was always crying with him, and through counselling he started to understand. He realised the harm that my father had done to me. In the beginning he used to tell me you hate your father too much, then when he saw me crying all the time and sobbing my heart out .., then we started doing some progress, we began to learn how to protect ourselves and care for us, thinking of where to go .., those .., for example… (Donna 1, p. 43).

For us, these experiences highlight the importance of looking at the couple system when working with clients who have gone through trauma experiences and exploring further how these same experiences may filter in the intimate relationship system (Catherall 2005).

Looking into Replicative and Corrective Scripts in the Lives of the Family Members: Struggling and Piecing Together the Puzzle Pieces When Becoming Parents

Another important, and persistent category in the women's narratives in the Sammut Scerri (2015)'s study was their strong yearning to not repeat their family of origin's script (Byng-Hall 1998). Many were afraid that because of their family backgrounds, they were destined to either become abusers or victims of family violence in the future. This perhaps reflects the embedded assumptions of researchers, clinicians and policy makers that children raised in violent homes tend to replicate what they have experienced in their family of origin (Widom 1989a, b).

A brief look into the current literature on intergenerational transmission of violence seems to indicate that the process is complex and influenced by a number of factors such as the age of the child at the time of the violence, whether the violence is maternally or paternally perpetrated, by the relationship of the child with her parents, and her siblings, and by the presence of other significant others who could offer a safe mental and physical space to the child, amongst others (Sammut Scerri 2015). More specifically, the process through which important adults deal with emotionally distressing interpersonal relationships and how they in turn help the children regulate their emotions, particularly their feelings of anger in intimate relationships continues to be underlined as important (Mikulincer et al. 2003; Moretti et al. 2014).

For those participants who were mothers, being a parent was seen as an important opportunity to provide their children a different life than the one that they had as children. They felt very protective towards their children and they did everything for them, determined that their children were going to be happy and not burdened by adult problems. Carmen and Jessica, both said that they still had a close relationship with their children even as their children became teenagers. Carmen highlighted how protective she was of her three sons

> … No one hurts my son, no one. And since you have gone through so many things in your childhood, you want to show your children how precious they are for you. I tell them 'don't let anyone hurt you' because if they hurt you, they will have to deal with me. No one hurts them. I tell you .., I don't even allow my husband sometimes to get angry with them, let alone… (Carmen, p. 56).

While the participants were reflective about their childhood experiences so as not to replicate the same experiences of violence with their children, it was also difficult for them not to go to the other extreme. In the case of Claire, being exposed to violence and experiencing violence, helped her immensely to control her temper (Chang et al. 2003) with her daughter and not vent out if she was distressed about work or about other things which did not relate to the daughter. At the same time, as a parent to a 6-year-old daughter, she was remembering more and more her childhood and connecting with anything in her daughter's life that reminded her of how powerless she felt when being physically abused by her father as a 6-year-old child (Courtois and Ford 2013). Such experiences then made her react aggressively towards the husband, to the extent that her husband told her that that she becomes a "monster" when commenting about how aggressive she was with him when he disciplined the daughter over something that she did wrong

> You might tell me-you don't cry about what happened to you? Rarely do I cry but on matters that concern my daughter – yes. That hurts me because I know- that hurts me because as parents they should have realised that they were doing something to me – that I had no control over, something that I could not fight. A while ago, my husband started getting angry with our daughter – he had come back from work, he was tired and he shouted at her. He tells me that I become a monster when something happens between him and our daughter. I don't even realise that I have lost control. I don't want anyone to shout at her for nothing. I: Are you very protective? P: Yes, a lot. Over-protective - a lot, a lot and this is because of what happened. I feel that this is because of what happened (Claire, p. 26-27).

This quote again further illuminates the implications for clinical practice—that the understanding of one's childhood experiences never stops and different life stages and the related developmental tasks trigger different memories. If these memories are not overwhelming in terms of their distress, they can be used to learn from adversity. At the same time, in such circumstances, the participants also reflected that despite their immense desire to make sure that their children were happy, they could not protect them from everything.

Looking for Turning Points and Examples of Agency and Resilience

Amidst all the suffering that these women went through both as children and as adults, they also recognised the psychological growth which was also part of their experiences (Smith 2013). Even here the dialectic of the trauma (Herman 1997) was apparent—suffering and growth, despair and serenity in the same interview. This, for us highlights the importance of keeping our attention also focused on any incidents, however small, that underline the clients' resilience together with honouring the suffering that they went through in the context of our work with them.

The participants volunteered detailed descriptions of what had been key turning points in their lives.

Change Through Observation, Social Comparison and Feedback as the Women Grew Older

A number of participants mentioned how, as they were growing up, they observed their teachers and modelled on them how they could be different from their mothers as girls and future women. From their teachers' occasional comments about their personal family life, the participants as older children also realised that family dynamics at home could be different and these observations were very meaningful for them. Donna explained how

> It could be that school was so helpful for me because this was the time where I could escape from home, mentally and physically. So in that space….a lot of students say "'what a pain – school!' But I really enjoyed school. It could be that I saw them as role models, no one in particular really. Role model in the sense that you see a woman, smartly dressed, like you know, with earrings, and she is in authority. So probably I used to say: Wow! Look at these!… and you know sometimes, they used to say…. Because my daughter….- and you get a hint about what is happening at their home. And so you say, - these people are serene in their family – serenity and peace does exist. It could be that I did this in secondary school. The guidance teacher was a like a mummy to me and my gosh, I used to observe her a lot. And when they share their personal experiences with you— you know- nothing elaborate, simple things, but for you, it is like they gave you a gift!.. even when they tell you – yes it is like that… they help you say: There are people who think in the same way that I do! Also I was proud of the fact that I did well at

> school, I used to feel…eh…for instance, I used to always want to help out with the books, that kind of role (Donna 2, p. 22-23).

Hannah, too, found her "news of difference" (Bateson 1979, p. 79) in books which she read for her studies The desperation that Hannah read about in women in the Second World War resonated with her desperation about her family situation and she became convinced that she was now responsible for her happiness and she had to be careful in her partner choice so that she does not perpetuate the sadness and desperation that she felt in her childhood into her adulthood. Interestingly, this finding is supported by research which shows that exposure to the literature arts such as poetry and fictional literature provide a novel context for thinking about one's life and identity and thus support the development of coherent life stories by organising personal experiences (Mackenzie 1989):

Such experiences continue to highlight the importance of a systemic approach when working with such families and looking for supportive relationships in the different client sub-system, for example, looking into of the teacher–student relationships and the school system as a venue for change in a person's life (Boyce Rodgers and Rose 2001).

Getting Support/Talking About the Violence, Bringing Things Out in the Open, Cautiously and Slowly

Seeking and getting support was not always very straightforward. In many cases, seeking help and support was met with a number of complicating factors especially when it was the children who were seeking help. However, these factors can also be important for adult survivors of childhood domestic violence experiences. The minimisation of the violence by the mother, the shame of not having a good family like other people had, the fear of reprisal by the father who may have always wanted to keep the violence a secret, and the extended family's fear of the father's violence and their reluctance to get involved all may come into the way of family members talking about their experiences of violence in their family.

The participants also feared that as children, they would be taken away from their mother by professionals, and they would have liked the professionals involved with the family's difficulties to intuit to "read their minds" that there were domestic violence issues, without them having to disclose what was happening at home. However, the participants also spoke about helpful social workers, residential care workers, psychologists, teachers and other mentors, as has been highlighted earlier.

Naming the Childhood Experiences as Domestic Violence

This was another important process. Some of the participants, like Sandra and Mary, spoke about their difficulties of naming their experiences as domestic violence. These participants spoke about their inability to recognise their childhood difficulties as growing up with domestic violence, unless they had help. Mary recalled that it was not until she started working in a domestic violence unit that she realised that what she went through in her family was as a result of domestic violence between her parents and this realisation helped her to start putting the puzzle pieces together:

> I started realising what this experience was all about when I started working in the domestic violence unit and I found myself working there because I had never wanted to work in the DV.., I wanted to work in child protection, with children.., I did not want to work in DV. And then when I found myself in the DV unit, it started dawning on me.., and we're talking about a time when I had already got married and had the children and that I had done my degree and look how long it took me to see it as DV. And there I started learning.., there I started understanding.., when I used to read on dv, and how children experience dv, I started saying.., oh.., this is the same as I used to feel because I had never seen it in this way……And I think, working in dv, reading and studying.., it was therapeutic for me because this was a way, I could understand and when you understand, you contain. (Mary, p. 31–32).

Such reflections perhaps illustrate the extent of the disconnection between the process of experience and the making-meaning process that is difficult for children and adults to do without help from an adult, possibly a social and healthcare worker, or an older sibling to help them make sense of what is happening. Naming and speaking aloud about what has happened are in fact very important starting points— for the processing of experiences, which till then are internal, often "unconscious, unintentional remembrances" (Smith 2013, p. 76).

In summary, the availability of having someone to talk to in their lives, and someone who loved them, someone who had a special place in their hearts for them, someone who went out of their way for them was an important source of resilience. Perhaps it was their mother, a grandparent, a teacher, their psychologist or a relative. All this supports and is supported by the resilience literature (DuMont et al. 2007; Ungar 2013). Perhaps it is in the nature of these relationships, including the therapeutic relationship, that the participants develop their reflective function despite the adversity that they experienced and because of these contexts, they can then start processing some of what they had gone through and gradually draw meaning from it.

Conclusion

The women's process of trying to make sense of their childhood experiences was a recurrent theme in these participants' lives. They talked about how the process was an emerging one that started to develop as they grew older, perhaps when they were likely to have the intellectual and emotional resources to support such understanding and reflection (Mullender et al. 2002). When they were young, they were focused on surviving day by day, which many a times when like trying to predict what was unpredictable (Swanston et al. 2002). As they grew older and with help, they started to embark on a process of naming their experiences, trying to understand the dynamics of their family relationships and some of the seemingly unreconcilable dilemmas.

Practitioners working with such families in turn need to contain the dissonance —responding both to the anger, hurt and possibly cut-off from the parent or sibling who has been abusive—and to their need for connection with the family member who has abused them. In the same way, workers also respond to the suffering of family members as children and adults and validating their sense of agency and their ability to carve out a life that is different than their parents.

References

Abela, A. (1997). *Marital conflict in Malta (Unpublished doctoral dissertation)*. United Kingdom: University of London.

Amato, P. R., & Afifi, T. D. (2006). Feeling caught between parents: Adult children's relations with parents and subjective well-being. *Journal of Marriage and Family, 68*(1), 222–235. doi:10.1111/j.1741-3737.2006.00243.x.

American Psychiatric Association. (2013). *Diagnostic and statistical manual of mental disorders* (5th ed.). Washington, DC: Author.

Asen, E., & Fonagy, P. (2012). Mentalization-based therapeutic interventions for families. *Journal of Family Therapy, 34*(4), 347–370. doi:10.1111/j.1467-6427.2011.00552.x.

Band-Winterstein, T. (2014). The impact of lifelong exposure to IPV on adult children and their aging parents. *Journal of Family Issues, 35*(4), 439–461. doi:10.1177/0192513X12472657.

Bateson, G. (1972). *Steps to an ecology of mind: Collected essays in anthropology, psychiatry, evolution and epistemology*. London, UK: University of Chicago Press.

Bateson, G. (1979). *Mind and nature: A necessary unity*. New York: Dutton.

Bateson, G., Jackson, D. D., Haley, J., & Weakland, J. (1956). Toward a theory of schizophrenia. *Behavioral Science, 1*(4), 251–264. doi:10.1002/bs.3830010402.

Bogat, G. A., Garcia, A. M., & Levendosky, A. A. (2013). Assessment and psychotherapy with women experiencing intimate partner violence: Integrating research and practice. *Psychodynamic Psychiatry, 41*(2), 189–217. doi:10.1521/pdps.2013.41.2.189.

Boszormenyi-Nagy, I., & Spark, G. M. (1973). *Invisible loyalties: Reciprocity in intergenerational family therapy*. Oxford, England: Harper & Row.

Bowlby, J. (1988). *A secure base: Parent-child attachment and healthy human development*. New York: Basic Books.

Boyce Rodgers, K., & Rose, H. A. (2001). Personal, family and school factors related to adolescent academic performance: A comparison by family structure. *Marriage & Family Review, 33*(4), 47–61. doi:10.1300/J002v33n04_05.

Briere, J. N., & Scott, C. (2015). *Principles of trauma therapy. A guide to symptoms, evaluation and treatment. DSM-5 update* (2nd ed.). London, UK: SAGE Publications.

Briere, J. N., & Lanktree, C. B. (2012). *Treating complex trauma in adolescents and young adults*. London, UK: SAGE Publications.

Buehler, C., & Welsh, D. P. (2009). A process model of adolescents' triangulation into parents' marital conflict: The role of emotional reactivity. *Journal of Family Psychology, 23*(2), 167–180. doi:10.1037/a0014976.

Byng-Hall, J. (1998). *Rewriting family scripts: Improvisation and systems change*. London, UK: The Guilford Press.

Byng-Hall, J. (2002). Relieving parentified children's burdens in families with insecure attachment patterns. *Family Process, 41*(3), 375–388. doi:10.1111/j.1545-5300.2002.41307.x.

Byng-Hall, J. (2008). The significance of children fulfilling parental roles: Implications for family therapy. *Journal of Family Therapy, 30*(2), 147–162. doi:10.1111/j.1467-6427.2008.00423.x.

Cassar, C. (2003). *Honour and shame in the Mediterranean*. Malta: Midseabooks.

Catherall, D. R. (Ed.). (2005). *Family stressors: Interventions for stress and trauma*. New York: Routledge.

Chang, L., Schwartz, D., Dodge, K. A., & McBride-Chang, C. (2003). Harsh parenting in relation to child emotion regulation and aggression. *Journal of Family Psychology, 17*(4), 598–606. doi:10.1037/0893-3200.17.4.598.

Chase, N. D. (Ed.). (1999). *Burdened children: Theory, research, and treatment of parentification*. CA, US: Guilford.

Connell, R. W. (2005). *Masculinities* (2nd ed.). Berkeley: University of California Press.

Cooper, J., & Vetere, A. (2005). *Domestic violence and family safety: A systemic approach to working with violence in families*. London, UK: Whurr Publishers.

Courtois, C. A., & Ford, J. D. (2013). *Treatment of complex trauma: A sequenced, relationship-based approach*. New York: The Guilford Press.

Crittenden, P. M. (2008). *Raising parents: Attachment, parenting and child safety*. Devon, UK: Willan Publishing.

Crittenden, P. M., & Kulbotten, G. R. (2007). Familial contributions to ADHD: An attachment perspective. *Tidsskrift for Norsk Psykologforening, 44*(10), 1220–1229. Retrieved from http://www.psykologtidsskriftet.no/?seks_id=31533&a=2.

Dallos, R., & Vetere, A. (2009). *Systemic therapy and attachment narratives: Applications in a range of clinical settings*. London, UK: Routledge.

Dallos, R., & Vetere, A. (2012). Systems theory, family attachments and processes of triangulation: Does the concept of triangulation offer a useful bridge? *Journal of Family Therapy, 34*(2), 117–137. doi:10.1111/j.1467-6427.2011.00554.x.

DeBoard-Lucas, R. L., Fosco, G. M., Raynor, S. R., & Grych, J. H. (2010). Interparental conflict in context: Exploring relations between parenting processes and children's conflict appraisals. *Journal of Clinical Child and Adolescent Psychology, 39*(2), 163–175. doi:10.1080/15374410903532593.

Diamond, M. (1995). Biological aspects of sexual orientation and identity. In L. Diamant & R. D. McAnulty (Eds.), *The psychology of sexual orientation, behavior and identity: A handbook* (pp. 45–80). Westport, CT: Greenwood Press.

DuMont, K. A., Widom, C. S., & Czaja, S. J. (2007). Predictors of resilience in abused and neglected children grown-up: The role of individual and neighborhood characteristics. *Child Abuse and Neglect, 31*(3), 255–274. doi:10.1016/j.chiabu.2005.11.015.

Earley, L., & Cushway, D. (2002). The parentified child. *Clinical Child Psychology and Psychiatry, 7*(2), 163–178. doi:10.1177/1359104502007002005.

Fosco, G. M., & Grych, J. H. (2010). Adolescent triangulation into parental conflicts: Longitudinal implications for appraisals and adolescent-parent relations. *Journal of Marriage and Family, 72*(2), 254–266. doi:10.1111/j.1741-3737.2010.00697.x.

Gerard, J. M., Buehler, C., Franck, K., & Anderson, O. (2005). In the eyes of the beholder: Cognitive appraisals as mediators of the association between interparental conflict and youth maladjustment. *Journal of Family Psychology, 19*(3), 376–384. doi:10.1037/0893-3200.19.3.376.

Gibney, P. (2006). The double bind theory: Still crazy-making after all these years. *Psychotherapy in Australia, 12*(3), 48–55. Retrieved from http://www.psychotherapy.com.au/fileadmin/site_files/pdfs/TheDoubleBindTheory.pdf.

Gorell Barnes, G., & Henessy, S. (1995). Reclaiming a female mind from the experience of child sexual abuse: A developing conversation between writers and editors. In C. Burck & B. Speed (Eds.), *Gender, power and relationships* (pp. 69–85). London, UK: Routledge.

Herman, J. L. (1997). *Trauma and recovery: The aftermath of violence–from domestic abuse to political terror*. New York, NY: BasicBooks.

Hlazo-Tawodzera, C. N. (2006). *Narratives of sexual orientation: Towards an understanding of how individual women come to know themselves as lesbian, heterosexual, bisexual, asexual and/or in other ways (Unpublished doctoral dissertation)*. London, UK: University of East London & Tavistock Clinic.

Johnson, D. R. (2004). Critical interaction therapy with couples. In D. R. Catherall (Ed.), *Handbook of stress, trauma, and the family* (pp. 513–532). New York, NY: Brunner-Routledge.

Jory, B., Anderson, D., & Greer, C. (1997). Intimate justice: Confronting issues of accountability, respect, and freedom in treatment for abuse and violence. *Journal of Marital & Family Therapy, 23*(4), 399–419. doi:10.1111/j.1752-0606.1997.tb01053.x.

Jurkovic, G. J., Jessee, E., & Goglia, L. R. (1991). Treatment of parental children and their families: Conceptual and technical issues. *The American Journal of Family Therapy, 19*(4), 302–314. doi:10.1080/01926189108250862.

Kaufmann, J. (Ed.). (2002). *Loss of the assumptive world: A theory of traumatic loss*. London, UK: Routledge.

Lawrence, J. A. (2014). Managing dissonance: Implications for therapeutic practice with partner668 violence. *Partner Abuse, 5*(2), 119–151. doi:10.1891/1946-6560.5.2.119.

Mackenzie, P. (1989). The contribution of 'story' to children's development. *Early Child Development and Care, 46*(1), 63–75. doi:10.1080/0300443890460106.

Mikulincer, M., Shaver, P. R., & Pereg, D. (2003). Attachment theory and affect regulation: The dynamics, development, and cognitive consequences of attachment-related strategies. *Motivation and Emotion, 27*(2), 77–102. doi:10.1023/A:1024515519160.

Mikulincer, M., & Goodman, G. S. (Eds.). (2006). *Dynamics of romantic love: Attachment, caregiving, and sex*. London, UK: The Guilford Press.

Minuchin, S. (1974). *Families and family therapy*. Oxford, England: Harvard University Press.

Moretti, M. M. M., Bartolo, T., Craig, S., Slaney, K., & Odgers, C. (2014). Gender and the transmission of risk: A prospective study of adolescent girls exposed to maternal versus paternal interparental violence. *Journal of Research on Adolescence, 24*(1), 80–92. doi:10.1111/jora.12065.

Mullender, A., Hague, G., Imam, U., Kelly, L., Malos, E., & Regan, L. (2002). *Children's perspectives on domestic violence*. London, UK: SAGE Publications.

Nielsen, L. (2014). Young adult daughters' relationships with their fathers: Review of recent research. *Marriage & Family Review, 50*(4), 360–372. doi:10.1080/01494929.2013.879553.

Peled, E. (2000). Parenting by men who abuse women: Issues and dilemmas. *The British Journal of Social Work, 30*(1), 25–36. doi:10.1093/bjsw/30.1.25.

Rivett, M., Howarth, E., & Harold, G. (2006). 'Watching from the stairs': Towards an evidence-based practice in work with child witnesses of domestic violence. *Clinical Child Psychology and Psychiatry, 11*(1), 103–125. doi:10.1177/1359104506059131.

Sammut Scerri, C. (2015). *Living with contradictions of love and violence: A grounded theory study of women's understanding of their childhood experiences of domestic violence*. (Doctoral dissertation). University of Surrey, Guildford, United Kingdom.

Smith, G. (2013). *Working with trauma: Systemic Approaches*. London, UK: Palgrave Macmillan.

Swanston, H. Y., Parkinson, P. N., Oates, R. K., O'Toole, B. I., Plunkett, A. M., & Shrimpton, S. (2002). Further abuse of sexually abused children. *Child Abuse and Neglect, 26*(2), 115–127. doi:10.1016/S0145-2134(01)00311-8.

Ungar, M. (2013). Resilience, trauma, context, and culture. *Trauma, Violence, & Abuse, 14*(3), 255–266. doi:10.1117/1524838013487805.

Van der Kolk, B. A. (2007). The complexity of adaptation to trauma: Self-regulation, stimulus discrimination and characterological development. In B. A. van der Kolk, A. C. McFarlane, & L. Weisaeth (Eds.), *Traumatic stress: The effects of overwhelming experience on mind, body, and society* (pp. 182–213). London, UK: The Guilford Press.

Van der Kolk, B. (2014). *The body keeps the score: Brain, mind, and body in the healing of trauma*. New York, NY: Viking Penguin.

Van der Kolk, B. A., McFarlane, A. C., & van der Hart, O. (2007). A general approach to treatment of posttraumatic stress disoder. In B. A. van der Kolk, A. C. McFarlane, & L.

Weisaeth (Eds.), *Traumatic stress: The effects of overwhelming experience on mind, body, and society* (pp. 417–440). London, UK: The Guilford Press.
Watzlawick, P., Beavin, J. H., & Jackson, D. D. (1967). *Pragmatics of human communication: A study of interactional patterns, pathologies, and paradoxes*. New York: W. W. Norton.
Whiffen, V. E., & Oliver, L. E. (2004). The relationship between traumatic stress and marital intimacy. In D. R. Catherall (Ed.), *Handbook of stress, trauma, and the family* (pp. 139–160). New York, NY: Brunner-Routledge.
Widom, C. S. (1989a). Does violence beget violence? A critical examination of the literature. *Psychological Bulletin, 106*(1), 3–28. doi:10.1037/0033-2909.106.1.3.
Widom, C. S. (1989b). The cycle of violence. *Science, 244*(4901), 160–166. doi:10.1126/science.2704995.

Chapter 3
How to Help Stop the Violence: Using a Safety Methodology Across the Life Span

Introduction

This chapter outlines a systemic safety methodology for safe relationship therapy with couples, parents and families where physical violence is of concern. A step-by-step guide is offered here for the first time in publication. This systemic approach to safety in family relationships was developed over 20 years in the Reading, UK, 'Safer Families' family violence intervention service and is grounded in relevant theory and research (Cooper and Vetere 2005; Vetere 2012, 2015). The safety methodology has a number of features: (a) it is based in a tailored safety plan designed to help predict and prevent violent escalations in family members' interactions; (b) it involves liaison and cooperation with the family–professional network and creates a safe 'watching' network; (c) it holds family members responsible for their behaviour that harms others, and for safety; (d) it pays attention to the intergenerational and developmental legacy of violence in the family, including trauma responses; and (e) it promotes healing and repair in family relationships where possible. Whilst 'healing and repair' in relationships is the main feature of Chap. 4, this chapter will outline the role of relationship repair and the necessary skills in the context of ending the violence and finding ways to go on.

Sometimes a couple will decide to separate once the physical violence has stopped—it is as if living with violence and the energy needed to cope emotionally is so overwhelming and preoccupying of our mental capacities, that we do not reflect on the meaning of the relationship and whether we wish to continue in the relationship until it is safe enough to do so. In this chapter, we suggest ways in which we can support couples in managing a safe separation. We also include findings from research on what constitutes a good outcome in this therapeutic work, from the different perspectives of family members, therapists, managers and commissioners of services. The chapter ends with an outline of the contraindications for relationship therapy with couples and families.

C. Sammut Scerri et al., *Intervening After Violence*,
Focused Issues in Family Therapy, DOI 10.1007/978-3-319-57789-0_3

The systemic safety methodology outlined in this chapter differs from other published approaches in that it is both theoretically and practically integrative and interdisciplinary in its approach, whereas other approaches tend to be dominated by one or two theoretical frameworks and focused on unidisciplinary practice.

Steps Towards Safety: An Overview of Safety Planning with Couples and Families Where Physical Violence Is of Concern

> …a wide variety of interventions appear to reduce or eliminate IPV among perpetrators and victims. Thus, there is no empirical justification for agencies, state organisations, judges, mental health professionals, or others involved in improving the lives of those impacted by IPV to limit the type of services offered to clients, or to restrict the theoretical and ideological underpinnings of such methods…..practitioners and policy makers should consider and attempt to implement a variety of different intervention methods for both perpetrators and victims in order to reduce IPV. (Eckhardt et al. 2013)

Our Safety Methodology: The risk of future violence, responsibility for violence and for safety and collaborative practice.

We work therapeutically with couples and families to help them stop physical and emotional violence in their intimate relationships. Over the past 20 years of practice in our dedicated family violence intervention service, we have developed a visible safety methodology for safe therapeutic practice with couple and family relationships. We are both systemic psychotherapists, and Arlene is also a clinical psychologist, and Jan is a former social worker. During this time, we have been invited to both supervise and train other practitioners, in the health and social care professions, in the public and voluntary sector areas of practice. One question we are repeatedly asked is—can you tell us more about the steps in your safety methodology? Or, how do we know we are doing it right? In writing this chapter, we are responding to this request, albeit with some caution. This is because we do not wish to be overly prescriptive as we recognise that practitioners need to develop their own approach and style of working. Similarly, violence in all its forms, in our intimate relationships is complex and multifaceted both in explanation and in finding solutions. We have found we need to formulate interpersonal violence within an integrative theoretical framework and use a range of therapeutic approaches and responses to assessment and treatment, under a systemic 'umbrella'. Thus this work does not easily lend itself to detailed specification.

Our approach to safety in therapeutic relationship work is grounded in a systemic understanding of the triangular relationship between the risk of future violence, responsibility for behaviour that harms others, and collaborative practice. We have written extensively of our safety methodology for relationship therapy elsewhere (Vetere and Cooper 2001; Cooper and Vetere 2005: Vetere 2011, 2012). In this chapter, we shall briefly summarise our method of working before moving on to the key aspects of our safety methodology, finally offering the 'requested' overview of our initial six safety planning meetings with the couple and or family.

In thinking about our method of working, we took into account the fact that this client group has often been the subject of intense negative scrutiny. Therefore, it seemed most appropriate to work together in the therapy room and combine 'live supervision' with a 'reflecting process'. We divide the work equally between the role of lead therapist and in-room consultant with the lead therapist doing most of the talking and the in-room consultant making notes and reflecting on the process. This means that both therapists are equally responsible for the session. Each therapist in turn changing their roles with each new referral. In this way, this particular weave of questions, discussion, reflection and note taking provides a collaborative process and a shared commitment to safety and change.

The 'lead therapist' is in many ways the manager of the session, outlining the policy of confidentiality and establishing the no-violence contract supported by the in-room consultant. She will ask the in-room consultant from time to time for comments so both therapists can discuss a particular issue in front of the family and then ask for their feedback. Contrastingly, the in 'room consultant' has essentially a listening role, which means that she can reflect on the process in the room and also translate that into the written word. There is an intellectual rigour that goes with the in-room consultant's task while at the same time maintaining a readiness to be able to contribute to the conversation in the room. These different positions allow for differences in perception, emotional responsiveness and intention as well as opinion in the therapist's discussion and feedback between sessions. We always offer a minimum of six meetings with family members to establish whether a safety plan can work or not (Fig. 3.1).

We shall summarise the key aspects of our safety methodology first, before offering the 'requested' overview of our initial six safety planning meetings with the couple and/or family. We work together in the room with the couple or the family, with one of us taking the role of lead therapist, and the other taking the role of in-room consultant. We change roles when we start working with a new couple or family. We offer a minimum of six meetings with family members to establish whether a safety plan can work.

Managing the Risk of Further Violence

We separate our consideration of the risk of further violence in family relationships into both the management of risk and the assessment of risk. We manage the risk of further violence by establishing a no-violence contract with the family, which can be written or spoken, and by identifying the risks for interpersonal violence as part of the safety plan with agreed safety strategies. We aim to help couples and family members understand, predict, de-escalate and prevent unhelpful and dangerous

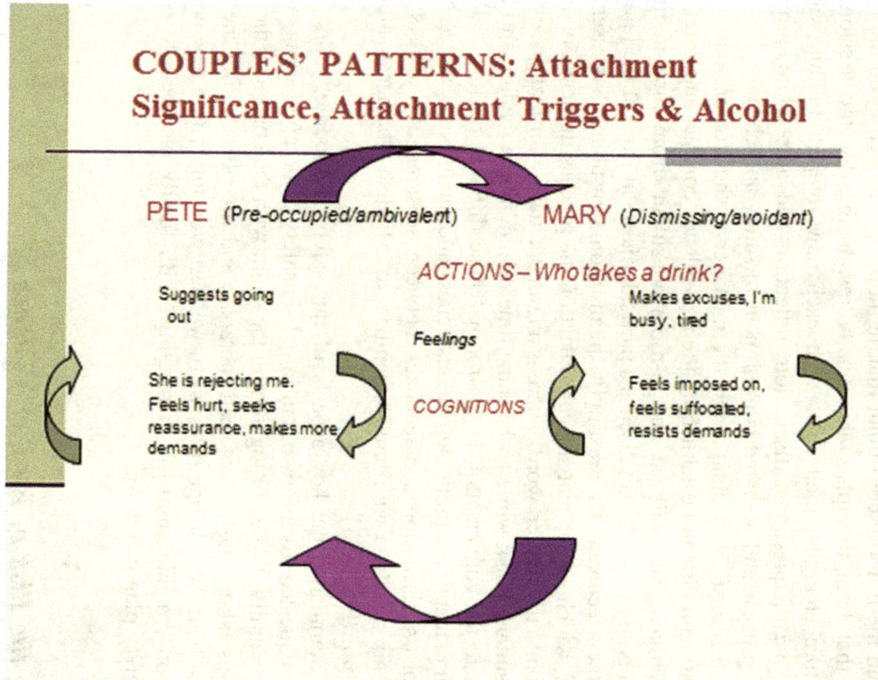

Fig. 3.1 Example of systemic tracking of a couples' interaction pattern

patterns of interactions, and to promote more realistic problem solving and satisfying relationships.

We work with the worst or last episode of violence to understand the triggers for violent behaviour, both internal, such as, attachment-based fears (for example, threats of rejection or abandonment, fears of shaming, feeling invisible and unheard by attachment figures) and non-conscious trauma triggers, (for example, implicit procedural and sensory memory resonances) and external triggers, such as stress at work, debt, conflict in the wider family and problems for children in school. Whilst tracking the escalation of unhelpful arousal and behaviour in the chosen episode of violence, we are also looking for family members' resources, such as, examples of resilient responding, previous attempts to stop the violence, the intention to do things differently and better for your own family than was done for you, and those people in the family and social community who are trusted as confidantes.

We systemically track the chosen episode of violence as a pattern of interaction between the couple or family members, including thought, feeling, intention and action, to help understand how the violence occurs and what happens next. We track this episode slowly and carefully, and continue to refer to it. We draw the pattern on a large sheet of paper, use colour as appropriate, and use it as a joint focus of attention for ourselves and the family. We find that drawing these patterns literally helps family members 'see' what is happening over and above talking about it. We are trying to actualise all representational systems of memory (thought, feeling, action and intention) when we do this tracking, so all of a person's mental resources can be at their disposal. (As an important caveat, we recognise that systemic tracking of patterning in relationships carries the risk of holding all participants equally responsible for the violence, so at the same time, we are constructing and enabling conversations of responsibility—responsibility for behaviour that harms others and responsibility for safety—we elaborate this further below.)

We help people to understand and manage their emotional responses and unhelpful physiological arousal and to challenge entitlement based self-talk, i.e. the entitlement to control others and to treat them as you wish. We ask questions that help people to understand how their bodies function when physically tense and unhelpfully physiologically aroused, and to learn how to calm and soothe themselves. This can be very difficult for some people who were never helped as children to learn to comfort and soothe themselves when unhelpfully aroused, or to understand and manage their emotional lives. If family members use drugs and/or alcohol to help them manage difficult and unbearable feelings, we require them to attend our local drugs and alcohol service at the same time. We work alongside the alcohol key worker to help families understand and change the emotional dynamics and contexts that may trigger and maintain violent responses. Many people we meet do not pay attention to their own safety, believe themselves undeserving of safety, believe themselves deserving of assault and punishment and may have no embodied sense of what physical and emotional safety feels like. We stay alert to trauma responses, especially those that are masked and misunderstood. Thus, we also track how this felt lack of entitlement to emotional safety developed, and what happened to them when they were growing up for this to develop.

Initial safety strategies in the safety plan usually involve the use of 'time out', because when we are physiologically flooded, we often need to take ourselves away from others in order to begin to calm down. 'Time out' has to be agreed by all family members, and 'time out' can be called by any family member, regardless of whether they perpetrate violence or are victimised by violence. Rehearsal is key to a successful safety plan, because when people are anxious, afraid and unhelpfully aroused, people are not creative problem solvers—they become preoccupied by their own arousal, information processing slows down, and reading relationship cues becomes harder. So rehearsal gives people a good chance of remembering the safety plan when they need it. We anticipate where people will take 'time out' and what they will do to soothe themselves and to calm down. We help people expand their repertoire of coping responses. We often suggest they do not return to the argument or disagreement that triggered the violent behaviour, but rather bring it to us, so we can support them in problem solving in a safer, calmer context. We explore how they reconnect after 'time out' so that they can resolve and heal any hurt, disappointment or loss. Clearly effective problem solving and repair in relationships is the longer term strategy for safety for the couple and family.

We offer a minimum of six meetings with family members to establish whether a safety plan can work.

The role of the stable third. Our approach to safety in family relationships needs to be highly visible to all members of the professional network and the family system. Such visibility helps reassure others that we take safety seriously and helps manage their anxiety about therapeutic practice with families where violence is of concern. All our safety planning is done with the help of a stable third or our referrer, i.e. someone who knows the couple and the children, visits the family home, and can corroborate what the family members tell us about safety and the cessation of violence.

We actualise the systemic theory of triangular relationships to form a secure base for our work with the family/couple: ourselves, the family or couple and the stable third (Dallos and Vetere 2012; Vetere and Dallos 2009). The stable third helps us plan for safety in relationships based in their knowledge of the family and their commitment to the process. We do not work without someone in the stable third position—often this can be a social worker, but it could be someone trusted within the family–professional system (e.g. a faith leader, community worker, grandparent, etc.) The stable third attends our first or second meeting with the family and then our third or fourth meeting to help us review the safety plan. We liaise closely and carefully with the professional network involved with the family, because if they do not trust us to take safety seriously, they will not support our work with the family. Thus, our approach to safety and safety planning needs to be visible to all.

The crucial attachment significance of comforting in family relationships. The accessibility and responsiveness of other family members, when we are frightened or distressed, form the building blocks of trust (Gottman 2011). When we are upset and frightened, the sound of a reassuring voice, a kind smile and a cuddle are sometimes the only responses that calm us down. The safety planning addresses each family member's capacity to comfort and soothe themselves, and to de-escalate unhelpful physiological and emotional arousal, in constructive ways. Many people we work with were not comforted as children, and may have learned to use psychoactive substances to escape unbearable feelings of shame, fear and sadness (Vetere 2014). So, comforting and the giving and receiving of reassurance are at the heart of a felt experience of safety in our close relationships.

Opening up and exploring a conversation around comfort can be poignant for people who have learned not to trust others. From a systemic perspective, we help develop the conversation by asking about intergenerational learning in families—how do we mutually influence each other across the generations, and teach and learn in families, about caregiving, care receiving and so on. So, we might start by asking the parents to reflect on their childhood experience—'when you were upset, or frightened, as a child, what happened?'. 'How did you get to feel better?' 'Who helped you do this?' 'What have you learnt from this for your own family?' If this conversation is too emotionally painful, we might ask what they think their parents (or carers) learned from their parents, i.e. by going back one more generation in the conversation, to give more emotional distance. We ask what they want to do the same, and what they want to do differently—how do they comfort each other in their own family and how do they comfort their children. We also explore how children learn to comfort their parents and what happens if this relationship becomes unbalanced for the children. Finally, we ask systemic questions about the future of the children and the parents' aspirations for them—for example, what do you hope your children will learn from you about comforting, and for the future of their children?

Assessing the Risk of Further Violence

Our assessment of the risk of future physical violence involves consideration of episodes of repeat violence and the contexts in which violence occurs, for example, at home, at work, in the street, at the sports hall, and so on, and in what relationships. We assess family members' ability to regulate their affect and their unhelpful physiological arousal. If in our view, a family member has an untreated substance use problem, we insist they access the help of our local substance use service, with permission for us to liaise closely. We look for the capacity for emotional empathy, i.e. to stand in the emotional shoes of the other, the ability to reflect on and learn from experience, and some recognition that violence is a problem and has to stop. If a family member continues to blame others and will not acknowledge that their violent behaviour both harms others and impacts in their family relationships, we will not offer relationship therapy, although we might offer individualised support.

We draw a distinction between violent behaviour that occurs in the context of unhelpful and unregulated physiological arousal, albeit accompanied by 'entitlement self talk' (i.e. how dare she look at me like this—why is my dinner not on the table, and so on) and violence that appears solely designed to control and coerce others, i.e. calculated, cool, instrumental aggression. Clearly, aggression in the context of dysregulated arousal may also be designed to coerce and control, but that may not be the sole intention. Our respective trainings and our joint training as family therapists equips us to help people understand and manage their affect and to challenge beliefs about the entitlement to treat others as they wish. We are not forensically trained, so we do not work therapeutically with aggression that is primarily instrumental.

We offer an example of an apparent inability to reflect on experience. A child protection social worker asked us to meet a family of two parents and two daughters, aged 6 and 8 years for an assessment of safe parenting. The paediatrician had referred the family to social care because the 8-year-old girl had a raised and reddened scalp, as if someone had lifted her by her hair and swung her by her body weight. The father said he did not do it and his wife did not do it. The mother said she did not do it and her husband did not do it. The girls said nothing. When we met the parents, the father told us there was no point in asking him about his childhood and his experiences of being parented because he could remember nothing before the age of 18. As far as we knew, there was no organic or traumatic reason for such global memory loss. Thus, our systemic response was to carefully track the consequences of not remembering, for him as a father now, and for his development as a father. For example, if you do not remember your childhood and adolescent experiences, what has helped you become a father? Who has helped you? What did you learn? How did you learn, and so on.

In another example, we offer the story of a couple where the husband was unable to manage and regulate his arousal and agitation. This also offers a potent example of how the ability to read and write is a source of power and influence in a couple relationship. The wife could read and write and the husband could not—and we did not know this. We made an assumption they could both do this. In making this mistake, we also learned how to pay more attention to this relationship dynamic. The social worker referred the couple to us for a safety assessment. The wife was pregnant with their first child. Apparently they had had a terrible argument, and he has physically assaulted her, putting both the wife and the unborn child at risk of serious harm. The child protection system was considering the possibility of removing their child at birth, so understandably, they were both anxious and afraid. We sent them a letter inviting them to meet us at our office, enclosing a map. They had an argument before coming to meet us, and on the way they got lost. They stopped at a petrol station and he asked her to go inside and ask for directions. She was still angry with him and refused to go inside. To his credit, he did go and ask for help, and apparently the cashier laughed and said, 'Can't you see—it's right there!' They had stopped outside our office without realising. We imagine the cashier's laugh was a polite, silly laugh but the husband experienced the laugh as deeply shaming—as if the cashier knew he could not read and write and was laughing at him. So, when the husband came into the waiting room, he was highly agitated and disturbed the others in the waiting room. The receptionist was troubled by this and asked us to see him immediately. It took us over an hour to help him calm down and tell us what had happened. Under those circumstances, we considered it was too dangerous to meet them together as a couple.

Developing Responsibility for our Behaviour that Harms Others: Holding Ourselves Accountable

We support and encourage family members to take responsibility for safety, for themselves and for others, and for their behaviour that harms others. We recognise our responsibility to help family members stop the violence, and their responsibility to stop it. We explore the relational and intergenerational impacts of violence in the family, such as unresolved trauma reactions and unresolved losses, the experience of well-being, problems with interactive affect regulation and other developmental impacts for all family members and for their relationships. We look for corrective and replicative scripts as examples of intergenerational learning in families, i.e. the conscious intentions and attempts to do things better in their family than was done for them in their childhoods, and/or the intention to repeat patterns of caregiving in an unquestioning way (Byng Hall 1995).

Too often we hear that violent means of influence, coercion and control are accepted or trivialised in so many families we work with in our project. When we encounter such 'taken-for-granted' beliefs about how we treat people and/or expect to be treated in our family relationships, we take a step back and invite family members to deconstruct with us how these beliefs have come to be so pervasively held. We always ask, 'What happened to you…..that you grew up believing you deserved to be hit? Or, ….that you grew up believing you are entitled to hit people, and treat them as you choose?'. Family members, especially parents, also talk about 'corrective scripts'—their reflections on how they were brought up and their attempts to do things differently for their relationships and for their children. Paradoxically, the intention to make things better for the next generation is often not enough—it is as if parents do not have a template for what safety in a relationship might look like, or feel like, in an embodied sense. They may not know what to do to make things safe in the family and for the family. We always notice and affirm family members' intentions to look after safety differently to how it was for them as children or for their own parents—we give people credit for trying, whilst recognising that being a pioneer in the family and challenging practices of caretaking that involve harsh and physical methods of discipline is never easy or straightforward. Ironically, this is further complicated in that we are more likely to ask for help as parents in looking after our children, when we are in safe and secure relationships, rather than we feel uncertain, psychologically threatened and defensive. We try to help parents and family members move out of a defensive stance by asking systemic future questions (Penn 1985).

For example, we might ask a father who has physically assaulted his son, the following future oriented questions in his role as a father: 'John, as a father, when your son becomes a man, and perhaps a father in his own right, what do you hope your son will learn from you about how to keep his children safe? 'John, as a father, when your daughter becomes a woman and perhaps marries a man, what do you want her to learn from you about how to keep herself safe?'.

Family members who live in an emotional context of constant and chronic over arousal are often likely to find themselves overwhelmed, cognitively, emotionally and practically. This leaves little mental space for curiosity and reflection and leads to over simplified explanations of other family members' behaviour, such as blaming statements like, 'he is a cold fish', or 'she is the problem'. Such blaming of others when confronted with frightening and complex family dynamics and events is more likely under these circumstances, and also then likely to become patterned, ingrained and subsequently taken-for-granted as a person's identity. In our initial six safety planning sessions, we try to help people soften from a blaming and defensive stance, so that they can develop some empathic curiosity about their own and others' actions. If after six meetings, a family member continues to blame others for their own behaviour and struggles to recognise the impact of their behaviour on themselves, on others and in their relationships, we would consider this a clear contraindication for systemic relationship therapy. Instead, we would offer another response, such as individual therapy, group therapy, or perhaps a legal response.

We do not meet the children with their parents/carers during the six initial safety planning meetings, until we are convinced the adults are taking safety seriously. We might meet the children separately or as a sibling group, depending on the referral or the Family Court instruction. We talk with the children about their understanding of safety and may well do a safety planning meeting with the children, or advise other professionals, for example, school teachers, on how to talk with the children about their safety (Cooper and Vetere 2005; Vetere and Cooper 2017). We are influenced by the work of Hester, Pearson and Harwin (2000) in this regard. We speak with the children about the frequency of violent episodes, the last episode of violence, and about the details they remember. We ask if weapons were used or threatened and if substance use is involved. We ask if their mother, or other family members, have been locked in a room and/or prevented from leaving the house. We ask if the police have ever come to their house and what happened. We ask what the children do during an episode of violence, whether they try and intervene, and what happens. We ask where the siblings are during a violent assault. Based on this information, we check who the child can go to and talk about what happens, if they have a safe place to go to, and if they know how to contact emergency services.

Although we try to impress upon children that it is neither safe nor their responsibility to intervene to protect family members during a violent episode, we recognise the double bind that traps and constrains children's choices. In our experience, it can be the children who take responsibility for safety when a family member or members behave with physical violence, for example, they may call the police, or run to the neighbours and ask for help. This history of taking responsibility can lead to some distress for children and adolescents when they take shelter in a domestic abuse refuge/hostel with their mothers. Here, the children are excluded from safety planning meetings because the staff wish them to reconnect with more age appropriate childhood activities and responsibilities. However, some children argue that they were the ones who looked after safety so they wish to know what is happening in the safety planning meetings and to make a further contribution to family safety.

We talk with parents about the effects on their children's development and well-being as a result of exposure to violence in family and community relationships. We ask, what are the children learning? Sometimes we meet mothers who tell us that they 'take' the violence from their adult partners and that they protect their children from knowing. These are poignant conversations when we challenge the mothers' attempts to comfort themselves with the idea that their children do not know about the violence. We talk about the research that estimates that upwards of three-quarters of all violent incidents in the home are witnessed in some way by the children, whether they are hiding in another room, sitting on the stairs and listening, or actively intervening to protect their mothers (Moffitt and Caspi 1998). We tell parents that we believe from our experience that the children always know, although they might not know the details. Children are acutely sensitive both to the well-being of the parents/carers looking after them and crucially to the well-being of the parent's relationship. Some children may be traumatised by their exposure to violence in the family and their behavioural and psychological responses may be both misunderstood and misdiagnosed if fear is not understood to be at the heart of their difficulties. The impact on children has been well documented to include: somatic symptoms, lack of interest in activities, regressive behaviour changes, lack of interest in activities, difficulties falling asleep and staying asleep, nightmares, numbing and inability to comfort self, repetitive play, distractibility, poor concentration, constant moving about and a high activity level (Perry and Szalavitz 2006).

Finally, in helping people to take responsibility for their behaviour, we pay close attention to how people talk about and describe their violent behaviour, for example, do they use language that minimises their violence, for example, a person might say—'I only hit him', or, 'I just hit her'. We notice how the words 'only' and 'just' minimise the impact of their behaviour and its effects. So we respond by asking about 'only' and 'just', for example, we might ask, 'If I was there, what would I see? What does 'only' look like? Where did you hit him? How did you hit him? What did you hit him with? How many times did you hit him? What did he do? What happened next?' And so on. In this way, we slowly walk around in the descriptions of violent behaviour and make clear their actions and their impact. In another example of minimisation, a woman might say, 'Well, things were a little tense'. She has a broken jaw. A father who physically assaulted his daughter in an argument with her, told us, 'She knows I love her, the silly cow, she knows I won't hit her again'. We would ask, 'What does she know?'. The father has put the knowledge he will not hit her again in the framework of love, whereas, she has been hit—so that is what she knows.

As well as tracking and catching the use of minimising language, we also listen for the use of the active voice and the language of personal agency, for example, if a partner says, 'I hit him', we have agency—a noun, an action verb and an object. We support these agentic descriptions of behaviour that harm others. When we hear the use of the passive voice in language, we challenge it. For example, a man might say of his angry and aggressive outburst—'the red mist came down'. Again, our response would be to walk around in the red mist and ask, 'What is the red mist? Where does it come from? What do you do with it? How do you make it go away?' And so on, thus supporting the use of the active voice when talking about violent behaviour. A man said to us, 'How can you hold me responsible for what I have done to my children, if you only knew what my father did to me?' We would responded with compassion for his childhood experience and let him know we wanted to hear his story AND we hold him accountable for his behaviour towards his children, to whom he has the responsibility of care as their father.

In these ways, we see most clearly how we interweave conversations about explanation for violence and why it happens, and taking responsibility for violence and safety. Thus explanation for violence cannot be used to escape responsibility or slide away from it (Goldner et al. 1990).

Collaborative Practices

Finally, in this brief overview of our safety methodology, we encourage and support collaborative practices with the family and within the family–professional network. We aim to be transparent with family members about our relationship with social control and how we work within the legal framework of child protection, for example, what we do in our work, who we know in the professional network and who we talk to about safety in the families we work with. We are clear that we believe that all of us are entitled to live without fear of the people we love. In so saying, we also recognise the emotional and attachment related dilemmas that can beset us all. We acknowledge our own moral dilemmas around violence and that as parents ourselves, we have engaged with and struggled over issues such as the bullying of our children at school. We acknowledge that there are different and contradictory discourses around violence and discrimination at different levels of our society. Our responsibility is to help family members stop the physical and emotional violence, and their responsibility is to stop, and to accept support in finding more mutually satisfying ways of healing and bonding in relationships.

As described above, we use a reflecting process in the room when we work with families, both during assessment and therapy, and in this way undertake to make our thinking known to all. One of us works as the lead therapist and the other as the in-room consultant, keeping the roles constant for the same family. We make a commitment to talking about risk and safety in front of the family and not when they are out of the room. We do not think there are easy solutions to the problems of violence, but our systemic practice is to identify the issues and continue to discuss them as straightforwardly and directly as we can, in the belief that a solution is more likely to emerge as a result.

We do not offer confidentiality in our work with couples and family members rather we agree to negotiate confidentiality when we know that the information told to us does not pertain to family safety. Finally, and crucially, we support families in their ability to see professionals in the child care network as potentially helpful to them and their family, and to sustain their ability to cooperate with the professional network during what can often be a lengthy and bruising emotional process. If this is all we do, so to say, we consider we have helped the family. The experience of living in the goldfish bowl of others' (sometimes hostile) scrutiny is wearing, demoralising and sometimes, demotivating. Supporting family members in understanding how complex professional networks function, understanding the various roles and responsibilities of the workers, and in finding advocacy when intimidated within the professional network, can be enough to sustain their cooperation and more active involvement in finding solutions for themselves and their families.

Overview of the Minimum of Six Safety Planning Sessions

The above summary of our method of working and safety planning methodology is provided to contextualise the oft requested overview of our six minimum safety planning and assessment meetings that we outline below. When working with individuals, couples and families, we present ideas, strategies and information around safety planning as much as possible in the form of questions. We find questions and questioning a prompt to thought and reflection, and they help both the therapists and the family to not reach for certainty too quickly. However, we would caution again that the overview offered below can only ever be a draft, and needs to incorporate the contraindications for relationship therapy work with couples and families presented at the end of this chapter.

We suggest you create your own safety plan with the couple/family, tailored to their specific circumstances, and make decisions as you go along, guided by listening and by feedback. This helps to develop a trusting and working partnership between the therapist, the family members and the stable third. The stable third might attend sessions 1 or 2 or 3, or 4 as agreed.

It is always helpful to meet family members separately and together. If possible, we try to begin by meeting both partners/parents together. If violence has been discussed in other professional meetings before people come to us, we may have an idea that it is safe to start by acknowledging what we know. If the violence is suspected and not talked about previously, we would welcome the couple/parents together, explain our approach, meet them separately to check on safety as far as we can, then meet together to agree a contract. Thus our initial six meetings might follow this schedule: meet one partner/parent; meet the other partner/parent; meet both partners/parents together; meet the children separately, and when the safety plan appears to work,... meet the children with parents; and include the 'stable third' at meetings 1 or 2, and 3 or 4.

The six sessions could, of course, involve just meeting parents/partners with a view to establishing a safety plan and meeting children separately. Or any other combination that is appropriate. All sessions should use and develop questions that both explore and help family members integrate their feelings, thoughts, intentions and actions as far as possible. This is a guide, apart from the task of the first session described below, as all the issues will probably come up again and may be repeated.

Overview of the First Safety Planning Session with a Couple or Family

The main tasks here are to, establish a working relationship, assess risk and responsibility, establish a no-violence contract with the help of the 'stable third' and prioritise any untreated substance use problem. We do not proceed with relationship work if the client/s refuse help with substance use.

We make people welcome with introductions and refreshment. We outline our safety planning project and the likely meetings, and our position of no-confidentiality around issues of safety. We share the information we have about the couple/family and the concerns contained in the referral with the couple/parents. During this conversation, we assess their acknowledgement of responsibility for safety and responsibility for behaviour that harms others. Importantly, we assess the commitment of both partners/parents to working in this family intervention project.

As we describe above, we begin to explore and carefully track the last incident of violence or the worst incident. This may link with specific information in the referral and this helps us, and them, begin to understand the triggers for violence (often with attachment significance), the role of unhelpful physiological arousal, unresolved conflict and unprocessed trauma responses, sources of stress and the family's resources, i.e. previous success in stopping the violence, confiding and supportive relationships in the extended family and community, and so on. We explore the contexts of violence: when and where does it happen, how does it happen, who does what, if we were there, what might we see and so on?

We agree and make the no-violence contract (either spoken or written), begin safety planning based on information from tracking an example of violence and agree the use of a time out strategy to help de-escalate conflictual and physiologically arousing interactions. It is essential to have both partners'/parents' agreement to the plan. This takes time and could well take up the rest of the session, and continue into the next sessions. It is useful to allow at least 1.5 h for the first meeting.

There may be time to start talking about what happens in a violent interaction, e.g. 'the red mist came over me', or 'I lost it' and so on, and thus challenge the lack of agency and minimisation of violence in the talk—this encourages people to begin to take responsibility for their actions that harm others. It is important to understand this and begin to get a sense of reciprocity, empathy and empathic appreciation in the couple/family relationships.

Overview of the Second Safety Planning Session

In the second meeting, we continue to develop and take feedback about the safety plan and the safety strategies. We take this very slowly and look for signs of safety and for success. It is important to validate and support family members' intentions and efforts to do things better. We ask what action the couple/parents have taken to ensure safety for themselves and others? This allows us to explore how they are calming down and learning to self-soothe, and how they are learning to understand and regulate their reactive emotional responses. As described above, we offer help with challenging unhelpful 'self talk', for example, entitlement to treat others as they wish and to blame others for the violence, or beliefs that they deserve the violence and are to blame for communication difficulties in the family

We want to know if the couple/parents are they still committed to this change and to this work with us? We explore their internal motivation for change and their curiosity and reflection on their own and others' behaviour? For example, are they beginning to talk in a more direct and straight forward way about the violence and the importance of safety, for them, for their family relationships, for their children, and for the future of their children?

Crucially, we ask what difference has the safety plan made: to them, to their children and the wider family? Thus we ask for examples, and the best examples are small everyday examples. These are all reflective conversations and track the development of empathy. There may be a three-generational history of violence in the family for the couple, so we explore the legacies of violence and their corrective and replicative scripts, and their hopes for the future.

If the stable third attends this second session, we include them in the thinking, and seek their feedback to help with the safety planning.

Overview of the Third Safety Planning Session

Usually we start the meeting by taking feedback on the safety plan. Again, we take it very slowly and look for examples of success, e.g. de-escalation of a difficult interaction that could have escalated to violence in the past. How are they calming themselves, comforting and self-soothing? We support active problem solving and it may be this occurs first with the therapist's help and with the help of the stable third—this promotes trust and relationship repair.

We ask if there been a breakdown in the safety plan? What would they do if there was a breakdown in the safety plan? We need to be honest and clear about what we would do, what they would do and who we would all talk to about safety.

This session reaffirms and further develops what goals the couple/parents want to set? In our experience, they must be easily achievable and our work helps to develop opportunities for change. Again, we continue to focus on the development of empathy, reflection and of mutual appreciation and listening. For example, do they seem to be developing the capacity to reflect on difficult experiences? Are they finding ways, however tentative, to express negative feelings without resorting to shame and blame? We seek out positive feelings and success and ask for small everyday examples.

If the 'stable third' is present at this meeting, we seek feedback on their views about safety and underline family member's success.

Overview of the Fourth Safety Planning Session

Take feedback on the safety plan and take it slowly, tracking success, dilemmas and concerns around safety, well-being and risk.

We continue to explore their development over time, both as individuals and in their family relationships, with systemic intergenerational questions designed to gently open conversations that promote both reflective and relational thinking. The following questions are examples of what we might explore. What is in their family history that helps us understand their views and beliefs about safety, entitlement, power and control, and so on? How do they give, seek and receive comfort in the family? Do they feel undeserving of others' care? What happened to them as children and young people? How have they learned to calm and sooth themselves—how do they help their children? What do they hope for their children's future? How do they understand their own history as a couple and/or co-parents, for example, are they open to each other's influence? Is there still a sense of unhelpful 'entitlement' to treat others as they please? How are they understanding and managing unhelpful emotional/physiological arousal? What more help do they need? Are they developing both personal and parental agency around safety and problem solving, for themselves, for each other, and for their children? Do they understand the risks to their children's development of being 'exposed'/caught up in, their violent behaviour? Do they know what their children 'see' and learn about violence, safety and problem solving in relationships? How do they help their children understand safety and make meaning around difficult experiences? How do they listen to their children, and to each other? In this way, we begin to open the possibility for trauma focused work as well as relational therapy if the no-violence contract can be maintained. Previous successes, current successes and hoped for future successes can be supported and validated.

Overview of the Fifth Safety Planning Session

Again, we take feedback on the safety plan and we track events slowly. If the 'stable third' is present at this meeting, we seek their views on safety and the viability of the safety plan. We check the safety strategies with regard to: the couple, the parents/carers and the children. We focus on what problem solving strategies are working for them. How are they healing and repairing experiences of hurt, rejection and loss in their relationships? We explore trust in their relationships and in their relationship with us and discuss how and when to take emotional risks in the work. It is a form of 'talking about talking' at a process level that helps smooth the way for relationship therapy if it is indicated.

We overview with the couple/parents how they are able to cooperate with other professional practitioners and what helps them sustain their cooperative positioning? We explore whether they see others as potentially helpful to them and their family, and we support the development of trust in the family–professional network. We reflect with the couple/parents and the stable third on what further work needs to be done. In particular, we focus on whether there are unresolved trauma responses and unresolved losses that need assistance?

Overview of the Sixth Safety Planning Session

We wish to emphasise here that six sessions for safety planning is only a minimum number to establish whether the safety plan and the safety strategies can work for the family, before progressing to work therapeutically on other psychological dilemmas and social issues for the couple/family, for example, emotional risk taking in relationships, healing and repair in relationships, promoting safe and more satisfying bonding experiences, healing rifts and cut-offs in the extended family, the development of and re-engagement with social support networks, addressing the impact of exclusion and marginalisation, and so on.

We set enough time aside for careful feedback from our clients and the 'stable third' about their experience of the six sessions and working with us in these ways. This is over and above the session by session feedback we take each time we meet. We address these topics in turn:

Where are they with the safety plan now and the changes required in the six sessions?

What effect do they think the six sessions have had: on them; on their children; on their wider family?

Do they believe that safety has been achieved? We track this carefully, for example, what does 'safety' look like? What does safety feel like? What do they think about safety now? What are their intentions, now and for the future?

Are they overreacting or underreacting to safety, risk and danger? Or does it seem a balanced view?

How do they see their future in terms of family safety: as a couple, for their children and for their children's future?

The 'stable third' can give feedback and make recommendations for further therapeutic work. This reviewing process forms the basis for everyone to decide if we continue with the safety planning and/or progress the safety planning into relationship therapy and processes of family reunification, for example.

Meeting the Children

During our first six safety planning sessions, we may meet with the children separately, or in a sibling group, but we do not meet them in the company of their parents or carers unless we are convinced the adults are taking safety seriously. The following questions inform the separate discussions we have with children about their safety. The children's social worker may also be present.

Overview of Separate Session/s with the Children

We start with introductions and settling down. We offer a clear explanation of the family violence intervention project and the work together in a developmentally appropriate manner. We give a clear explanation of our Duty of Care/no-confidentiality on safety concerns. We use drawing and play materials as relevant and helpful, including solution focused scaling questions.

We ask the children when and how they saw their parents during the recent and/or past violence? What are their worries and where do they take them? Who notices? Who helps? Have they noticed any changes at home? If so, we ask for everyday examples. What difference have the changes made for them: at home, at school, with friends, and so on? We give a clear acknowledgement of the efforts that their parents have made.

In working with safety planning with children we focus on what to do and where to go if safety breaks down. We explore and support relationships with siblings? Have they taken responsibility for safety in the past, for example, calling for help with neighbours, extended family, the police and so on? What has happened? We offer encouragement and reassurance as appropriate. If possible, we help children understand the social work process and the future plans for safety in the family.

Seven Questions to Ask of Yourself (and Your Supervisor) at the End of a Safety Planning Meeting with a Couple or Family Group……

The following seven questions were developed to help practitioners in their safety planning meetings with families, and in their post-meeting discussions and supervision sessions to review the signs of safety and signs of concern in family relationships. In addition, the seven questions were developed to help the in-room consultant and the lead therapist acknowledge the differences between the two roles and to discuss how they can blend the differences in perception, emotional responsiveness and intention to further the understanding in the work with couples and families. They offer an opportunity to review their observations about change in family relationships and the potential for change. Bruner says that there are always feelings and lived experience not fully encompassed by the dominant story (1990). Thus the discussion generated in response to these questions, allows practitioners and supervisors to consider the 'dominant story' within a wider context of possible meanings. These discussions also help bridge understanding between written documents about the family and the spoken word in meetings. We have found that paying attention to the differences of opinion between us and the different emotional responses evoked in the work with the family, to be the most productive. We amplify these differences, in order to understand them, and importantly, in order to help protect against a mutuality that is too comfortable, which is always a risk in any well-established working partnership.

The Seven Questions:

1. What interests/challenges you in your thinking about this couple/family?
2. Discuss from your different points of view (for example, therapist and co-therapist or in-room consultant) your understanding and assessment of the safety plan and 'time out'?
3. At this particular time what is your assessment of the safety of the children?
4. What do you think are the intergenerational effects of domestic violence for the children and adults in this family?
5. Highlight one or two issues where you agree and where you disagree?
6. What more do you need to know to work with this family?
7. Do you need to contact your stable third?

Thus, these questions act as prompts for continuing discussions around safety and safe practice in supervision and peer reflection. The continuous nature of these reflections helps pre-empt crisis responding or reactive responding in the work, as success is continuously acknowledged alongside continuing concern. It is the balance in these reflections between success and concern that enables practitioners, in our experience, to tolerate a level of doubt and uncertainty in their work with couples and families with less risk of practitioner 'burn out'. We discuss these questions of practitioner self-care, the role of supervision and the potential risk of secondary traumatisation in Chap. 7.

Domestic Violence Perpetrator Programmes: What Counts as Success

In this section, we describe some findings from a pilot study that explored what success looks like to key stakeholders in group programmes designed to help perpetrators of domestic violence to stop the violence (Westmarland et al. 2010). These findings both support our thinking around safety and the complexity in defining good outcomes and in addition, help us assist couples with a process of safe separation, should they decide to part. We discuss safe separation in the section below this one.

The participants in the pilot study were self-selecting and came from five UK domestic violence perpetrator programmes. The views of four groups of participants were sought: (a) 22 men who were on or had completed perpetrator programmes; (b) 18 women partners/ex-partners of men on programmes (not all of whom were linked to the men interviewed); (c) 6 funders/commissioners of programmes; and (d) 27 programme practitioners (including perpetrator group work facilitators, women's support workers and managers). A total of 73 interviews were undertaken. All participants were involved with organisations that provide an integrated support service to the partners and ex-partners of men attending the perpetrator programmes. The programmes in the pilot study work with men mandated by family courts and child protection as well as self-referred and asked to attend by partners.

The interviews focused on all participants' expectations and relevant experiences of perpetrator programmes and, importantly, on what success meant from their perspective. For example, funders/commissioners were asked about how they define and expect programmes to measure success. Practitioners, who have the most extensive experience, were asked to reflect on what they thought success meant for perpetrators, their partners, children and funders/commissioners. Group participants and their partners tended to speak about what worked for them.

All the interviews were transcribed and thematically analysed using NVivo—a computer-assisted qualitative data analysis programme. The core themes will be described from the four perspectives.

Six themes emerged from the analysis of the women partners' transcripts in relation to the meaning of success: (a) respectful/improved relationships; (b) expanded space for action (agency); (c) support/decreased isolation; (d) enhanced parenting; (e) reduction or cessation of violence and abuse; and (f) the man understanding the impact of domestic violence. The researchers presented the themes in order of how frequently they were talked about in the interviews.

Three core themes emerged from the analysis of the transcripts of the men on programmes. In relation to the meaning of success, the themes most often mentioned were: (a) enhanced awareness of self and others; (b) reduced cessation of violence and abuse; and (c) improved relationships with better communication.

Analysis of the interviews with the funders and commissioners of services in relation to success on programmes led to three main themes: (a) safety for women and children (including safe child contact); (b) increased well-being for all family members; and (c) quantifiable measures of success.

Four themes emerged from the interviews with the practitioners. Success to them meant: (a) safety and freedom from violence and abuse; (b) empowerment/having a voice; (c) enhanced/safer parenting; and (d) improved well-being for all.

In a separate study, we conducted qualitative research interviews with men who had attended a men's group for men who had physically assaulted their women partners, and with women, who had attended a parallel partners' group. We were interested to explore what both men and women thought had helped to stop the violence. Interestingly, both men and women research participants spoke about a growing ability to take responsibility for safety and how their wish to continue their relationship had helped them make the commitment to stopping the violence—for the men, responsibility for violence, and for the women, recognising their entitlement to be safe (Bonham and Vetere 2012).

Contraindications for Relationship Therapy When Physical Violence Is of Concern

As we describe above, if the no-violence contract breaks down, we do not abandon people. Initially, we review the circumstances and effects of further violence with the family, the stable third and the professional network. It may be agreed at this meeting that we continue to work for safety with the safety plan, and we may adjust the safety plan. It is likely that we will work individually with the relevant family members and not bring them together in a meeting until the no-violence contract and the safety plan appears to work. Alternately it may be considered unsafe to work for safety for relationship therapy, and individual therapy, group therapy or a legal response may be the preferred way forward.

The following factors, in combination, contraindicate the advisability and safety of relationship therapy with couples and families. We do not offer these factors as a checklist or as a heuristic, but rather as a guide to clinical decision making around safety in relationships.

If the family member/s who perpetrates violence continues to blame others for their behaviour, we do not offer relationship therapy. As we describe in this chapter above, we offer a minimum of six sessions for safety planning with the couple/family and we expect to find some acknowledgement that their behaviour is a problem and has multiple impacts on development and for well-being, for them, for others, and for their relationships. For example, we met a father of two daughters, aged 11 and 13 years. The father had been to prison because he has sexually and physically assaulted his wife and tried to strangle her. The two girls had overheard the attack on their mother while hiding in the bedroom of the older daughter. When the father was released from prison, he asked the child protection professionals if he could have contact with his daughters. The wife had separated from him during his time in prison. Both daughters said they did not want to meet their father. The child protection social work team asked us to meet the father and give a view on whether we thought it could be safe for him to meet his daughters if they were to agree to this in future. When we met the father he refused to discuss his attack on his wife with us, and refused to acknowledge that the attack had an impact on his daughters **and** on his relationship with his daughters. We were not able to find a way to help him discuss this with us. He told us that he had been to prison, that he had 'done his time', and thus did not need to talk about it further. We concluded that it would not be safe for him to meet his daughters until he was able to acknowledge the impact of his behaviour.

If we think a family member has an untreated substance use problem, we ask them to access treatment at our local drugs and alcohol treatment agency. We are prepared to work in parallel with alcohol key workers, for example, so that they pay attention to the substance use, and we pay attention to the emotional dynamics in the family and affect regulation problems that maintain the substance use (Vetere 2014). If the family member is unwilling to seek help from the substance use service, and psychoactive substances are implicated in dangerous escalations of conflictual interactions in the family, we do not offer relationship therapy as such. We might offer individual work and consult with other family members about how to help their family member access the substance use services. This could of course be an example of an inability or unwillingness to make a commitment to the resolution of the problem of violence. Thus, an unwillingness to accept any responsibility for safety and for actions that harm others, no acknowledgement of their behaviour or that violence is a problem, lack of internal motivation for change and little understanding of the relational impact of violence contraindicate any form of relationship therapy. This is sometimes part of a wider problem of lack of respect for practices and policy around social control.

Along with the above, we are looking for the ability to reflect on past experience and to emotionally empathise with the victim/s of violence and to listen to another point of view. If we struggle to support the development of these capacities within our six session safety planning framework, paired with a perpetrator's consistent blaming of others, such as family or professionals, we do not undertake relational work that makes others emotionally vulnerable to further physical and/or psychological attacks.

In this chapter and in Chap. 4, we make clear that we can work therapeutically with violence that erupts out of unregulated physiological and emotional arousal. We do not work with violence that is cool, calculated and solely instrumental in the intention to control and dominate others. However, we might occasionally meet a family member whose developmental struggle to contain and manage their unhelpful arousal means that they cannot be helped to calm themselves enough to talk about what has happened to them—they remain angry, entitled and very frightening to others. In these circumstances, we would not consider it safe to talk together with all the family members, but we might offer an individualised response, if appropriate.

Conclusion

It takes courage for family members to sustain a commitment to a resolution of physical violence and to heal its intergenerational and developmental legacies in the family. Whilst our safety planning sessions are not relational therapy per se, they are therapeutic in their use of systemic therapy ideas and practices, and in creating a context for the development of trust, empathy and good listening in family relationships. This forms the secure base for effective problem solving and more straightforward communication of feelings, needs and intentions. Once the violence stops, we need to know how to go on.

References

Bonham, L., & Vetere, A. (2012). A qualitative study using a systemic perspective exploring the remediation of abusive interactions in intimate heterosexual couples. *Journal of Interpersonal Violence, 27,* 916–929. doi:10.1177/0886260511423253. (Sage Online First).

Byng Hall, J. (1995). *Rewriting family scripts*. New York: Guilford.

Bruner, J. (1990). *Acts of meaning*. London: Harvard University Press.

Cooper, J., & Vetere, A. (2005). *Domestic violence and family safety: A systemic approach to working with violence in families*. Chichester: Wiley.

Dallos, R., & Vetere, A. (2012). Triangles and triangulation: A possible bridge between systemic theory and attachment theory. *Journal of Family Therapy, 34,* 117–137.

Eckhardt, C., Murphy, C., Whitaker, D., Sprunger, J., Dykstra, R., & Woodard, K. (2013). The effectiveness of intervention programs for perpetrators and victims of intimate partner violence: Findings from the partner abuse state of knowledge project. *Partner Abuse, 4,* 175–195.

Goldner, V., Penn, P., Sheinberg, M., & Walker, G. (1990). Love and violence: Gender paradoxes in volatile attachments. *Family Process, 29,* 343–364.

Gottman, J. (2011). *The science of trust: Emotional attunement for couples*. New York: Norton.

Hester, M., Pearson, C., & Harwin, N. (2000). *Making an impact: Children and domestic violence*. London: Jessica Kingsley.

Moffitt, T., & Caspi, A. (1998). Annotation: Implications of violence between intimate partners for child psychologists and psychiatrists. *Journal of Child Psychology and Psychiatry, 39,* 137–144.

Penn, P. (1985). Feed-Forward: Future questions, future maps. *Family Process, 24,* 299–310.

Perry, B., & Szalavitz, M. (2006). *The boy who was raised as a dog: And other stories from a child psychiatrists' notebook*. New York: Basic Books.

Vetere, A. (2011). Family violence and family safety: An approach to safe practices in our mental health services. *Partner Abuse, 2,* 246–256.

Vetere, A. (2012). Supervision and consultation practice with domestic violence. *Clinical Child Psychology and Psychiatry, 17,* 181–185. doi:10.1177/1359104511433563.

Vetere, A. (2014). Alcohol misuse, attachment dilemmas, and triangles of interaction: A systemic approach to practice. In R. Gill (Ed.), *Addictions from an attachment perspective: Do broken bonds and early trauma lead to addictive behaviours?* London: Karnac.

Vetere, A. (2015). Working systemically with the legacies of inter-personal violence: A case study of couple therapy. *Partner Abuse, 6,* 243–251.

Vetere, A., & Cooper, J. (2001). Working systemically with family violence: Risk responsibility and collaboration. *Journal of Family Therapy, 23,* 378–396.

Vetere, A., & Cooper, J. (2017). Children who witness violence at home. In A. Vetere & E. Dowling (Eds.), *Narrative therapies with children and their families* (Second ed.). London: Routledge.

Vetere, A., & Dallos, R. (2009). Family mirrors: Reflective practice in systemic therapies. In J. Stedmon & R. Dallos (Eds.), *Reflective practice in psychotherapy and counselling*. Maidenhead: OU Press.

Westmarland, N., Kelly, L., & Chalder-Mills, J. (2010). What counts as success? London: Respect.

Chapter 4
Helping Couples Separate Safely: Working Towards Safe Separations

Introduction

When the physical violence stops, we often find that is when the couple contemplate a separation. It is as if they live under conditions of chronic crisis during the times, if not years, when violence was prevalent, and accordingly manage and cope on a day-to-day basis as best they can, and often dare not risk reflection on their options. Sometimes such reflection can be dangerous. It may not be safe to discuss possible separation for fear of violent reprisal or further attempts to coerce and control. We also work with younger couples, who might be described as impulsive and ambivalent about their relationship, and have little shared history of commitment and loyalty in their relationships. Sometimes, for a woman who is financially dependent upon a partner, and, with children to look after, there are other reasons to stay, including social pressures in some communities from extended families. However, when the violence stops and it becomes safer to reflect on what happened in the relationship, and what the future could or might look like for them as individuals, as a couple and as a family, one or both might seek separation. And for us as systemic psychotherapists, a safe separation is a good outcome, given the higher risk of physical violence for women during separation, divorce and contact handover, when safety is not being monitored or maintained within statutory services (Johnson and Hotton 2003).

There is not much written in the systemic family literature on helping couples separate safely following the cessation of physical violence. This is a gap that we attempt to address here. In our experience, many women are advised to leave their partners/husbands when violence has occurred, or is suspected. Such advice, though well meaning, does not fully acknowledge that separation and divorce are emotionally fraught and painful processes in their own right—both for the partners and for their children, if they have any. Separation involves multiple losses and transitions, such as, legal, financial and residential settlements, perhaps a move of accommodation, and change of school for the children, loss of friends and a familiar

C. Sammut Scerri et al., *Intervening After Violence*,
Focused Issues in Family Therapy, DOI 10.1007/978-3-319-57789-0_4

community, adjustment to changed roles and changed relationship and community status, impact in the extended family system and faith community, and so on. At the heart of these processes are changes in our primary attachment relationships with the accompanying profound emotional experiences of loss, sadness, fear, shame and anger. Such processes are linked to unhelpful physiological arousal and challenges to self-regulation that often need time to navigate and resolve, from the different perspectives of those involved. So, although separation and divorce can also provide opportunities for change, growth and development, the earlier stages of separation invariably involve poignant triggers to arousal and challenges to self-control. Thus we consider it essential that we support couples and partners in managing these deeply ambivalent processes, and when working therapeutically with individuals who are in the process of separation, we help by keeping a clear relational focus in our work, and consulting with ex-partners wherever possible.

As therapists we explain it is not our job to advise the couple to separate or to stay together, as those are their decisions. It is though our job to help couples and families to live safely—for both partners and for their children. This is our statement of intent to our clients, and we return to it from time to time in our meetings when we feel pulled by one or other partner to ally with them.

Safe Separation and the Use of Systemic Relational Questions

We work for safe separation by using a continuous process of creating systemic, relational questions that position the partners as competent and resilient people with a clear sense of their own agency. The questions are designed to promote reflective spaces in which partners can more calmly experience themselves and each other as thoughtful decision makers. For example, we might ask, 'What decisions did you and your partner make when you separated?' An early response to such a question could indicate a felt sense of disempowerment, so we would expand the questions by asking for everyday detail, such as, 'Who got the children ready for school?', 'How did you do that?', and so on. Such questions seek clarity about the minutiae of everyday decision making that many of us take for granted—but such detailed exploration underlines the parents/partner's agentic positioning. We can further develop these questions by including specific reference to the everyday familial roles that people play, such as, 'As a father, how did you decide what to give the children for breakfast?', or, 'As a mother, what did you decide to cook the children for supper?', and so on. These are all important questions about the 'here and now' that affirm the complexity of looking after ourselves and our children in emotionally challenging circumstances. We can ask intergenerational questions that explore learning in families, and how aspects of family culture are either handed on, or changed for the next generation. For example, 'As a father, what did you learn from your father about looking after sons that you want to repeat, strengthen, or alter?'.

Such questions of intergenerational learning in families can be placed into the future of the partners and/or their children. Future oriented questions make it possible to speak of aspirations and hopes, and to recognise that choices are sometimes possible!

Using Systemic Questions to Anticipate the Early, Middle and Later Stages of the Process of Separation

When working to support a safe separation, we find it helpful to create and ask questions for the early, middle and later stages of the process of separation and divorce. The following questions are examples of what we weave into the conversation with couples and parents that will help us all think and plan, for now, and for the future.

The early stages of separation. We ask these questions both to the couple and to them individually as seems appropriate, for example, we ask, what decisions have you already made about separating? Are you clear about the reasons you want to part and have you talked about this? Here we are looking to see if their thinking, intention and behaviour are reactive or reflective. What would you like to achieve in this first (or any other) session with us? What kind of separation are you planning: is it to clear the air, to give yourselves some time to think and plan for the future, or are you feeling 'this is a definite commitment to be apart'? In these questions, we are trying to access their decision making and their emotional states. We try to be sensitive to whether this is a mutual arrangement, or if there is a 'leaver' and a 'left', so to say, with perhaps a 'new' partner on the horizon.

We ask—Did your safety plan work or not (this may have already been discussed) and have you discussed a safety plan for living separately? Again, we wish to emphasise the need for constant rehearsal and review of the safety plan (Cooper and Vetere 2005; Vetere 2011, 2012) (see Chapter 3 this volume).Will your safety plan work if you meet in the street, when you have contact with your children or if you meet when out socialising? Who will support you in this new safety plan? Here we are exploring the wider system of friends and family as a helpful resource, and recognise the potentially reactivating and re-traumatising impact of the social media.

We acknowledge that splitting up is sad for them and for their children. We try to be validating and containing in our approach. We explicitly recognise that however complicated separation is, it is bound to feel like a big loss and really strange and difficult for some time. We ask, have you told your children, and who else knows, for example, grandparents, carers, faith leaders, school, nursery, and so on. Has the wish to separate been held as a secret? Can your children talk to both of you about the reasons you are separating? What do your children know about the violence? We want to know if the parents can put the children's developmental needs first and think about their children's safety. This demands empathy and a willingness to co-operate. We ask, have you thought about and made arrangements for the children to see you both? What about telephone calls with the children? As therapists, we are aware that texting and telephone stalking is common. We ask, what would happen if you met at a family social event? Would you try to avoid each other for the first few weeks? Domestic violence may have been a secret in the family and maybe family members are hearing of it for the first time. These questions begin the process of acknowledging the timing of separation, in that one partner may have been thinking of leaving for some time, unbeknownst to the other. Such differences in timing can lead to differences in emotion regulation, and one partner can appear more reactive as a result.

The middle stages of separation. We anticipate the middle stages of separation and ask questions that help couples plan and predict. For example, who will go to parents' evening at school? Can you go together or would it be best to go separately? How would you know? What would be happening? Have you discussed finances and how is that going? Are there any continuing safety issues for you, the children and for anyone else in the family? Who will support you, both of you? If your children wanted to talk to someone else, perhaps outside the family, who would it be and could you encourage that connection?

The later stages of separation. In the longer term, we anticipate and explore the following: Do you think you will you be able to talk to each other in the future? How will you be able to support your children as they grow and develop? They may need to ask different questions about what happened as they grow up? They may need more information as they grow older and you may want to talk to them in a different way. Sometimes parents remarry and make relationships with new partners. These can be challenging times for all family members and the following questions are demanding. We ask future oriented questions, such as, thinking of the future, you may need to support them if or when you make relationships with other people and maybe they will also have their own children to support. If your son or daughter came to you because they were in an unsafe relationship, what would your advice be?

For each member of the family we ask, how do you see yourselves in three months and this time next year? Will you be able to talk to each other in the future, as parents around your children? Will you be able to support your children as they grow, as they may need to ask different questions at different times? And you may want to talk to them in a different way? You may need to support them if, or when, you make relationships with other people? And in these new relationships, maybe you or they will have other children to support?

Conclusion

In this section we wish to emphasise that supporting safe separation for couples is a good outcome. There are higher risks of emotional and physical violence during the processes of separation and divorce as our primary attachments are disrupted and re-organised, accompanied by increased risk of unregulated and unhelpful physiological arousal, and fears of abandonment and rejection. For children, who also have to navigate the processes of loss and family separation, their vigilance around their parents' well-being and the well-being of their parents' relationship is enhanced. The strain on them may well be reflected in their behaviour, and not always well understood by others. If the children remain resident with their mother or mother figure, consideration needs to be given to the children's relationship with their paternal grandparents who may wish to help with child minding, for example, as these relationships are often more complex and conflicted during the time of separation. Finally we support children in their wish to understand why their parents parted, according to their age related needs (Blow and Daniel 2002, 2017). We assist the parents in agreeing a narrative of why they parted, and this is often accompanied by the narrative of how they met and what they have appreciated in each other. Children often tell us they are 50% of each parent, and if their parents continue to hate each other, they ask us, what does this mean for their other 50%? This narrative offers an explanation to the children and an affirmation of their 100%, and begins a slow process of repair and recovery that has the best interests of all family members at heart.

References

Blow, K., & Daniel, G. (2002). Frozen narratives? post-divorce processes and contact disputes. *Journal of Family Therapy, 24,* 85–103.

Blow, K., & Daniel, G. (2017). Children involved in contact disputes. In A. Vetere & E. Dowling (Eds.), *Narrative therapies with children and their families: A practitioner's guide to concepts and approaches*, pp. 167–181.

Cooper, J., & Vetere, A. (2005). *Family violence and family safety: Working systemically with family violence*. Chichester: Wiley.

Johnson, H., & Hotton, T. (2003). Losing control: Homicide risk in estranged and intact intimate relationships. *Homicide Studies, 7,* 58–84.

Vetere, A. (2011). Family violence and family safety: An approach to safe practices in our mental health services. *Partner Abuse, 2,* 246–256.

Vetere, A. (2012). Supervision and consultation practice with domestic violence. *Clinical Child Psychology and Psychiatry, 17,* 181–185. doi:10.1177/1359104511433563.

Chapter 5
Healing and Repair in Relationships: Working Therapeutically with Couples

Introduction

This chapter is concerned with healing and repair in couple relationships—helping couples to reconnect and re-bond, if that is their wish, after the physical violence has stopped. Using examples from our therapeutic practice, we shall outline the continuing negative impacts in couples' relationships of relational traumas, defined here as unprocessed and unresolved losses and hurts, for example, fears and experiences of rejection, shame and abandonment. Accessibility and responsiveness in a partner forms the basis of trust in our close relationships. Thus, this chapter will draw on the extant theory and research that guides us as practitioners to help couples feel safe enough to explore ways of resolving their relational losses, hurts and trauma responses. The goal of which is to help rebuild trust and develop reciprocity and more satisfying ways of interacting and problem solving for the couple, (Gottman 2011; Johnson 2014). This includes developing a narrative of how they healed their relationship and developing their vision of a violence free future for themselves and for their children.

Although this chapter is about couple relationships, we are always mindful of the impact of the couple's relationship dynamics on the developmental pathways of their children, and we always ask and take action around, what the children are learning, as they observe and participate in, relationship conflict and relationship repair (Dallos and Vetere 2009). The research on positive bonding and adult romantic attachments is the basis on which we explore relationship repair and positive problem solving for couples, so that their interpersonal resources and their repertoire of coping can be developed and expanded (Hazan and Shaver 1987). As systemic therapists we are interested in intergenerational learning in family systems—both household systems and kin networks—thus we shall consider the impact on *all* family members' development and their family relationships of healing and enhanced cooperation between partners/parents/carers/grandparents/siblings, for now and for their joint futures (Byng Hall 1995).

C. Sammut Scerri et al., *Intervening After Violence*,
Focused Issues in Family Therapy, DOI 10.1007/978-3-319-57789-0_5

Sometimes we help couples to separate safely once the violence has stopped since not all couples wish to remain together. And sometimes, they cannot take the decision to separate until it is safe enough to do so, both emotionally and physically. A safe separation is crucial as the risks of physical violence are elevated during the process of separating and the subsequent contact with children (Wilson and Daly 1993). We consider a safe separation to be a good outcome, particularly if we can promote co-operative parenting on behalf of the children. We outline our approach to helping couples separate safely in Chap. 4 of this book.

There continues to be controversy over whether couples therapy is indicated in the context of physical violence in the couple relationship, whether the violence is from one to the other, or from both. In Chap. 3 above, we outline our systemic safety methodology designed to help individuals, couples and family members stop the physical violence (Cooper and Vetere 2005; Vetere 2011, 2015). Researcher therapy teams have been in agreement that couples therapy may be indicated when the physical and emotional violence experienced is low to moderate, when partners voluntarily seek therapy and make a commitment to ending the violence, and when the violence is from both partners (Stith et al. 2005; Vall et al. 2014). For the purposes of this chapter, we are assuming that the partners have made the commitment to ending the violence and that it has stopped for a sufficient period to reassure all members of the family-professional system that safety can be assured.

Empathy and the Therapeutic Alliance

Healing and repair in our relationships occurs in a context of emotional safety and trust. Thus the first task in the post-violence work is to further develop and establish a robust and compassionate bond in the therapeutic working alliance, with agreed goals and vision for the future. Collaborative practice involves both partners and their therapists in an agreement on how to achieve continuing safety and felt security in both the therapeutic triangle and in their relationship, for now, for their future, and for the future of their children.

The therapeutic relationship is accepted as necessary for change in all the major psychotherapies and is the key predictor of client outcome (Elliott et al. 2011). Lambert and Barley (2001) in their overview of psychotherapy outcome research estimate that the therapeutic relationship accounts for 30% of the variance in client outcomes. Empathy has been described by Norcross and Wampold (2011) as the 'evidence based component' of the therapeutic relationship. It is a conscious perspective-taking process, involving both affect and cognition, whereas sympathy is thought to be an emotional response to another's affective state. Rogers (1975) described 'accurate empathy' as a process of understanding the other and communicating this through reflective listening. Trust in the therapist and in the therapeutic process develops in the context of warm acceptance i.e. by listening, being present and focused and showing care. The therapist creates the context in which clients can begin to take emotional risks and make themselves emotionally vulnerable as they acknowledge and articulate their fears, hopes and wishes for their relationships and in their relationships. Empathic responding from the therapist helps clients identify and modify their own affective responding. If we believe our therapist can help us, we are more likely to make a stronger commitment to therapy and similarly, the therapist's hope in the usefulness of therapy is linked to client engagement. Thus the principal researchable healing components of the therapeutic relationship are empathy, genuineness, positive regard and validation, and these are said to form the basis of compassion (Kirschenbaum and Jourdan 2005). Violence ends with the development of the capacity for empathy. In the moment when rage or frustration or hurt makes us wish to strike out, it is empathy that stays our hand—when we see in our mind's eye the look on our partner's face and the harm we would wreak should we do so. This combination of empathy and seeing the consequences of an action before we take action, helps us stop the violence and prevent violence in the future.

In therapeutic practice, we might ask what empathy looks like in interaction, for example, what is the therapist doing, and what are the partners doing, for themselves and in their relationship. Thus, the therapist's task is to acknowledge, clarify and affirm both partners' experiences separately, and in the presence of both. This does not mean any agreement that violence is acceptable, rather that our experiences of fear, sadness and shame are entitled to be heard and witnessed. This often also involves a deeper consideration of the children's experiences during the episodes of violence and afterwards, once the physical violence has stopped. This models an acceptance for both partners as people, who are entitled to have their experiences heard and understood. Feeling validated, understood and listened to is calming, and forms the basis on which therapeutically, we can gently encourage and support partners in listening to the other. We cannot expect people to be curious, reflective and compassionate about the experience of their partner, if they do not also feel listened to, supported and understood in their own right.

Experiencing affirmation from the therapist can also lead to a 'softening', a soothing and calming experience, as the Emotion Focussed Therapists describe it, so that blaming the other is less likely (Johnson 2002). In our experience, physical violence is always accompanied by emotional violence, and stopping the physical violence may not always help stop the emotional violence, for example, name calling, intimidation and practices of humiliation. Blaming, especially character blaming, is often implicated in the escalation of difficult interaction into physically violent interaction, so interventions aimed at understanding and stopping the practice of blaming are particularly helpful to couples. Blaming can sometimes be reframed as a positive wish for change, and this is more likely from a felt position of being seen and heard in the therapy.

Once the violence has stopped, it may be necessary to revisit and reprocess the attachment hurts and losses that were discussed in Chap. 3 above, as part of the safety planning methodology, and explore their deeper and more powerful representational meanings, for the partners, and for their relationships. Again, as described in Chap. 3, this systemic tracking of meaning and experience needs to take place very slowly and safely, so that both partners can process and reprocess their experiences. The integration of remembered action, thought, feeling and intention is crucial for reflection and reflective functioning (Dallos and Vetere 2009). The combination of empathy, curiosity and the integration of memory system resources enables self-reflexivity to develop (see below). The capacity to give, seek and receive comfort is at the heart of attachment theory. The therapist's willingness to offer, model and encourage a more predictable process of comforting challenges the couple's previous experiences of comforting as dangerous, neglectful, unpredictable and/or shaming.

Intergenerational Patterns of Comforting

The experience of comfort and reassurance is at the heart of felt safety and is the vehicle for protection. This is a central process in attachment theory and seen as essential for relationship repair (Dallos and Vetere 2009).

Safety and protection are have central importance in attachment theory (Bowlby 1988; Crittenden and Landini 2011). The development of self- protective and self-defensive processes occurs in the relational context of feedback with our significant attachment figures. Comfort and comforting has special attachment significance in our close relationships, as described in Chap. 3, above. When we are upset and frightened, the sound of a reassuring voice, a kind smile and a cuddle are sometimes the only responses that can calm us down. Many people we work with therapeutically were either not comforted as children, or they were offered comfort in unpredictable and frightening ways and thus they may have learned to use psychoactive substances to escape unbearable feelings of shame, fear and sadness or alternatively, to feel alive if their way of coping with danger was to numb themselves (Vetere 2014a, b). The safety planning work described in Chap. 3 is designed to help stop the physical violence and in this work it clearly address each family member's capacity to comfort and soothe themselves, and supports the de-escalation of unhelpful physiological and emotional arousal, in constructive ways. The task here though, is to support people in the longer term to develop a repertoire of coping responses and resources, and to learn to see a few trusted others as a source of comfort, help and support. The capacity to give, to seek and to receive comfort may be constrained by entrenched and unhelpful views of the self, (internal working models) and we address this later in this chapter. So, for longer term repair, comforting and the giving and receiving of reassurance are at the heart of a felt experience of safety in our close relationships.

However, opening up and exploring a conversation around comfort can be poignant for people who have learned not to trust others, and especially for those family members who only ever experienced comfort from the very people who also abused them. When encouraging couples to take risks in seeking and accepting comfort, we might initially open the conversation in a more discursive way, using a framework of intergenerational learning in families, such as the exploration of corrective and replicative scripts (Byng Hall 1995). If family culture can be described as learned patterns of thoughts, expectations and behavior around key family tasks, such as care giving, skill development, affection exchange, and so on, our approach might invite the partners to reflect on their corrective and replicative scripts i.e. what is it they want to repeat and what is it they want to change in how they were comforted as children, or how they observed their parents/carers comfort each other. Thus, from our systemic perspective we help develop the conversation by asking about inter-generational learning in families—how do we mutually influence each other across the generations, and teach and learn in families, about caregiving, care-receiving, comforting, and so on. Taking an intergenerational perspective on learning and development in families affords a degree of emotional distance initially, from a topic that can often trigger arousal and a strong desire for self-protection, sometimes expressed as defensiveness or even hostility. So, we might start by asking the parents to reflect on their childhood experience, for example,—'when you were upset, or frightened, as a child, what happened?'. 'How did you get to feel better?' 'Who helped you do this?' 'What have you learnt from this for your own family?' If this conversation is too emotionally painful, we might ask what they think their parents (or carers) learned from their parents, i.e. by going back one more generation in the conversation, to give more emotional distance. Similarly we can frame the questions hypothetically, if that helps people have the courage to speak of painful matters in their histories. We ask what they want to do the same, and what they want to do differently—what do they value and want to strengthen, and what they are trying to change for the better, such as, how do they comfort each other in their own family and how do they comfort their children. Then we might focus specifically on their relationship with their children and also explore how they help their children learn to comfort themselves and to comfort them as parents and what happens if this relationship becomes unbalanced for the children. Finally we ask systemic questions about the future of the children and the parents' aspirations for them—for example, what do you hope your children will learn from you about comforting, and for the future of their children? Future questions often pave the way for a thoughtful and reflective conversation about the hoped for futures of their children and grandchildren. We find that most parents speak with aspiration for the future of their family and importantly, this allows us to frame their intentions in a positive light, even if their past efforts have not been so successful.

Internal Working Models and Strategies of Attachment

Our beliefs and expectations about our own and other people's behaviour are thought to develop and change in the context of our earlier and later attachment relationship experiences (Bowlby 1988). At the core of these beliefs are the constructs, sometimes referred to as schemas, of our acceptability and competence. Our views of ourselves might be expressed either more negatively or positively, as: How loveable, worthy and acceptable am I? Our views of others might be expressed as: How available and interested are others in me, and in caring for and looking after me? Do I matter to the people I love? These deep seated beliefs are said to guide our actions, thoughts and feelings, and importantly, how we try to keep ourselves safe, close to and loved by others. Negative beliefs about self and others can also act as blocks to trust and the development of intimate relating. In our therapeutic work it is important to help people identify these unhelpful ideas, develop curiosity about how they have grown over time, and support and encourage a gentle process of challenging such beliefs in the light of present day resources, wishes and needs.

Attachment theory is a developmental theory of the social regulation of emotion in families. From this perspective, our sense of felt security and our ability to trust others and to turn to them for comfort and support at times of need, is rooted in our earlier experiences with our parents or carers. If our parents were mostly consistently available when we needed them, our belief of being able to trust others, based in our awareness that our parents will be available, enables us to show both positive and negative emotions (Bowlby 1988).We are learning that we can use our thoughts and feelings to make sense of events. Mikulincer and Goodman (2006) summarise some of the adult attachment research that purports to show strong positive correlations between well-being and a sense of felt security in our close relationships, such as fewer difficulties with affect regulation (less reactivity, and over- and under-arousal), more willingness to seek support when needed, more openness to new information, curiosity and tolerance of uncertainty, more assertiveness, more collaborative and empathic in communication styles, and possessing a more elaborated sense of self, that is positive and richly articulated. And, of course, this is the focus of relationship therapy.

From a systemic perspective, our attachment strategies, or ways of keeping ourselves emotionally safe, can be seen as attempted solutions to the developmental dilemmas we experienced with our parents if they were preoccupied and/or unavailable to us, for whatever reason. A more dismissing or emotion deactivating and self-protective strategy might develop when parents are consistently not available when needed for comfort or reassurance. Under these circumstances we may learn to believe that we have to rely on ourself, and to be self-sufficient by learning to suppress and even deny our negative and/or more needy feelings. Any display of distress is expected to annoy or upset our caregiver so we might engage in pretending to be alright, or put on a false front. This can result in learning that expressing emotions cannot reliably elicit comfort or caring, and learning to distrust feelings as a guide to choice and action, as expression of the need for reassurance, for example, did not lead to comfort and safety. A defensive strategy develops of distancing or excluding emotions. Instead cognition is relied on to help distort or omit emotional and physiological information. However, some children learn that occasionally they get their needs for reassurance met, especially by pleasing and caring for parents. This can lead to patterns of caring for others, along with inhibition of our need for care (Crittenden 2008).

A more preoccupied strategy might develop when parents have been inconsistently available, such that children learn that exaggerating a show of negative feelings and needs elicits care, albeit a more negative form of attention—often said to be preferable to being ignored. Such an intermittent reinforcement strategy can occasionally result in the child learning they get their needs for attention and care met by coercing their parents or developing ‘clingy’ strategies. The expectation of inconsistent care and the inability to predict parental availability or trust their verbal promises leads to a distrust of words and cognition as useful in making choices or taking action—you cannot believe what people say! Since words fail to predict others’ responses, a person may increasingly rely on affective information and along with a growing difficulty in regulating arousal in difficult interpersonal interactions, may reduce the complexity of explanation by blaming others and avoiding consideration of their own contributions. During our development into adulthood and with our engagement in intimate relationships as adults, these learned self-protective strategies can act as blocks to developing trust and intimacy. If the adult romantic relationship does not provide the necessary feelings of safety and security it can be harder to be reflective about what needs to change, and could even further undermine a sense of felt security for the partners.

Extreme strategies often develop when the child lives with fear and is trying to adapt and survive when their parent or carer is confusing, inconsistent and unavailable, frightened and/or frightening. Neither self-reliance nor coercion work to elicit care so the child finds it difficult to develop and predict a consistent pattern and learns a distrust of words and feelings (Crittenden 2008). The child might learn to numb themselves in the face of danger and when this strategy breaks down in the face of overwhelming events, they might flip into an intensely preoccupied strategy that confuses them and others. Self harm as a strategy for managing and relieving unbearable and overwhelming feelings often develops in this context. This might take the form of excessive alcohol consumption and or reliance on other psychoactive substances, to help regulate arousal and escape unbearable feelings, such as fear, sadness and shame, as a form of ‘numbing out’ or even to feel alive, if numbness is the dominant survival and self-protective strategy (Khantzian 2014; Vetere 2014a).

So to summarise, a more secure attachment strategy is the ability to turn to parents or carers to protect us and help us manage our feelings, fears, anxieties and distress. Young infants and toddlers rely on their parents/carers to help them regulate their feelings as they cannot do it by themselves initially. Children gradually learn to manage their own feelings i.e. self control, by a process of imitation, modelling and internalising how their parents comfort them and how their parents regulate their own feelings. If children are looked after by two parents or carers, they may well develop different strategies of self control and emotion regulation with each parent. From a systemic perspective we can think of a network of attachments that both contain and support children’s learning and exploration. Children learn to develop their own internal conversations and to use images and their feelings to calm and soothe themselves when upset. The patterns of self-comforting that evolve embody aspects of their preferred attachment strategies, for example, turning inwards to their self in a pattern of self-reliance, or outwards to others with little experience of comforting their self, or a blend of both strategies in a more balanced approach to emotion regulation.

Our strategies of emotion regulation are activated when we perceive danger and our need for safety and reassurance is high, for example, when we fear rejection or abandonment from an attachment figure, or when we are rejected and abandoned. We respond with panic and protest, and often with anger. In adult couple relationships, we can experience mutual comforting and assist each other in managing, controlling and soothing unhelpful physiological arousal and difficult feelings. Similarly, we can engage in mutual patterns of escalation and de-escalation of affect and affective responding in both exciting and helpful ways and in ways that prolong unprocessed distress.

What are the Implications of Modern Attachment Theory for Therapeutic Practice with Couples in the Aftermath of Violence?

As we describe in Chap. 3, modern attachment theory informs our development of a safety plan and safety strategy with couples and families to help stop the physical violence. Physical and emotional violence often occur together, and because emotional violence in its more subtle forms is harder to define, working therapeutically with couples in the aftermath often involves a more detailed focus on the experiences of feeling controlled, coerced, shamed and humiliated by the other. Emotional violence sometimes develops in the context of self-defence, and often then holds a 'moral high ground' position of 'I have borne the brunt of physical assault for years, now it's my turn to make you feel the same'.

The implications of modern attachment theory for therapeutic practice are clear and comprehensive, regardless of the school or model of therapy followed. Couples therapy requires the co-construction of a secure base i.e. a sense of emotional safety within which it becomes possible to name troubling emotional experiences and to develop a repertoire for regulating unhelpful emotion and for interactive regulation. It needs to be safe enough to think about what is happening. Compassion for the self and for the other is promoted through a slow process of affirmation and validation of individual experience. Couple therapy requires co-presence and inter-subjectivity by showing our connections to each other with emotional mirroring. This then leads to curiosity about the other and the ability to stand in their emotional shoes. Thus comforting and soothing the self and the other is at the heart of healing. The embodied responses of the couple therapist, as a form of somatic counter-transference, often provides clues to where change and transformation is desired, albeit stuck or blocked. The reorganisation of our attachment strategies requires reflection and integration of our different representational systems, in the context of emotional safety. Couples therapy encourages the joint exploration of attachment based narratives from a secure base—from excursions to expeditions.

Thus both the form and content of our shared narratives of healing both express and continue to construct our attachment experiences.

We hold our attachment figures and attachment experiences in memory, as representations. Memory research suggests we hold these memories in inter-connected systems (Tulving 1983; Crittenden 2008). For example: (a) procedural memory is memory for how we do things in our relationships—how we give affection, how we argue and make up, and so on; (b) sensory memory is memory for sensation and emotion i.e. embodied memory—what touch feels like, the sight and smell of a lover, the sound of their voice and so on; (c) semantic memory is memory for our thoughts, values and beliefs—the meaning of our attachments; (d) episodic memory or autobiographical memory is memory for inter-connected experiences i.e. what happens to us—the stories we tell of events; and (e) integrative memory both integrates our experiences across all representational systems, and is the platform on which we reflect on what has happened to us, and others, and what is happening now. Left brain or explicit processes of memory are said to be involved with semantic representations and with episodic and integrative representations. Right brain or implicit memory processes are said to be involved with procedural and sensory representations, and with episodic and integrative representations (Schore 2012).The couple therapy process aims to bring implicit memory into conscious awareness so that it can be named, explored, understood and processed.

Thus in therapy we can all think about the complex layers of our attachments and how we might explore what resources couples bring to their decision making, problem solving and healing. When we are upset, disappointed, humiliated and otherwise anxious and unhelpfully aroused in our relationships, our ability to process negatively laden information slows down, we become preoccupied with our arousal and our ability to read relational cues is impaired. In these difficult moments, we are likely to fall back on a preferred strategy, as described earlier, such as a dismissing strategy or a preoccupied strategy. In the couples therapy it is important to explore what representational systems are activated for each partner in these difficult moments. For example, if a partner employs a deactivating strategy, they may rely on semantic representations; alternately, if a partner becomes physiologically flooded, they may rely on sensory representations. These are the self-defensive and protective processes we employ to keep ourselves safe. The couple therapist can then engage with them in their preferred representational system, to begin the slow process of exploration and illumination of their experiences, before exploring warded off or marginalised representational experience. Thus we help people ‘warm up’ and take emotional risks to explore dismissed affective responses; and we help people ‘calm down’ so that they might be able to think about what is happening to them, their partner, and in their relationship. The aim of the couple therapy is to help both partners draw on *all* their representational memory systems as a resource when exploring difficult relational moments, so that they might eventually integrate and reflect on what is happening to them, the other, and their relationship.

Trauma and Loss

Fight. Trauma and loss are an inevitable part of all our lives. The fight-flight-freeze system is often activated in these difficult moments in our relationships (van der Kolk 2014). A fear of abandonment or rejection leads to anxiety, physiological arousal and vulnerability, experienced as sadness, fear and/or shame. Self-defensive anger and aggression often fronts this sadness, fear and shame and can be accompanied by blaming of the other. Bowlby (1988) described this as the anger of hope and observed that it signalled a wish for connection i.e. protest anger ('where are you!!') and the anger of despair ('I don't want you anymore!!'). These responses can become patterned over time and can maintain a felt sense of insecurity and being unlovable. An over reliance on a pre–occupied strategy in these moments can leave a person overwhelmed by carrying too much sensory information forward into the future with them. This can leave them remaining anxious, hyper-vigilant and chronically over—aroused.

Flight. Emotional withdrawal in relationships can be seen as a form of flight. An over reliance on a dismissing strategy risks discarding too much information with the further associated risk of remaining unsafe because the person ignores relevant cues to potential future danger. Both dismissing and pre-occupied strategies also have implications for how we parent our children and teach them to keep themselves safe, and what children learn from observing their parents' responses to difficult, frightening and/or conflictual interactions. When we learn to predict rejection from a key attachment figure, we may also learn to avoid risk-taking to seek comfort and connection in our adult relationships, and this of course, reduces the possibilities for change. We learn not to trust others and come to believe that eventually, we will be let down and disappointed. In trans-generational traumas, the child can be abused by a parent/carer, can learn to care for a traumatised parent, and can experience themselves as an abuser if the parent acts frightened by the child's actions i.e. their own trauma responses and unresolved memories are triggered by their interaction with their child. It is this lack of resolution with trauma memories that can lead some parents, and in turn as partners, to increasingly and rigidly repeat attempts to protect themselves, and/or to correct interactions and scripts that do not have the desired effects. Under these circumstances, when we are trying to make things better in our current relationships than was done for us when we were younger, or our parents did for themselves, that our efforts fail because we do not hold a representation of what 'better' might look like or be like. As our anxiety and need for safety rises further we tend to repeat our solutions even though we know they are not working as we hope because, simply, we do not know what else to do. Thus a rigidityin relational responding enters the couple and family system in these desperate attempts to solve problems.

Freeze. But freeze is different. It signals a stronger and more implicit trauma response and the person needs help to re-inhabit and re-possess their own body, so to speak. Freeze develops at a much earlier developmental age when fight or flight as a self-protective response is neither possible nor available, for example, the babe in arms whose mother is physically assaulted, or the young child who is sexually abused who can neither protest nor escape (van der Kolk 2014). Their experience of intrusive and uncontrollable ideation and memories, such as visions, smells and feelings, may intrude into their primary attachment strategies and disrupt their coping attempts.

Couple therapy seeks to help both partners achieve a more balanced resolution, whereby they are able to both carry forward and also to discard irrelevant information, and able to connect information from their different representational systems (Crittenden and Landini 2011). In addition, couple therapy aims to help the partners interactively co-regulate their responses. Empathy, mentalisation and mindfulness require us to be aware of our own mental states and those of others. Our understanding and expectations of how relationships work need to be open to reflection and revision, including an awareness of contradictions and inconsistencies within and between our representational memory systems. As explained previously in this chapter, reflection and integration needs to involve and integrate all the memory systems.

The development of unresolved trauma states is often shaped by the reactions of significant others, such as family, a partner, and friends. Our social support network and our key attachment figures are centrally important. They assist in processing our experiences of dangerous and extreme events by both validating and acknowledging our experience, helping to overcome feelings of disorientation and confusion, and they assist in developing coping strategies for future safety. Thus their involvement in any psychotherapy aimed at resolving trauma states is crucial, and in the context of couple therapy, the couple relationship is a resource to heal traumas that occurred for one or both partners prior to their relationship (Johnson 2002).

In couple therapy, we help partners to identify and name experiences that have led to trauma responses, such as sexual and physical abuse. The secure base in therapy involves making clear that we shall only explore what the partner is willing and able to discuss and that at any time they can signal to stop the discussion. This involves validating their experiences and any distress experienced then and now. Gentle exploration of the impact of these experiences on their sense of self, their embodied experience and in their relationships with their family, partner and friends helps us consider and begin to revise how they have attempted to cope. The therapy then supports each partner and for them as a couple to anticipate how they might avoid danger in the future and to identify what resources they will be able to draw on. If the partners are also parents, we help them anticipate for the future emotional and physical safety of their children and what they need to be doing now to help secure that future.

Attachment Injury

'Attachment injury' is a helpful phrase developed by Susan Johnson and her colleagues in their Emotion Focused Therapy for couples to describe an unprocessed and unresolved loss or hurt in an intimate couple relationship (Johnson et al. 2001). The attachment injury is thought to occur during a time when one partner has a very high need for comfort, acknowledgement and reassurance and experiences the other as emotionally unavailable to them in that moment. This can result in extreme disappointment and a sense of their partner as 'not being there for them'. If this experience is repeated or builds on an earlier unvoiced disappointment, it can also lead to a self-defensive strategy of not trusting their partner to respond to their need for comfort and reassurance again, so they never ask again. An emotional distance creeps into the relationship that is unacknowledged, unresolved and without a chance for repair. It may be their partner did not realise their need in that moment, or perhaps was preoccupied with their own emotional state, or even that they thought their response as it was, was sufficient. Clearly in this exchange, the apparently emotionally unavailable partner did not intentionally mean to hurt or disappoint their partner. This is not deliberate emotional abuse, although it feels most hurtful to the person who was let down.

Susan Johnson and her colleagues recognised that if these unresolved hurts were not aired, acknowledged and healed, they caused an impasse in the couple therapy, making any attempts to deepen intimacy and develop trust much harder for everyone. She emphasises that it is the attachment significance of the moment that is key, not the content as such.

In couple therapy, we identify with the partners a difficult event, episode or pattern. We articulate the experience in the pattern for each person separately, whilst we help and support the other to listen. We direct the focus to the critical part of the interaction, for example, the outburst of anger, hurt feelings and disappointment, feeling criticized, frustrated and misunderstood, and so on. We help identify the feelings, thoughts, actions and intentions at the critical moment in the episode, working slowly and carefully. The therapist supports the other in continuing to listen and staying responsive. We reverse this experience before inviting them to turn to each other, so that both feel understood and supported. We always negotiate where we start in this process and seek permission of the other, continuing to hold and contain as we go. Susan Johnson advises that where blaming is taking place in the relationship, it is important to help prevent further blaming, through a process of 'softening' and validating experience before inviting curiosity about the other's experience in the interaction. Through the process of systemic tracking of the episode, we try to trace the thoughts and feelings that fuelled the actions back to the person's underlying 'internal working model' of self and relationships (Bowlby 1988). We invite them to be curious about where their working model derives from, for example, some previous history in their family of origin or previous adult romantic relationship. We ask what happened to them. We work slowly as we consider previous experiences of hurts, humiliations, insults and disappointments that may have become part of their working model.

In the following example, we see how a couple resolved an attachment injury in the making, so to say. We work therapeutically with a man and a woman couple, and their little boy. The couple were told by the child protection services that they must meet with us regularly if they wish to continue to care for their child. We shall call the woman Jane (44 years old), and the man, John (48 years old), and the little boy we shall call Tommy (two years old). This is a white British family with extended family in the local community. Jane was married previously and had four children, all of whom have been long term fostered and she is permitted to see them infrequently by child protection services. Her previous husband was frequently physically violent to her and she says she developed her alcohol misuse problem as a way of coping. Her reliance on alcohol led to the child protection services removing her children from her care. John experienced severe physical abuse and neglect as a boy and became involved with a heavy drinking group who engaged in criminal activities. He never had a committed romantic partnership nor did he have children.

Jane and John met and fell in love in a hospital based alcohol detoxification programme. When they were discharged from hospital they continued their relationship and wished to marry and have a child. Their abstinence from alcohol proceeded well and the child protection services staff told them they would support Jane's pregnancy if the couple agreed to work therapeutically with us. This is how they came to us and we had been meeting with them for two years, every two to three weeks, sometimes with Tommy present and sometimes as a couple.

So, what do we mean by attachment injury in the making? One day, they came as a couple, walked into the room with us, and before we had a chance to sit down, John began talking rapidly and urgently—to give you a flavor…… "Ok, Arlene, you want an update—well, we took Tommy to the health visitor for his developmental check and he was fine—and I had a crap birthday—and we took Tommy to the dentist and I sat in the chair so he would see it was nothing to be frightened of…." I was overwhelmed by the rush of words, but heard 'crap birthday' and asked John what he meant. He carried on talking over me, with the same rush of words as to how they took Tommy to the health visitor, and so on. I asked again if we could pause and what did he mean by 'crap birthday'…..the words continued unabated, so I asked again, if we could pause and discuss what he meant by 'crap birthday'. Reluctantly John agreed, if I insisted, which I did! I then realized I had not been looking at Jane. She looked crushed, staring at the floor. I acknowledged this and asked her if we could speak about this, and I explained why I thought it best to start with John. She gave me her permission.

John's story: it was his birthday. He was sitting on the settee, in the morning, waiting for his birthday present as promised. He was happy. Jane came to the living room door, opposite where John was sitting, and apparently turned sideways in the door, and without looking at him, slung his present into his waiting lap. John said he picked it up, tore the paper off, put it on the side table, where it remained, and neither of them spoke about it until our current meeting. He was clearly hurt, puzzled and disappointed. They had not spoken of this.

Jane's story: She loves John very much. Six months earlier she had been wondering what to get John for his birthday. They have little money to spend as a couple. John smokes cigarettes that he rolls up and usually has one sticking out of his top shirt pocket, somewhat bent over with threads of tobacco visible at the end. Both of them love to watch the 1930s Hollywood films on television, where the hero flips open a cigarette case and elegantly offers one to the heroine. Jane thought she wanted to get John a slim, silvered cigarette case for his birthday. For months before hand, she and Tommy went around local second hand shops looking for a cigarette case. Finally they found one they could afford. It was scratched so Jane took it to a local jeweler who re-silvered it and inscribed a love message on the back. Jane wrapped it with coloured tissue paper and looked forward to giving it to John on his birthday. She told me that he was right—that she did turn sideways in the door and sling it in his lap. It seemed that as she approached the doorway, she was overwhelmed and flooded with shame. In that moment, she had remembered her children who had been removed from her care and felt that she did not deserve this new found happiness and this second chance. She was confused and ashamed and still wanted John to have his present and could only sling it sideways.

John felt compassion and cuddled Jane. Jane acknowledged how it had seemed to him at the time, apologized and wanted to rerun the moment in a happier way. John accepted her acknowledgement and he comforted her in turn, telling her she deserved her new happiness and was entitled to it. We focused on exploring how they had not been able to resolve this hurt and told them how pleased we were that they felt safe enough to bring this episode to us for exploration, understanding and resolution.

Conclusion

In conclusion, adult attachment theory is about the mutual exchange of affection and caregiving, and it is both representational and sexual. Attachment theory does not pathologise dependency in our relationships. Rather it emphasises that effective dependency provides the context for openness, exploration and play in our relationships and fosters autonomy in 'knowing our own minds'. Gottman (2011) in his work on healing reminds us to support couples to turn to each other, to make and receive repair attempts and to create shared meanings in the stories we tell about our relationships. Fondness and admiration is nurtured in a context of mutual influence and comfort and support. Thus relational resilience supports the capacity to learn and to take emotional risks (Vetere 2014b). As Fosha (2009, pp) writes: "The roots of resilience… are to be found in the sense of being understood by and existing in the mind and heart of a loving, attuned, and self-possessed other."

References

Bowlby, J. (1988). *A secure base: Clinical applications of attachment theory*. London: Routledge.

Byng Hall, J. (1995). *Re-writing family scripts: Improvisation and systems change*. New York: Guilford.

Cooper, J., & Vetere, A. (2005). *Domestic violence and family safety: working systemically with family violence*. Chichester: Wiley.

Crittenden, P. (Ed.). (2008). *Raising parents: Attachment, parenting and child safety*. Portland: Willan.

Crittenden, P., & Landini, A. (2011). *Assessing adult attachment: A dynamic maturational approach to discourse analysis*. New York: Norton.

Dallos, R., & Vetere, A. (2009). *Systemic therapy and attachment narratives: Applications in a range of clinical settings*. London: Routledge.

Elliott, R., Bohart, A., Watson, J., & Greenberg, L. (2011). Empathy. *Psychotherapy, 48,* 43.

Fosha, D. (2009). *The healing power of emotion: Affective neuroscience, development and clinical practice*. New York: Norton.

Gottman, J. (2011). *The science of trust*. New York: Norton.

Hazan, C., & Shaver, P. (1987). Romantic love conceptualised as an attachment process. *Journal of Personality and Social Psychology, 52,* 511–524.

Johnson, S. (2002). *Emotionally focused couple therapy with trauma survivors*. New York: Guilford.

Johnson, S. (2014). *The love secret: The revolutionary new science of romantic relationships*. London: Piatkus.

Johnson, S., Makinen, J., & Millikin, J. (2001). Attachment injuries in couple relationships: A new perspective on impasses in couple therapy. *Journal of Marital and Family Therapy, 27,* 145–156.

Kirschenbaum, H., & Jourdan, A. (2005). The current status of karl rogers and the person centred approach. *Psychotherapy: Theory Research, Practice, Training, 42,* 37–51.

Khantzian, E. (2014). The self-medication hypothesis and attachment theory: pathways for understanding and ameliorating addictive suffering. In R. Gill (Ed.), *Addictions from an attachment perspective*. London: Karnac.

Lambert, M., & Barley, D. (2001). Research summary on the therapeutic relationship and psychotherapy outcome. *Psychotherapy: Theory Research, Practice, Training, 38,* 357–361.

Mikulincer, M., & Goodman, G. (Eds.). (2006). *The dynamics of romantic love: attachment, caregiving and sex*. New York: Guilford.

Norcross, J., & Wampold, B. (2011). Evidence-based therapy relationships: research conclusions and clinical practices. *Psychotherapy, 48,* 98–102.

Rogers, K. (1975). Empathic: An unappreciated way of being the Counselling. *Psychologist, 5,* 2–10.

Schore, A. (2012). *The science of the art of psychotherapy*. New York: Norton.

Stith, S., McCollum, E., Rosen, K., Locke, L., & Goldberg, P. (2005). Domestic violence focused couples treatment. In J. Lebow (Ed.), *Handbook of clinical family therapy* (pp. 406–430). New York: Wiley.

Tulving, E. (1983). *Elements of episodic memory*. Oxford: Oxford University Press.

Van der Kolk, B. (2014). *The body keeps the score: Mind, brain and body in the transformation of trauma* (2nd ed.). Penguin Books.

Vall, B., Seikkula, J., Latila, A., Holma, J., & Botella, L. (2014). Increasing responsibility, safety and trust through a dialogical approach: A case study in couple therapy for psychologically abusive behaviour. *Journal of Family Psychotherapy, 25,* 275–299.

Vetere, A. (2011). Family violence and family safety: An approach to safe practices in our mental health services. *Partner Abuse, 2,* 246–256.

Vetere, A. (2014a). Alcohol misuse, attachment dilemmas and triangles of interaction: a systemic approach to practice. In R. Gill (Ed.), *Addictions from an attachment perspective*. London: Karnac.

Vetere, A. (2014b). What supports resilient coping among family members? A systemic practitioner's perspective. In J. Ribbens McCarthy, C. Hooper & V. Gillies (Eds.), *Family troubles? exploring changes and challenges in the family lives of children and young people*. Bristol: Policy Press.

Vetere, A. (2015). Working systemically with the legacies of inter-personal violence: A casestudy of couple therapy. *Partner Abuse, 6,* 243–251.

Wilson, M., & Daly, M. (1993). Spousal homicide risk and estrangement. *Violence and Victims, 8,* 3–16.

Chapter 6
Working Systemically with Parents, Children and Adult Survivors When the Abuse Stops

Introduction

Child maltreatment is more common than we might imagine. According to a WHO report (Sethi et al. 2013), at least 850 children die every year as a result of child maltreatment in the European region alone. The same report reviews community surveys on child maltreatment in Europe and around the world and suggests a prevalence rate of 9.6% for sexual abuse, with girls being victims two and a half times as much as boys. No gender differences exist for physical abuse and mental abuse, the prevalence of which rises to 22.9% and 29.1% respectively. Physical neglect is also high, reaching 16.3%, whereas emotional neglect is 18.4%. The different types of abuse are interrelated and in the vast majority of cases it is the parents themselves who abuse their own children. This puts these children at increased risk.

Many parents feel very distressed when experiencing serious difficulties with their children and come forward to ask for help themselves, while others are referred to clinicians for help by child protection services. Therapeutic work with families whose children are placed in out-of-home care is often about repair and healing following maltreatment. Many others, who would have been abused as children, consult with a therapist when they become adults. This chapter is about therapeutic work with families when the violence from parent to child stops. It also touches on violence from child to parent and on violence between siblings. How do we go about helping parents and their children in such difficult situations once the violence stops?

The original version of this chapter was revised: See the "Chapter Note" section at the end of this chapter for details. The erratum to this chapter is available at 10.1007/978-3-319-57789-0_10

C. Sammut Scerri et al., *Intervening After Violence*,
Focused Issues in Family Therapy, DOI 10.1007/978-3-319-57789-0_6

Understanding the Processes at Play When Parents are Abusive Towards Their Children

Systems theory and attachment theory (Bowlby 2008) inform our thinking regarding the processes at play when parents experience great difficulty to connect empathically and to attune to their children and are dangerous towards them. Very often, such parents would have been traumatised themselves as they were growing up and the sense of safety, comfort and love that is normally associated with the relationship between the parents and their children is seriously dented (Lyons-Ruth 1996). A trauma-informed approach that takes into account a relational perspective to trauma (Briere 1992) is therefore helpful when considering the therapeutic implications. These theoretical frameworks also apply when there is child-to-parent violence and violence between siblings. The sociocultural context in which families are embedded also plays an important role. Various authors have noted that parents who are living in poverty feel more stressed than other parents who are more comfortably off, to the extent that the parental relationship may be disrupted (Van Ijzendoorn et al. 1999; Conger et al. 2000; WHO and the Calouste Gulbenkian Foundation 2014; Center on the Developing child at Harvard University 2016).

The focus on what happens afterwards and, above all, what can be done when the abuse stops, which is the focus of this chapter, leads me to keep in mind that the capacity to overcome adversity is ubiquitous and knowledge on resilience (Masten 2014; Walsh 2006) will be an important source of inspiration throughout this chapter. Understanding child abuse from a systemic perspective is also useful as it helps us take into account the fact that abuse and trauma in children occur in the context of relationships.

The Parents

Parents who abuse children often have their own history to contend with which precipitates an intergenerational cycle of abuse (Herzog et al. 1992). A longitudinal study by Lyons Ruth (1996) and Jones (1992) showed that some mothers whose child had a disorganised attachment, which is typical of children who have experienced abuse, were too preoccupied with their own stories to attend to their children and often behaved in an intrusive and hostile manner towards them. Some other mothers seemed helpless and fearful and looked out for comfort from their own children. She noticed that these parents were not doing this on purpose but found it difficult to attune to their children. While the intrusive and hostile mothers were more likely to have histories of physical abuse and/or of witnessing domestic violence, the latter group was more likely to have experienced sexual abuse or parental loss. In our study on the relationship between adolescents and their parents, some of the fathers resorted to intimidation and harsh criticism when setting boundaries for their children. Only those fathers who had reflected on the negative repercussions they had experienced during and in the aftermath of repeated physical and emotional abuse from their own fathers were determined to build a different relationship with their children (Abela et al. 2012).

Manifestations of Abuse on Children

The most frequent symptoms of abuse manifested in children are fear, terror, disorganised attachment, PTSD, behaviour problems and low self-esteem. Children who are sexually abused tend to manifest sexualised behaviour. Children exposed to trauma have twice the rate of psychiatric disorders, particularly anxiety and depression. Whereas the prognosis for a single trauma are good, children who are exposed to multiple traumas are more troubled (Copeland et al. 2007). Bentovim (1992) explains how abuse within the family is most often on going and children are subjected to different and interrelated forms of abuse.

Children may not recall actual memories of abuse; indeed, some children are led to believe otherwise and this makes it more complicated for them to develop a coherent narrative of their experience of abuse; however, these experiences are enacted during play. Children may regress and start bedwetting, or become very active or passive.

> One of the very first boys I (Angela) worked with in a residential home was suffering from elective mutism and encopresis. During the sessions he was spaced out and would gaze into nothingness. He would spend the time blowing consecutive long whistles on a flute. These eerie sounds and the silence in between created an air of fear in the room. Images of howling wolves hounding a terrorised deer in the woods would come to my mind's eye. Many months later it transpired that his mother who suffered from a mental illness used to put his head between the stair railings in an attempt to keep him quiet during the day.[1]

Van der Kolk and his colleagues forming the National Child Traumatic Stress Network argued in (2009) that 'whether or not they (meaning the children) exhibit symptoms of PTSD, children who have developed in the context of ongoing danger, maltreatment and inadequate caregiving systems are ill-served by the current diagnostic system as it frequently leads to no diagnosis, multiple unrelated diagnoses, an emphasis on behavioural control without recognition of interpersonal trauma and lack of safety in the etiology of symptoms, and a lack of attention to ameliorating the developmental disruptions that underlie the symptoms' (Van Der Kolk 2015, p. 359). The network proposed criteria for what they termed Developmental Trauma Disorder (DTD). This included those who had direct experience of or had witnessed prolonged adverse events over a period of at least one year, and children manifesting the following symptoms for at least 6 months were considered to be suffering from DTD. Symptoms would comprise those

[1]All vignettes are either taken from existing literature or are closely parallel to stories of clients. However, every effort has been made to conceal the true identity of the clients.

featuring on the posttraumatic spectrum but also affective, physiological, attentional, behavioural, self- and relational dysregulation as well as functional impairment. Children would exhibit such impairment in at least two different contexts such as at school, within the family or with their peer group. Others experience dysregulation when having to abide by rules and regulations in the work environment or even in their own body.

The above manifestations highlight the fact that children are often traumatised in the context of their ongoing relationships.

The Healing Process

Unfortunately, children who are traumatised are often diagnosed as having ADHD or as exhibiting oppositional behaviour and are given medication or are subjected to behaviour modification. Such an approach does not take into account the relational context within which the trauma and abuse of children occur. When child abuse takes place in the home, trauma 'is woven into the emotional dynamics of a family' (Dallos and Vetere 2009, p. 122).

Breaking the Silence of Abuse

> I still remember the mother of a 5-year-old girl lamenting with me about her behaviour. She described her as 'ADHD'. She then moved on to tell me about her relationship with her husband. The story unfolded painstakingly. The couple were verbally and emotionally abusive towards each other and the daughter would witness this on a daily bases. I worked with this family; sometimes focusing on the couple dynamics and sometimes bringing the focus on the girl. The parents were very critical of her disobedience. In my reflections with them I invited them to reflect on the effect this daily manifestation of abuse was having on the child. The girl felt safe in the clinic and insisted on coming more often. One day she expressed her disappointment at the fact that her mother would hit her with a broom.

Breaking the silence is not easy for a child and it is often the parents themselves —as was the case in my vignette above—or symptomatic behaviour that is noticed by other professionals in other contexts that bring children and parents to the clinic. Parental neglect and harsh treatment predict misbehaviour in the child at school and a difficulty in empathising with others, which in turn lead to further rejection by the parents and the school. These children are often referred to a psychologist or family therapist by the school.

The Importance of Working in a Team

Working systemically with parents and their children by getting the other professionals who are involved in the life of the child on board is very important. Systemic work with the family and the school system is more likely to bring about good results (Dowling and Osborne 2003), especially when the child is manifesting behavioural difficulties in both contexts as is typical of those with DTD. Furthermore, for children who are in residential care or in foster care, bringing these important networks of support on board is also important. Inter-professional collaboration and teamwork help to maximise the efforts of every person involved and avoid fragmentation, which often alienates children and their families who then end up getting lost in the meanders of the system.

The value of teamwork cannot be overemphasised and becomes increasingly important, the more complex and delicate the situation becomes. Good teams give valuable feedback to each other, and tend to have the necessary resources to provide crisis intervention, such as home visits, if necessary. Moreover, the school setting, residential home or foster family are better supported to provide a safe place for the child

> I remember how difficult my therapeutic work with the boy who was suffering from elective mutism and encopresis was in the beginning. Seeing how full of fear the child was, I approached the carer in charge of the dormitory to tell him how important it was that he tucked the boy in bed and made him feel safe as he was about to sleep. The carer was very sensitive and dedicated. He took special care of the boy and even bought him a bird as a pet. Some days later Peter broke his mutism in the home by interacting with the bird, chirping to it and expecting a reaction back.

The First Sessions: Building a Therapeutic Alliance with Families

The first meetings with families are of crucial importance as it is during these meetings that the therapeutic alliance between the family therapist and the family starts to be forged. The evidence from meta-analyses shows that the therapeutic alliance is an indispensable common factor for a good therapeutic outcome (Wampold 2015). Dallos and Vetere (2009) write about what they term as 'the therapeutic invitation' (p. 124) for families where there is abuse. They argue that very often, in such families, seeking help is experienced as an ambivalent experience by the family members as they may find it difficult to trust the helping professionals. Their past experience of abuse would have taught them that 'people who should offer them trust actually hurt them' (p. 124). Moreover, as McIlwaine and O'Sullivan (2015) point out, 'families feel distrustful of each other and are not confident about the other's capacity to listen and respond in helpful ways' (p. 314). Parents may come to therapy only because they have been pushed to do so or because they are at their wit's end and find themselves trapped in a vicious cycle of abuse.

It is important to gauge the capacity for trust of family members when getting to know them. Parents who are more trusting may possibly have developed their resilience through the support of significant persons in moments when they most needed it.

> The example of a mummy whose presenting problem was about her son's misbehaviour comes to mind. She described her son as "spiteful" and "mean" when talking to me over the telephone. In the very first session I introduced myself to the family made up of father, mother, daughter and son. I told them that my work was that of looking after the wellbeing of families and it would help me to get to know how they were doing. I made use of scaling questions to gauge the quality of their relationships. One could already notice from the very first session that the mother had a strong capacity for empathy and she was very sorry to discover that her son was feeling very alone, miserable and distanced from all the family members.

The importance of building a good therapeutic alliance with both the child/ren and the parents cannot be underestimated. When offering short-term psychodynamic psychotherapy for adolescents, (Whitefield and Midgley 2015) highlight the importance of the therapeutic alliance. In their project, parents and children have different therapists and children are provided with more sessions. However, not all psychodynamic therapists adopt this approach. Sometimes it is the same practitioner who sees the parents and the children. Children are seen more often than the parents are and conjoint meetings are not so frequent. These ways of working have implications in terms of the kind of therapeutic alliance that is built between the therapist and the child and the parents respectively. Whitefield and Midgley point out that 'there has been little empirical research into the nature of parent work itself and there appears to be much variance on how this work is undertaken in routine practice' (p. 272). They also cite Rustin's work about dialogues with parents. Rustin noted that 'developing work with parents took practitioners into new territory' (p. 274). The work may sometimes involve work with couples and adults, some of whom are referred for adult psychotherapy. Although this is not mentioned in the paper, the need for case conferences, meetings and ongoing communication between the different therapists is also essential.

In the absence of violent and abusive behaviour, or when the nature of the abuse is moderate or low and parents show remorse and are seriously committed to stop the abuse and to work on themselves, (Mcllwaine and O'Sullivan 2015) argue that 'there is a strong case for family work to facilitate the strengthening and rebuilding of relationships' (p. 314.). Parents and children are often seen together but also separately. Very often it is the same systemic therapist who sees the different family members, albeit with the support of the team. This has implications regarding the building of the therapeutic alliance. In such a context, the positioning of the therapist vis-à-vis the abuse is crucial and both the adults and the children need to be made aware of this. As Dallos and Vetere (2009) point out, the parents as perpetrators need to take 'responsibility for actions that hurt, frighten and intimidate' (p. 126).

Once such responsibility is ascertained, the therapist has to be very skilful in the way she or he engages with the children and the parents, empathising with both and facilitating a conversation between them. Escudero et al. (2012) alert us to the possibility of split alliances between family members towards the therapist in conjoint sessions. The authors present a session where a rupture occurred when the therapist invited the mother for an individual session to explore how her personal stress may be affecting her relationship with her daughter, who is described as 'rebellious' in the presence of the daughter. The therapist was very skilful in bringing about an emotional turnaround by enhancing his connection with each family member and by highlighting what they were both striving for in their relationship, thus helping them to keep connected.

Building a secure therapeutic alliance with the different members in the family may prove to be a challenging task for therapists in general and especially for systemic therapists, who must continuously make clinical judgements on when and how to intervene during conjoint sessions, in one-to-one sessions or in sessions for a particular subsystem (a parental subsystem, for example). Children need to be informed that at times it might prove helpful to share what they do in the one-to-one session with the parent/s. However, a conversation about the nature of the disclosure will take place between the child and the therapist first, and the child will have a say on how this is communicated. High-conflict couples who are at war with each other even post separation and divorce but who both have joint custody or, in some cases, supervised access may present more challenges (Dowling and Gorell Barnes 1999). In spite of the fact that as a general rule family therapists work with the whole system, this does not preclude them from referring family members for individual or couple psychotherapy.

In spite of the complexity involved when working with the whole family, the focus on the relational connection between family members and the ability of the systemic therapist to bring about change by consolidating relationships and strengthening the attachment bond between family members is considered to be a major strength when working with parents and children.

Taking an Empathic Stance with Parents

Psychologists working with children and their parents find working with parents more taxing than working with the children. This is because some parents may feel guilty, criticised or blamed for their child's presenting behaviour and find it hard to open up or may be critical towards the therapist (Brown 2008), especially when the latter is young (Whitefield and Midgley 2015). Professionals may not always be empathic with parents when working with them and they often forget about the intergenerational legacy of abuse and the experiences that lead parents to lack attunement with their children. It is a struggle that psychologists/therapists and other related professionals face when working with parents and their children. This is especially so when professionals are not trained from a systemic perspective. However, even professionals who are trained from a systemic perspective, struggle to be empathic with both. To this effect, both the WHO and the Calouste Gulbenkain Foundation report (2014) and the (Center on the Developing Child at Harvard University 2016) highlight the importance of building a skilled workforce to work with adults and children in difficulty. The self-regulation of the professional is considered important (See Chap. 8 on Supervision and Consultation about this). Research has also shown that supervision for trauma work helps clinicians empathise with clients (Wilson and Lindy 1994). This is especially so when such clients are experienced by clinicians as being uncooperative or difficult.

Mullins (2014) makes the point that: 'Empathy is very empowering for clients, especially to parents involved in the child welfare system who feel powerless, helpless, and unmotivated. An empathic worker has the opportunity to determine the outcome of a successful reunification. … When parents sense empathy from child welfare workers they may become more likely to comply with tasks and become more motivated to actively participate in the process to reunite with their children' (Mullins 2014, p. 250). She writes about a framework for cultivating empathy towards parents and points out that 'one of the most difficult challenges child welfare workers face is the ability to comprehend what parents are thinking and feeling and communicate that understanding, without judgement to the parents' (p. 243).

Mullins (2014) and Gerdes and Segal (2009, 2011) also highlight the importance of self-awareness, emotion regulation and perspective taking in the development of empathy by professionals: 'Active and deep listening, promotion of cooperation, understanding, providing validation, and support are all important attitudes and behaviours' (p. 245). Self-awareness on the part of the therapist entails personal work. Mullins (2014) and Walsh (2006) argue that it is much easier for professionals to empathise with clients who hold their same set of beliefs. When this is not the case, professionals need to suspend judgement and enhance patience.

Being a Good Listener, Making Good Conversation, Showing Compassion, Providing Validation and Comfort

This work is delicate and complex and can be very taxing on the children and on the parents as well as on the therapist. One way that can help the therapist remain attuned to the family members is by eliciting feedback from them. Asking the family about what is helping them in therapy and what is not so helpful is considered very positively by family members in spite of the fact that therapists need to be aware of the power differential that might inhibit families from being completely truthful, especially when the therapeutic alliance is still fragile. Such an intervention is a good way of building a collaborative relationship and strengthening the therapeutic alliance. We know from research in psychotherapy that the way the therapist connects with the clients in the first sessions is associated with progress later on (Cramer and Takens 1992). Stratton et al. (2013) also suggest that the clinical use of the SCORE instrument would be highly appropriate for assessing early improvement in therapy for families.

Helping parents understand how their own stories of neglect and verbal, physical or even sexual abuse are shaping their behaviour with their children is not an easy task. Seeking permission from parents about working around these stories can be experienced as very respectful by them. In systemic therapy, genograms, which are usually started in the very initial sessions, are an excellent tool that would help to create a conversation about the families of origin. As a student at the Tavistock Clinic, one of us (Angela) used to observe Byng-Hall work as a family therapist from behind the screen. He used to make use of real soft toys that would stick to a flannel graph when building the genogram. He then used to prop up the genogram in the clinic for the family every time they came in for the session. Each time new family members or significant others were mentioned, family members were invited to choose new figurines and stick them to the family tree on the flannel graph. It is always helpful to have the genogram available for easy reference, especially since the genogram may help to elicit new information even when a parent attends alone.

Very often, parents need to be cared for themselves. They frequently complain about having a low mood and other related somatic symptoms, such as migraines, and do not spend quality time with their children. They expect their children to thrive on their own and behave at all times. Trying to comfort them by exploring how they can look after themselves is a good starting point. Building networks of support through the school or childcare centres—if not through their own family—and incorporating this in the genogram can be really helpful.

When parents complain about their children, a good opening question to get to the parents' own stories of being parented is to ask: When you were young, was it similar or different to what you are telling me about your child? Many parents react to this question and are willing to reflect more on their own stories of loss and pain. Conversely, others might insist that they are very different from their children or that the children resemble their father who is now an ex-partner, the latter being someone who had been very cruel to them. These answers indicate that a lot of work needs to take place for attunement to be enhanced between the children and the parents. Some find the task of parenting so demanding that they would rather abdicate their responsibilities as parents and have their children parent them instead. They expect their children to be sensitive to their bad moods and are too absorbed to attend to their needs.

There will come a time, maybe during a moment of crisis, when some of the more closed parents will open up and allow us to see a part of themselves that they had left hidden to protect themselves from the pain and the risk of having to expose themselves to someone whom they deem as being alien to the reality they have grown up in. Helping a mother regulate her emotions after she threw a severe tantrum when her husband exposed her misdeeds during therapy was a major turning point in her ability to trust me. These moments are considered as key turning points in therapy and a lot depends on our sensitivity and the quality of our attunement with the parents.

To have come to this point, many parents would have already cross-examined our ability to empathise and be compassionate with them, not only by the way we respond verbally but also non-verbally. Neander and Skott (2006) interviewed parents, who struggled with their children, about professionals who they experienced as helpful. The parents emphasised non-verbal communication and mentioned the warmth with which they interacted with them, the smiles and the gentle tone of voice of the professionals. Our ability to empathise transcends our words and can be read by our clients, even from the way we look at them. The recent research on mirror neurons by Rizzolatti and Craighero (2004) has confirmed what we already knew on an intuitive level. It was Winnicott (1958) who first spoke about the mother's pupils acting as a first mirror to her child.

Our Empathy can Even be Experienced on a Somatic Level

> I remember a lone parent who had come to see me one morning. She narrated a very traumatic story of how her son was going to choke on a piece of foam that came out of the settee. The boy was turning blue and she froze and could hardly focus to call the doctor. Luckily she was at her parents' house and her father helped the child clear the air pipe from the material. The mother told me that she considered her father's act as lifesaving and this helped her to partly forgive him for his abuse towards her when she was a child. The amount of emotion that flowed as this mother narrated this story left me dizzy for hours that day and I felt as if someone had hit me on my head with a brick. When I told my client this in our next session, she promptly replied: "I can see that you have understood what I was talking about!"

Body-based senses are often at the core of what traumatic experiences are about (Van der Kolk 2015), and our ability to decipher them in ourselves and in our clients, even when they do not mention them, is a form of advanced empathy. They can be very therapeutic for parents, who often feel empowered and acquire a new sense of identity as they let go of some of the shame and frozen terror that would have accompanied them as children in the face of abuse. Such a process is not always easy for clinicians. I could sense that I had somehow experienced vicarious trauma as I empathised with this woman when I took this story with me to supervision. As soon as I started to talk about it, I felt as if I was choking on my saliva. In Chap. 7 of this book I will highlight how important it is for therapists to process vicarious traumatisation during supervision.

Taking into Account the Social Context of the Family

Systemic practitioners are also trained to take into account the context in which families are embedded and are mindful of the experiences that they go through. 'Parents who are involved in the system may have experienced a complex combination of socioeconomic, structural or personal barriers, such as poverty, racism, or lack of parental role model, that would have made their life more difficult' (Mullins 2014, pp. 249–250).

The Center on the Developing Child at Harvard University (2016) makes the point that it is important not to medicalise poverty, violence, racism and other threats. They call for 'science informed innovation at the neighbourhood systems, and policy levels, including investments in housing, income support and job training among other domains of influence on child well-being' (p. 6).

A lack of adequate income and other support services is a big source of stress and distress for parents who have a right to the appropriate resources to be able to function appropriately. This rights-based approach to dealing with poverty (Abela and Renoux 2014) is indispensable if professionals are to adopt a way of working that is socially just, 'thus demonstrating overall ethical responsibility to social context' (D'Arrigo-Patrick et al. 2016, p. 2).

Very often, families living in poverty are isolated and socially excluded (Ridge 2009). Therapists and other members in a transdisciplinary team can widen the system creating networks of support within the community for parents living in poverty. Liaising with schools and other systems, such as the extended family or the parish, can maximise support for parents and their children and provide an important source of connection.

Ways of Developing the Reflexivity of the Parents

When parents have a space to think and not have to face unexpected crises on a daily basis because of the precarious conditions in which they live, this will enhance their reflective functioning. Furthermore, the increased understanding and validation that they receive empower them to be more proactive towards their children.

Brown (2008), who is a Bowen Family Systems therapist, notes that little has been written about how to help parents see their part in the family system when problems emerge. This is a sensitive issue because many parents would rather have the therapist focus on the children rather than on themselves. She draws from feedback which she elicits from two sets of parents on what 'facilitates a parent's willingness to consider their own contribution to the circular relationship patterns in which symptoms emerge' (p. 61). In one of the families, the two adolescent daughters were violent towards each other. Simple questions, like asking parents to give their reaction on what was going on in the family, rather than focusing on what the symptom bearer/s were doing, were considered helpful. The questions helped to develop more awareness and helped parents to think about the impact of their behaviour (Read more in Chap. 1 on sibling violence).

Brown points out that the therapist has to be very skilful in the way the questions are posed—to not take a 'blame the parents' tone, while at the same time asking questions around parent and couple issues. Moreover, she explains the value of waiting for the members of the family to provide explanations for the current behaviour in the family system rather than acting as a 'mouthpiece' for any one of the members. In this respect, the therapist too has to focus on self-awareness in the therapeutic relationship and remain engaged with the different members without getting drawn into alliances.

As mentioned earlier on, individual sessions with each of the parents (when both are available) are sometimes necessary as at times one of the partners may fear criticism and blame by the other partner.

> A mother who asked for family therapy after their house broke down following a bomb explosion nearby was particularly concerned about her younger son's challenging behaviour. She found it impossible to keep calm with him and they were having frequent rows. At the same time, she idealised her eldest son. One day, she came to see me on her own in the morning as her husband could not make it and the children were busy preparing for their exams. After giving me a short update of how they were faring in their rented apartment, the conversation drifted to her childhood. Once again she described her father's preferential treatment towards her siblings when they were young and how painful it felt for her not to feel validated by him and her eventual rebellion. It did not take much probing for this woman to put two and two together and to become aware of the resonance between her painful story with her father and the one that she was living with her son.

A capacity for awareness and reflexivity is an important resource for parents to help them build an intimate experience with their children. Some stories include conversations about the experiences parents would have gone through during their childhood. Many systemic therapists make use of attachment theory to make sense of the stories that are narrated. The parents' ability to have a coherent story (Main et al. 1985) about their experiences of being parented is considered as being a good indicator of whether the parents had processed their adverse childhood stories. In situations where the parent is still feeling vulnerable and the work is more like therapy work as opposed to parent work, Whitefield and Midgley (2015), who work from a psychoanalytic perspective, highlight the importance of working 'hard to draw back the parent to think about how her past related to her relationship with the child' (p. 277). This is because once parents open up, those who are still very raw about their own experiences need to come to terms with their own stories to be able to attend to their children. In this respect, asking them to do both simultaneously is a complex endeavour and necessitates therapists who are able to express compassion and understanding in their regard while keeping in mind the needs of the child. It is only when parents feel such attunement that they can let go of some of their pain and find space in their head to start to think about their children.

Some parents may need more time to process their trauma and loss. Comforting clients is very therapeutic during such moments. This is why it is important for parents to have sessions for themselves where they can open up without having to be mindful of what they say because of the children. Once parents process their pain by talking about it in the presence of the therapist, who can witness their pain, I like to make use of interventions that encourage resilience, such as the ones proposed by Walsh (2006). She suggests asking the persons involved what they needed to overcome their traumatic experiences and then move on to ask them how they could make use of such wisdom by passing it on to their children.

The use of language is very important. Metaphors can help parents to persist in being creative and invent new and more constructive ways of relating to each other and towards their children when the latter misbehave. One of my favourites is that of validating their efforts and likening them to pioneers who courageously strive to invent new loving ways of being together. Byng-Hall's (1986) notion of corrective scripts for parents is very pertinent here.

Working with the Child During Individual Sessions

Emilia Dowling highlights the importance of giving children a voice (Dowling 1993) in contexts where the parents may not have the space to attend to their children's needs and may need help themselves. Children who are abused often need therapy sessions on their own to be able to overcome and heal from an abusive experience. A number of studies report that initially, children may feel reluctant about attending therapy (Foster and Hegedorn 2014) and it is therefore very important that they can feel comfortable and able to trust the therapist. In systemic work, the first sessions are often held with the whole family. It is only at a second stage that the child or, in some cases, the siblings are invited for sessions on their own, which often alternate with sessions where the parents are present. Broaching the subject of abuse with a therapist is not easy for children, even when there is a very good relationship between the therapist and the child. In a study on the experience of therapy for children who had been sexually abused, Isidora (8 years old) confirms this: "we talked about the topic with the psychologist and I didn't like it very much … but we also had to talk about it for her to help me" (Capella et al. 2016, p. 11). Although children admitted that talking was helpful, they preferred playing to just talking.

> During individual sessions, a boy who I used to see and who was physically and emotionally abused would pretend to be going around driving a car and then crashing during sessions. He would then ask me to call an ambulance and take him to hospital where I would become a doctor and have to attend to his bone fractures. He would then want me to bandage him and take care of him. I could see that he found the whole operation very comforting.
>
> He also sought validation by pretending that he was a famous footballer; a hero, in fact. My role would be that of a commentator announcing his entry into the football arena and then highlighting his extraordinary tackles and goals and inviting the spectators to applaud him. Given his mother's wish to do well at school, and his low marks during tests, he used to lie

to me about his results at school. I empathised with him and with his wish to do very well at school. Following my intervention he did not feel the need to pretend that he was doing well at school when he was not.

Although children in their teenage years are more likely to talk about the abuse rather than play, they still find that talking about it is not easy. Besides the discomfort that talking about difficult situations provokes, children are extremely loyal towards their parents and find it very hard to disclose information about the abuse. One adolescent girl spent a lot of time talking to me about her difficult relationships with her peers before she actually spoke to me about the abusive way in which her parents treated her.

Joint Work Between Parent/s and Their Children

Systemic work gives a lot of importance to joint work. During these sessions, the therapist has the opportunity to meet the child and the parent or both parents (depending on who has the custody of the child) to continue working on the relationship between them. Usually, this is an opportunity where the concerns, hurt and pain pertaining to their relationship, including those that would have emerged in their respective sessions, would be processed further.

These sessions are very healing. Parents and children have opportunities for therapeutic conversations, which may be facilitated through play techniques in the presence of someone who can help regulate their emotions. This in itself is a learning experience. Many families have a history of relating in a very hostile way to each other or glossing over experiences that may be painful for family members. Conversations in the clinic can be an opportunity for parents and children to slow things down and speak intimately to each other. Parents and children may be yearning to use and even more listen to their loved ones, addressing them in tender and affectionate language but they are shy to do so. In such circumstances, structural interventions such as the ones suggested by Minuchin (1974), where the therapist asks family members to give each other a hug, hold hands or say sorry, are good emotional experiences for family members.

It is often revealing for parents to see that children react positively to tender and warm interaction by the therapist and that they comply more in such circumstances. When parents witness the children behaving and relating well to the family therapist, they are sometimes in disbelief and attribute the child's behaviour to the fact that the child is still getting used to the therapist and therefore not being his or her true self.

When hyperarousal takes place at the clinic or is reported back, it may help to externalise it with the family by mapping the cycle of arousal. The family may be asked to find a name for such a process and the undesirable behaviour of family members. This distance may help them better understand and describe the process and gives them more control over their dysregulated behaviour (White 1988/1989).

The use of photos can also be very helpful when doing attachment work

> An adolescent girl was devastated and felt very abandoned by her parents who had left her behind with the grandmother when they moved house and took her younger sister with them. She joined the family home when she was fourteen but was inconsolable. She dropped out of school and spent her day eating chicken nuggets from a takeaway nearby with money she would steal from her parents or from her sister's moneybox. Attachment-based work making use of photos depicting the daughter spending time with the family, especially the mother, along the years helped the mother and daughter to narrate stories of their relationship and to achieve a certain amount of closeness. At the end of therapy, a much thicker story emerged for the daughter that helped her appreciate the challenges and the dilemmas that her mother had to face trying to keep a full-time job and take care of her husband who struggled with mental health problems along the way. She developed a sense that her mother did love her after all and, although she experienced bouts of loneliness and longed for her mother's affection, she was willing to go back to school.

Conversations between parents and children are extremely helpful in the healing process. Children need to make sense of disappointment, loss and abandonment to be able to regulate their emotions. Children who experience sexual abuse by family members (e.g. stepfather, sibling, relative or biological father) find the support of their parents, or the other parent, who is most likely to be the mother, very important. Capella et al. (2016) noted that a lack of support hindered the recovery process to a great extent, whereas disclosing the abusive experience and receiving support from family members marked a turning point in the recovery process. Such support needs to be talked about during the joint sessions.

Therapeutic talk at this level is never an easy process and is even more difficult when children feel like they want to rebel rather than get closer. This process of distance regulation becomes even more complicated as parents themselves are still struggling to attune themselves to their children's emotional states, to the extent that parents and children often report having clashed in the course of therapy. Joint sessions may be considered as excellent therapeutic spaces where the difficulties in the relationship may be processed further.

Mcllwaine and O'Sullivan (2015) talk about helping family members increase their awareness of the link between the eruptive behaviour that takes place and the emotional state that precedes the eruption by identifying their bodily responses through body mapping. They cite the example of a mother (Mary) and her son Jamie (12) who were referred because of Jamie's violent behaviour towards his mother

> Body mapping with Mary and Jamie helped Mary identify that she 'gets tight in the chest and finds it hard to breathe' when triggered by Jamie's behaviour. Jamie identified his early warning signs, such as his heart beating fast and a hot sensation in his hands and feet. By mapping their responses using an outline of a gingerbread drawing and using colour, shape and texture, Mary and Jamie deepened their awareness of themselves and each other. Jamie was able to put words to those feelings. With growing insight, and by identifying early warning signs of being stressed, anxious and upset, Mary and Jamie agreed that they would assist each other to calm down and take responsibility for their own early warning signs by stopping the conversation. During sessions, they practised throwing a ball to each other as a way of calming themselves and each other (p. 320).

This may be considered as an excellent way of identifying and possibly breaking vicious circles. Besides regulating their emotions, each family member needs to think about what he or she can do to change the escalation.

I also find that giving feedback to parents and children when they are behaving warmly to each other reinforces positive behaviour during joint work and validates family members, thus freeing them from the guilt and shame that they carry. Spontaneous feedback like: 'It's lovely to see you giving a hug to each other!' creates an immediate sense of well-being among family members. Other affirming play activities include the use of narrative approaches such as the one where family members have to imagine that they were to be shipwrecked on a deserted island with other family members with whom they usually clash. They then have to say why they would be grateful to have them on the island with them.

When Separation from the Parents is Necessary

When the abuse is severe and ongoing, the only way that children can be protected is by separating them from their parents. This is a very drastic intervention that may be experienced as being traumatic for the child and the parents, in spite of the fact that it may be considered necessary. In such circumstances, the children may experience being placed with their next of kin—if they are close to the extended family—as being less traumatic. An adult who was interviewed about his experience of being placed in residential care as a child because of his mother's severe mental illness exclaimed that: '… it's difficult, I wished to die when I was in care…' and then he exclaimed 'but it's true, they dumped me there. Because no one out of 3000 relatives from my parents' side, cousins and uncles and aunts, no one took care of me and my sister! … It's true I was naughty at that time, but … it's hard to accept!' (Galea 2009, p. 67).

Even in contexts where the nature of the abuse is so severe that it merits the separation of the child from the parents, restoring the parent–child relationship continues to be an ideal goal in therapy. The importance of not taking a punitive stance towards parents and to help them gain some control over the situation may work wonders. Mullins (2014) gives a very good example of how social workers can interact with parents when they are distressed because children are taken away from them: 'You're right, this is a difficult situation. Let's work on having them back with you' (p. 247).

Adopting a family-centred approach when children are in out-of-home care would entail working with a bigger team of professionals, as I indicated further up, including foster carers, who are considered to form part of the professional team and at the same time need ongoing support with the placement.

How do we Help Families Heal and Repair and Move from Reflecting to Acting?

In spite of their best efforts and their regular attendance to therapy, parents may still find it difficult to contain a child. In the face of misbehaviour, their affect is aroused in an unhelpful way. Parents often start criticising each other instead and put each other down for not being able to elicit the desired behaviour from their child. They also attack the child verbally, trying to refrain from physical punishment because of the promise they would have made to stop the abuse. These incidents remind us that this work requires patience and perseverance and how important it is to keep an eye on the progress achieved in spite of the fall-backs.

These stories narrated by parents during therapy continue to give us an opportunity to have a conversation with them about what would help them to regulate their behaviour when things go wrong. Children and parents always come up with little ideas that help. Usually, the soothing behaviour that they come up with is not relational but relies on their own solitary endeavours, such as smoking a cigarette, going for a walk or playing with the cat. When the parents are alone, either as a couple or individually, it would help to ask them about the patterns of comforting that used to help them as children when they felt agitated or in distress. Some may remember happy moments when their parents listened to them, played with them or allowed them to do things together in the kitchen, or gave them a cuddle or a hug. These are precious memories that may enhance their empathy towards their child and each other if the parents are coming to therapy together. When these memories are not forthcoming, exploring with them the sort of behaviour they would have enjoyed receiving from their parents in moments of distress is very therapeutic (Hughes 2007).

At the same time, it is important that the therapist highlights positive change. Families enjoy being validated for what they do well.

> During the session, a mother takes a call from her mobile because it is her son who is calling. The boy starts to complain because he does not want to stay with the babysitter but the mother remains calm and explains that she has an appointment. She ends the call by telling him that she loves him.

This kind of interaction is very different from how the mother and son had interacted in the initial sessions and needs to be validated. In moments when the relationship between parents and children is not going well, it also helps to remind them of the good moments

> You remember how happy and content your son was when he came down from the session; he hugged you and told you "I love you"!

This form of coaching may be necessary for families who are severely deprived. Van der Kolk (2015) notes that at the Trauma Centre in Brookline in Massachusetts (trauma.center.org) where he works, they have developed programmes to coach parents in connection and attunement.

Helping Adult Survivors of Abuse

Many children who suffer abuse never seek help or only do so when they grow up. Rutter (1999) noted that not all children are affected in the same way by adversity and more than half of the children did not suffer from any particular disorder, irrespective of the risk involved. Others seemed able to suppress the abusive experiences and cope relatively well in their daily lives until something happens which acts as a trigger and the person's defensive system breaks (Van der Kolk 2015), while others are more severely affected. Herman, Perry and Van der Kolk (1989) report that 81% of the patients diagnosed with borderline personality disorder at a psychiatric hospital in the United States had been severely abused or neglected. Most of these children had gone through this experience before the age of 7. He also notes that these studies have been replicated by others (See van der Kolk (2015, p. 140).

In the case of sexual abuse, many clients are usually women who would have been abused as children in their own homes. Given the taboo surrounding incest, it is not easy for these women to speak about an experience that usually takes place in secrecy and where words are hardly exchanged. Elsa Jones' (1992) rich account of her work with adult survivors of child sexual and even physical abuse is an excellent point of reference when working in this area. Her ability to interweave a feminist, systemic perspective of the client's personal experience of abuse makes it possible to take into account the larger family and societal context when helping clients make meaning of their traumatic experience. In her work, she provides an awareness of power abuse mostly by men towards women and towards children irrespective of gender.

Creating a Safe and Containing Place

Disclosing the abuse is an important step for recovery (Anderson and Hiersteiner 2008) and, therefore, creating 'a safe and containing space where the unthinkable and the unsayable can be expressed' (Jones 1992, p. 8) is very important. I would like to think that my humble clinic, which is a little old converted house with honey-coloured limestone walls situated very close to the village core, may provide a welcoming setting for my clients; nevertheless, the setting is just a detail, and genuineness, empathy and positive regard—as espoused by Rogers (1977)—are key in the building of the client–therapist relationship.

Jones' (1992) non-expert approach when working with adult survivors is respectful of the clients who remain in charge of their story at all times in the course of their therapeutic experience. Her belief in the resilience and resourcefulness of her clients creates a sense of safety for them. From my experience, clients are more willing to confide when the therapist signals to them that they are not obliged to disclose every single detail of their story but only what they consider to be relevant and appropriate to tell.

> One of my early clients was sent to me by an orthopaedic surgeon. She had consulted with the latter because of the massive pain she was experiencing all over her body. When she came into my clinic she was looking very scared and would not give me eye contact. She told me that she had already been seeing a psychiatrist for a number of years because of her uncontrollable anxiety. She would talk very little and, to be honest, I did not have much hope that I could help her. We wrote a letter to her psychiatrist together to inform him that she was to start seeing me. Then, something extraordinary happened. She started writing letters to me by hand where she disclosed horrible episodes of her sexual abuse by multiple perpetrators. I would read the letters during the session with her permission. She gradually found a voice and was able to talk and elaborate on what had happened. Her ability to bounce back from adversity was a real lesson about resilience.

Bessel van der Kolk (2015) points out how important it is to break the silence about abuse. In his book, he confesses that

As long as I had no place where I could let myself know what it was like when my father locked me in the cellar of our house for various 3-year-old offences, I was chronically preoccupied with being exiled and abandoned. Only when I could talk about how that little boy felt, only when I could forgive myself for having been as scared and submissive as he was, did I start to enjoy the pleasure of my own company (p. 233).

Processing Feelings of Intimidation, Stigmatisation, Isolation, Helplessness and Self-blame and Anger in the Family Context

Clients who would have experienced sexual and/or physical abuse as children go through a rollercoaster of emotions during the abuse itself, but also afterwards. The notion of blame persecutes many clients (Jones 1992), especially those who are trapped in incestuous relationships. Many seek reassurance and want to hear that they are not to blame for the abuse. Their story is often complicated by a sense of guilt and shame vis-à-vis their mother, who is expected to be their protector. Others may feel angry for not having been believed and protected by their mother and may wish to use the therapy space to understand and make sense of the experience.

Giving New Meaning to the Abuse

Understanding the family context may bring about new meaning of one's trauma. Clients may develop compassion even towards their abuser, while others may wish to position themselves differently to those who brought them up.

> One of my clients brought her father in for therapy to tell him in front of me how much the abuse had affected her. She pondered for quite some time about the idea of telling her mother about what had actually happened. She imagined that her mother would leave her father if she were to know. In the end she chose not to tell her, for fear that her mother might break down when hearing the shocking news. Nevertheless, over time this woman became more respectful of herself and although she brought up her children on her own following a breakdown in the relationship with their father, she kept a job and was given increasing responsibility at work, and had a small network of friends who loved her. She also kept very close contact with her mother and was able to see her father's good points in spite of the fact that she did not experience any affection towards him.

Working with Survivors in the Context of Their Couple Relationships

Sue Johnson (1989) was among the first to suggest that couple therapy over and above individual therapy was needed for adult survivors of abuse, especially for those who were living in the context of a couple relationship. Her way of working (Johnson 2002), which aims at strengthening attachment bonds and also draws on trauma research, may be considered as a treatment of choice for couples where one or both are trauma survivors.

This is because the quality of the relationship with one's partner is an important determinant of well-being. Ford and Courtois (2013) explain how survivors sometimes choose partners who are immature, needy or downright abusive and very similar to their perpetrators. Others may choose partners who are more dependable and loyal but who are emotionally unavailable and are unable to offer them comfort or remain emotionally engaged in moments of distress. These types of couple-fit create an impasse, making it very difficult for couples to re-edit their life story and create a better version of their existence.

While couple therapy is contraindicated for couples where there is domestic violence, it may be very beneficial for those who are not as it helps them understand how the traumas that they went through in their lives affected them, both as individuals and as a couple, and can help them work together as a couple to develop a secure attachment between them. On the other hand, resilient survivors who choose partners who are secure may improve their sense of self enormously through the relationship and develop an 'earned secure' attachment style. Some survivors, however, may find that engaging in a healthy relationship is too overwhelming and may run away from it. In this respect, they may also need couple therapy to learn how to engage in such relationships.

Given the breadth of this chapter, there will not be a lot of detail about the course of therapy. A whole chapter in this book (Chap. 5) is dedicated to couple work after the violence between the partners' stops. These couples too are trauma survivors and may also have gone through other traumas in the past, including sexual and/or physical abuse or neglect. In the latter case, couples will be helped (without being pushed) to disclose more about the experience, especially about those which they would have kept secret for fear of being stigmatised. These shared stories will make them realise that they are in the same boat and will enhance mutual empathy and understanding. With the help of the therapist, couples will be helped to decipher hyperarousal and stonewalling as 'post traumatic re-enactments of traumatic events in the relationship' (Ford and Courtois 2013, p. 217) and as a cry for love and attention. Affect regulation is fundamental when working with this client population as it would be difficult to do further therapeutic work if couples are not able to soothe themselves and each other and show compassionate understanding towards each other. From my experience this can be quite a challenging task for the therapist, especially because couples are not always synchronised in terms of their readiness to trust the therapeutic experience and open up. Whether the other person in the couple relationship will open will most likely depend on the safety of the therapeutic environment, the therapist's capability for attunement, and her ability to intervene as skilfully as she can.

Conclusion

It takes enormous courage for parents, children and adult survivors to open up about their trauma and enter into a therapeutic alliance with the therapist on a journey that promises relief and relationships with loved ones that are safe, warm, loving and supporting. The therapist needs to be well prepared to contain and accompany families on this challenging journey given the intergenerational legacy of trauma and the need to work with different family members in the process. We believe that attachment theory, trauma theory and systems theory provide a rich theoretical framework that best informs therapists on the motions family members go through. Translating these theoretical frameworks into helpful therapeutic techniques and ways of working requires specialised training and a lot of skills, savoir faire and supervision. It is not enough that family members relate their stories around the trauma. Family members need to come to terms with the pain and the hurt, gain new meaning and position and see themselves differently as they walk the walk towards recovery. Of course, integrating such experiences is an ongoing process and continues after the end of therapy. The personhood of the therapist, her ability for attunement with the different family members and her capacity for self-awareness are very important ingredients in the therapeutic experience. Very often, good therapists become important attachment figures about whom family members continue to think and with whom they have conversations in their minds long after therapy is over. Working in a team and in full collaboration with the family is another important prerequisite. The work necessitates resourceful professionals with a compassionate heart who can support each other and have the patience to persevere even when progress slows down or seems to be at a standstill. As the family members pluck up their courage and come to us for the next session, they will feel relieved to find us there with renewed interest in continuing our conversation with them in the hope that they may regain better regulation of their emotions and a sense of dignity and self-worth.

References

Abela, A., Farrugia, R., Galea, M., & Schembri, D. (2012). The relationship between parents and their adolescent children with special reference to consensual and contentious separations. *International Journal of the Jurisprudence of the Family, 3,* 111.

Abela, A., & Renoux, M. C. (2014). Families living on the margin in affluent societies. In A. Abela & J. Walker (Eds.), *Contemporary issues in family studies: Global perspectives on partnerships, parenting and support in a changing world* (pp. 302–316). London: Wiley Blackwell.

Anderson, K. M., & Hiersteiner, C. (2008). Recovering from childhood sexual abuse: Is a "Storybook Ending" possible? *The American Journal of Family Therapy, 36*(5), 413–434. doi:10.1080/01926180701804592.

Bentovim, A. (1992). *Trauma-organised systems: Physical and sexual abuse in families*. London: Karnac Books.

Bowlby, J. (2008). *A secure base: Parent–child attachment and healthy human development*. New York: Basic Books.

Briere, J. N. (1992). *Child abuse trauma: Theory and treatment of the lasting effects*. CA, US: Sage Publications Inc.

Brown, J. (2008). We don't need your help, but will you please fix our children. *Australian and New Zealand Journal of Family Therapy, 29*(2), 61–69. doi:10.1375/anft.29.2.61.

Byng-Hall, J. (1986). Family scripts: A concept which can bridge child psychotherapy and family therapy thinking. *Journal of Child Psychotherapy, 12*(1), 3–13. doi:10.1080/00754178608254780.

Capella, C., Lama, X., Rodriguez, L., Aguila, D., Beiza, G., Dussert, D., et al. (2016). Winning a race: Narratives of healing and psychotherapy in children and adolescents who have been sexually abused. *Journal of Child Sexual Abuse, 25*(1), 73–92. doi:10.1081/10538712.2015.1088915.

Center on the Developing Child at Harvard University (2016). *From best practices to breakthrough impacts: A science-based approach to building a more promising future for young children and families.* Retrieved from: http://www.developingchild.harvard.edu.

Conger, K. J., Rueter, M. A., & Conger, R. D. (2000). The role of economic pressure in the lives of parents and their adolescents: The family stress model. In L. Crockett & R. Silbereisen (Eds.), *Negotiating adolescence in times of social change* (pp. 201–223). UK: Cambridge University Press.

Copeland, W. E., Keeler, G., Angold, A., & Costello, E. G. (2007). Traumatic events and posttraumatic stress in childhood. *Archives of General Psychiatry, 64*(5), 577–584. doi:10.1001/archpsyc.64.5.577.

Cramer, D., &Takens, R. J. (1992). Therapeutic relationship and progress in the first six sessions of individual psychotherapy: A panel analysis. *Counselling Psychology Quarterly, (5)*1, 25–36. doi:10.1080/09515079208254447.

Dallos, R., & Vetere, A. (2009). *Systemic therapy and attachment narratives: Applications in a range of clinical settings*. London, New York, USA: Routledge.

D'Arrigo-Patrick, J. P., Hoff, C., Knudson-Martin, C., & Tuttle, A. (2016). Navigating critical theory and postmodernism: Social justice and therapist power in family therapy. *Family Process*. doi:10.1111/famp.122236.

Dowling, E. (1993). Are family therapists listening to the young? A psychological perspective. *Journal of Family Therapy, 15*(4), 403–411. doi:10.1111/j.1467-6427.1993.00768.x.

Dowling, E., & Gorell Barnes, G. (1999). *Working with children and parents through separation and divorce: The changing lives of children*. UK: Palgrave Macmillan.

Dowling, E., & Osborne, E. (2003). *The family and the school: A joint systems approach to problems with children* (2nd ed.). Eastbourne, UK: Routledge.

Escudero, V., Boogmans, E., Loots, G., & Friedlander, M. L. (2012). Alliance rupture and repair in conjoint family therapy: An exploratory study. *Psychotherapy, 49*(1), 26–37. doi:10.1037/a0026747.

Ford, J. D., & Courtois, C. A. (Eds.). (2013). *Treating complex traumatic stress disorders in children and adolescents: Scientific foundations and therapeutic models*. NY, USA: Guilford Press.

Foster, J. M., & Hagedorn, W. B. (2014). Through the eyes of the wounded: A narrative analysis of children's sexual abuse experiences and recovery process. *Journal of child sexual abuse, 23* (5), 538–557. doi:10.1080/10538712.2014.918072.

Galea, M. (2009). *The experience of growing up with a parent who has a mental health problem: A retrospective account* Unpublished master's dissertation, University of Malta, Malta.

Gerdes, K. E., & Segal, E. A. (2009). A social work model of empathy. *Advances in Social Work, 10*(2), 114–127.

Gerdes, K. E., & Segal, E. (2011). Importance of empathy for social work practice: Integrating new science. *Social Work, 56*(2), 141–148. doi:10.1093/sw/56.2.141.

Herman, J. L., Perry, J. C., & Van der Kolk, B. A. (1989). Childhood trauma in borderline personality disorder. *American Journal of Psychiatry, 146*(4), 490–495.

Herzog, E. P., Gara, M. A., & Rosenberg, S. (1992). The abused child as parent: Perception of self and other. *Infant Mental Health Journal, 13*(1), 83–98. doi:10.1002/1097-0355(199221)13:1<83:AID-IMHJ2280130111>3.0.CO;2-6.

Hughes, D. (2007). *Attachment focused family therapy*. New York, USA: W.W. Norton & Company.

Johnson, S. M. (1989). Integrating marital and individual therapy for incest survivors: A case study. *Psychotherapy: Theory, Research, Practice, Training, 26*(1), 96–103. doi:10.1037/h0085411.

Johnson, S. M. (2002). *Emotionally focused couple therapy with trauma survivors: Strengthening attachment bonds*. New York, USA: Guilford Press.

Jones, E. (1992). *Working with adult survivors of child sexual abuse*. London, UK: Karnak Books.

Lyons-Ruth, K. (1996). Attachment relationships among children with aggressive behavior problems: The role of disorganized early attachment patterns. *Journal of Consulting and Clinical Psychology, 64*(1), 64–73. doi:10.1037/0022-006X.64.1.64.

Lyons-Ruth, K., & Block, D. (1996). The disturbed caregiving system: Relations among childhood trauma, maternal caregiving, and infant affect and attachment. *Infant Mental Health Journal, 17*(3), 257–275. doi:10.1002/(SICI)1097-0355(199623)17:3<257:AID-IMHJ5>3.0.CO;2-L.

Main, M., Kaplan, N., & Cassidy, J. (1985). Security in infancy, childhood and adulthood: A move to the level of representations. *Monographs of the Society for Research in Child Development, 50*(1–2), 66–104. doi:10.2307/3333827.

Masten, A. S. (2014). *Ordinary magic New York*. USA: Guilford Press.

Mcllwaine, F., & O'Sullivan, K. (2015). 'Riding the wave': Working systemically with traumatised families. *Australian & New Zealand Journal of Family Therapy, 36*(3), 310–324. doi:10.1002/anzf.1114.

Minuchin, S. (1974). *Families and family therapy*. Oxford, England: Harvard University Press.

Mullins, J. (2014). A framework for cultivating and increasing child welfare workers' empathy towards parents. *Journal of Social Service Research, 37*(3), 242–253.

Neander, K., & Skott, C. (2006). Important meetings with important persons: Narratives from families facing adversity and their key figures. *Qualitative Social Work, 5*(3), 295–311. doi:10.1177/1473325006067357.

Rogers, C. (1977). *On personal power: Inner strength and its revolutionary impact*. NY, USA: Delacorte Press.

Ridge, T. (2009) *Living with poverty. A review of the Literature on children's and families' experiences of poverty* (Research Report no. 594). London: Department for Work and Pensions.

Rizzolatti, G., & Craighero, L. (2004). The mirror-neuron system. *Annual Review of Neuroscience, 27,* 169–192. doi:10.1146/annurev.neuro.27.070203.144230.

Rutter, M. (1999). Resilience concepts and findings: Implications for family therapy. *Journal of Family Therapy, 21*(2), 119–144. doi:10.1111/1467-6427.00108.

Sethi, D., Bellis, M., Hughes, K., Gilbert, R., Mitis, F., & Galea, G. (Eds.) (2013). *European report on preventing child maltreatment.* Copenhagen, Denmark: WHO Regional Office for Europe. Retrieved from: http://www.euro.who.int/en/publications/abstracts/european-report-on-preventing-child-maltreatment-2013.

Stratton, P., Lask, J., Bland, J., Nowotny, E., Evans, C., Singh, R., et al. (2013). Detecting early improvement in therapy: Validation of the SCORE-15 index of family functioning and change. *Journal of Family Therapy, 36*(1), 3–19. doi:10.1111/1467-6427.12022.

Van der Kolk, B. (2015). *The body keeps the score: Brain, mind, and body in the healing of trauma*. Great Britain: Penguin Books.

Van der Kolk, B. A., Pynoos, R. S., Cicchetti, D., Cloitre, M., D'Andrea, W., Ford, J. D., Lieberman, A. F.,… Teicher, M. (2009). *Proposal to include a developmental trauma disorder diagnosis for children and adolescents in DSM-V.*

Van Ijzendoorm, M. H., Schuengel, C., & Bakermans-Kranenburg, M. J. (1999). Disorganised attachment in early childhood: Meta-analysis of precursors, concomitants and sequalae. *Development and Psychopathology, 11*(2), 225–250.

Walsh, F. (2006). *Strengthening family resilience* (2nd ed.). New York, US: Guilford Press.

Wilson, J. P., & Lindy, J. D. (1994). Empathic strain and countertransference. In J. P. Wilson & J. D. Lindy (Eds.), *Countertransference in the treatment of PTSD* (pp. 5–30). New York, US: Guilford Press.

Wampold, B. E. (2015). How important are the common factors in psychotherapy? An update. *World Psychiatry, 14*(3), 270–277. doi:10.1002/wps.20238.

White, M. (1988/1989). *The externalization of the problem and the re-authoring of lives and relationships*. Dulwich Centre Newsletter, Summer.

Winnicott, D. W. (1958). *Collected papers: Through paediatrics to psycho-analysis*. New York: Basic Books.

Whitefield, C., & Midgley, N. (2015). 'And when you were a child?': How therapists working with parents alongside individual child psychotherapy bring the past into their work. *Journal of Child Psychotherapy, 41*(3), 272–292. doi:10.1080/0075417X.2015.1092678.

World Health Organisation & the Calouste Gulbenkian Foundation. (2014). *Social determinants of mental health* (NLM classification: WM 101). Geneva: World Health Organisation. Retrieved from: http://www.who.int/mental_health/publications/gulbenkian_paper_social_determinants_of_mental_health/en/.

Chapter 7
Working in the Territory: Therapists' Experiences of Working with Violent Behaviour in Couples and Families

Introduction

> "Lest we forget, it is the therapist who makes psychotherapy, and other helping professions, effective. Accumulating research demonstrates that in practice, as well as in clinical trials, much of the variability in outcomes is attributable to the therapist, regardless of the treatment being delivered." Wampold (2011, p. 1)

The quotation above from Bruce Wampold reminds us of the significance of the therapist and the therapeutic relationship in helping to actualise the client's resources for change and the maintenance of change. At the time of writing this chapter many statutory health and social care agencies are facing deep economic cuts in resources and staffing. The organisational contexts for our practice are constantly shifting and reorganising with consequent threats to staff morale. Guidance for evidence-based practice frequently ignores the scientific literature on the therapeutic relationship as the vehicle for change, making it harder sometimes to care for our practitioners in terms of the best fit between them and the model of psychotherapy. The guidance often assumes that any therapist can deliver any recommended intervention with any person with a diagnosed mental health condition without due consideration for the fit. Compassion fatigue and secondary traumatisation (Figley 2002) are well recognised to be risks in our work so the question of looking after ourselves in the best way to sustain ourselves over professional time has become more urgent.

Skovholt (2008) has conducted research in the area of practitioner resilience for a number of years. He argues that our everyday work is very complex, dialectical and emotionally demanding. So, in thinking about how we develop and sustain our resilience as practitioners, he raises some profound questions for our consideration. For example, how do we practitioners, who use our own self as a means of change for the benefit of others, prevent 'burn out' experiences and maintain our professional energy and commitment? How do we establish and maintain a balance between our care of others and our care for ourselves, especially as our training in

C. Sammut Scerri et al., *Intervening After Violence*,
Focused Issues in Family Therapy, DOI 10.1007/978-3-319-57789-0_7

the health and social care professions is almost unique in its emphasis on helping us take the perspective of others? And crucially he asks, what is practitioner resiliency—what does it look like? Feel like? And what is it that we do that maintains our receptivity to others?

> We are open to absorbing profound loss, hurt and mistrust from our clients but also to the stimulation of those states, present in us all." Berger (2001)

In this poignant quotation from Hatti Berger she reflects on the double-sided nature of the possible impact on us of doing therapeutic work over time—the impact of being present with our clients' distress in their overt and covert manifestations, and potently, the possibility that it may resonate with our own as yet unprocessed experiences. Hatti Berger writes from within the context of a specialist trauma service. In this chapter we shall consider the impact on therapists and their professional colleagues of working with children and families where violence, in its many forms, is of concern. This focus in our work raises many questions around the meanings our work holds for us, and how those meanings can strengthen and/or alter over time. We shall pay attention to the role of supervision and other collegiate support, such as team work, and positive work structures in helping to maintain the balance between self-care and the care of others.

In this chapter we shall raise questions for supervisees and supervisors alike. We are interested in why we do this work, the many meanings it holds for us and how our investment in our work changes over time. We assume that the meaning of our work is in a dynamic exchange with both our working practice and our 'out of work life' experiences. Our capacity for empathic engagement, our cognitive and perceptual flexibility and our tolerance of high levels of uncertainty is based in our professional resilience and is supported by positive working structures and our wish to make life better for others.

The Many Impacts of the Work on Us, as Practitioners and Supervisors

Too often, we therapists neglect our personal relationships. Our work becomes our life. At the end of our workday, having given so much of ourselves, 'we feel drained of desire for more relationships' Yalom (2002).

So why do we do this work? Norcross and Guy (2007) highlight in their research that we practitioners and supervisors enjoy the variety of roles and experiences in our work, take pleasure in assisting others, and find opportunities for intellectual stimulation and emotional development with work that is consistent with our core values.

At all times in our practice as therapists and supervisors we are simultaneously working within the present moment and with our histories and anticipated futures. We can experience both joy and disappointment in our work. These experiences have an impact on us, our colleagues, and on our 'nearest and dearest'. We cannot simply shrug them off, so to say. Skovholt and Trotter-Mathison (2011) write movingly of the continuous flow of our work, from greeting every new client, situation and colleagues with energy and enthusiasm, to maintaining trust and connection, and actively engaging with problem solving, and to refreshing and renewing for the next piece of work. Their research acknowledges the paradox in our training and practice, that occupationally we are trained to take the perspective of the other and this can make boundary regulation between the needs of others and our own needs fraught at times. The supervision space is an opportunity to reflect on the different ways in which we talk about these impacts, for example, privately to ourselves, our family members, our friends and our professional colleagues, for example, 'moved by'; 'shocked by'; 'resonated with'; 'traumatised by'; 'triggered something in me'; and so on. How do we understand and monitor our arousal and other embodied responses, such as somatic countertransference, and how do we talk about them? Do we have permission to speak, or do we fear the critical gaze of others as we reveal our mistakes and our prejudices? Whilst supervision is advocated here as a safe space for talking about the unsayable and the 'not yet said', we acknowledge that supervision can involve surveillance and scrutiny of our work with both implied and specific ideas of what is good practice.

In supervision we can both reflect on those impacts that are easier to recognise and respond to, and wonder about those impacts that are harder to recognise and respond to—how would we describe this to our professional colleagues and what might happen if we could experiment with other ways of describing these embodied meanings? Our professional experiences evolve over time and our modes of talking about the impact may not always reflect a good fit. For example, when do we discuss our work based processes and experiences with a partner or friend? What impact might this have on their wellbeing? Are there implicit or explicit rules in these relationships about such discussions? When can the rules be challenged, and by whom? Who are the rules designed to protect?

Creating positive work structures and identifying protective factors helps us all look after ourselves and each other in the work. In supervision, we focus on the activities, strategies and approaches that we have developed to sustain us in our working professional lives and in our personal lives away from work, and on how these strategies may have changed as the meaning of our work evolves over time and with experience. We find it important to name these strategies, both professional and personal, for example, talking with colleagues and supervisors, walking the dog, gardening, and so on. We try not to take these relationships, strategies and activities for granted in our supervision conversations, and always ask how well these activities, strategies and approaches work. How do they mutually influence, inform and combine across all walks of life… and how do they work for those you are close to? We offer a reflective space to consider those activities, strategies, and approaches for sustaining professional resilience that have not yet been explored or supervisees feel unable or not yet ready to explore.

When supervising individual practitioners or teams of practitioners, we explore responses within the professional teams to the named impacts of doing this work.

We might enquire about working as part of a team and what responses to 'impact' are possible currently within this context and in this economic and political climate? We focus on what works well and what sustains reciprocity and mutuality in the work. And of course, we explore what responses practitioners would like to see develop in their teams, what might be possible and how they might work.

We have developed the following activity to enable supervisee/s to explore their deep worries, anxieties and experience of somatic countertransference in their therapeutic work using an attachment narrative focus (Dallos and Vetere 2009; Vetere 2017). We invite the supervisee to fully describe their example of 'risk informed' work. We try to create a context for reflection and emotional processing. We think with our supervisee about how they are creating a secure base in their work with their client/s. What has been the experience of emotional risk-taking—for them and for their client/s. How do they talk about trust and security in their work—are descriptions of thinking, feeling, action and intention held in equal regard and integrated across their account of the work? We explore how comfortable, secure or anxious the therapist might feel in the work and in particular what might trigger such responses. We ask what defensive processes does the therapist notice and start to use? We try to connect with the therapist's attachment experiences and wonder what attachment figures and relationships do the client/s arouse for the therapist AND the therapist for the client/s? We consider how the client/s defensive processes are impacting, influencing, and connecting with the therapist? And what has been talked about and what can be talked about… and how might this happen? We ask what feelings and thoughts might be defended and/or excluded? We explore whether the supervisee prefers thought, feeling or action when aroused and worried in their work—we ask if they notice if their anxiety might be blocking their thought? We consider what is triggered for us as supervisors in this conversation, and thus for the therapeutic triangle of client/s, therapist and supervisor.

Thus, reflective practice explores the relationship between reflection and intuition, especially the experiences of somatic countertransference in the therapeutic relationship. Trust, safety and calming is needed to promote this form of reflexive exploration so that we can consciously come to know *how* we know, i.e. our procedural knowledge, and what we do *not* know, and very interestingly, how we can wonder about what we do not know we do not know! As George Kelly described them—the unknown unknowns.

Our previous experiences in supervision may well guide how we try to keep ourselves safe in the supervision relationship, particularly if previous experiences have involved unhelpful criticism. These experiences guide our actions, thoughts and feelings, and how we try to keep ourselves safe, close to, appreciated and loved by others. Bowlby (1988) wrote about our internal working models of relationships, i.e. we come to learn about how relationships work and what we might expect of them, and in them, of ourselves, and of others. Internal working models are thought to be that collection of thoughts and beliefs about our own and other people's behaviour in relation to acceptability, lovability and competence. For example, in my view of myself, do I believe I am loveable and deserving of others' comfort and care? In my view of others, how available are others to me and are they interested in me? Damasio (2008) developed Bowlby's ideas and renamed these working models as 'dispositional representations'. Our representations of self and others are thought to guide our actions—they predispose us to action based on our memories of previous repeated experiences and their consequences, both predictable and unpredictable. These mental representations involve action, thought, feeling and sensation—integrated into coherent accounts of our experiences that can be communicated and understood by others (Crittenden 2006). This integration provides a platform for reflection on what is happening—in the here and now, and on past experience, and as a guide for future action. However, we may have learned to protect ourselves by deactivating arousal and relying on words, i.e. our feelings have not been a good guide to action in the past; alternately we may have learned we cannot trust what people say and find ourselves easily overwhelmed when we perceive a threat. Here, we wish to raise the question of how this understanding of protective and self-defensive processes and how they might have developed in our life long history of learning from experience have implications for both therapeutic practice and for supervisory practice—for both supervisors and their supervisees.

Mikulincer and Goodman (2006) have helpfully summarised the research on the relationship between self-reported felt security in close relationships and psychological wellbeing. For example, felt security correlates positively with less arousal reactivity in arousal regulation; a greater likelihood of support seeking at times of need; greater toleration of uncertainty, and more curiosity and openness in information processing; a developed capacity for meta-communication, self-disclosure, collaborative working, assertiveness and empathic listening; and a more articulated and positive sense of self.

Clearly, a sense of trust in the accessibility and responsiveness of others and a 'felt' security in close relationships supports wellbeing (Gottman 2011). Thus, we might ask: how does this work with our colleagues and clients and in supervision? Our practices of joint working, consultation, peer supervision, and group supervision provide opportunities for the development of trusting relationships and opportunities for therapists and supervisors to look after each other. Thus in supervision, we always ask about our supervisee's wellbeing and we make it clear from the outset that we will always ask.

Stress in Our Professional Work with Violence in Family Relationships

In our experience of working therapeutically in a family violence prevention and intervention service, stress in our professional work stems from the following factors: (a) hearing gruelling accounts of cruelty and neglect, both intentional and unintentional; (b) our disappointment when violence continues in the face of therapy or rehabilitation work, and this can be felt collectively within a team;

(c) our risk of an inflated sense of responsibility around our work, particularly in the absence of personal and organisational support for our work; and (d) navigating the tensions around introducing systemic/therapeutic ideas into a conservative legal system with no tradition of acknowledging the role of emotion or passion in people's thinking and behaviour. These stresses can of course, be exacerbated by holding too high a case load. Such stresses can also create a number of difficult dilemmas for practitioners. For example, getting overwhelmed and overloaded with information without managing to find any clarity of purpose or understanding—this could result in seeking simplistic solutions; practitioners becoming isolated by not sharing their concerns with colleagues, especially in the absence of positive work structures, with a resulting preoccupation with the work and/or the family; living with the tension of constantly being asked to judge and risk assess unpredictable behaviour; practitioners losing sight of their competencies and their sense of professional resilience; and finally, overempathising with the victim and repeating victim/rescuer positions with resulting anger and frustration over agency responses, services or management decisions (Vetere and Cooper 2008; Vetere 2012).

What Are the Main Responsibilities of the Supervisor?

Supervision for our work that aims to help stop and prevent future violence in family relationships is central to practitioner wellbeing in our view. Clearly the supervision relationship needs to be based in mutual trust, where the practitioner is assured of the supervisor's accessibility and responsiveness to their concerns, both spoken and embodied. The supervisor's responsibilities are many in this context and they are complex. Thus we advocate for regular supervision of supervision, so that supervisors may pay attention to their self-care. Many supervisors are also practitioners and have the advantage of seeing the different perspectives and impacts of the work, but also carry the load of responsibility. So, what are these responsibilities?

Supervisors have responsibility for the creation of calm and safe spaces for reflective rather than reactive thinking, within a trusting collaborative relationship where indecision, reflexivity and action will be held in equal regard. This means that practitioners can explore their concerns and anxieties as useful information, not as signs of 'weakness', knowing that an action plan will emerge as a result of more effective problem solving. So supervisors encourage clarity about shared accountability within family–professional systems and the shared responsibility within the supervision relationship allows tension and anxiety to be contained while still encouraging the development of creative ideas. We have long believed it is helpful for supervisors to share with their supervisee some ideas about their style of supervision and their supervisory role. It is then possible to discuss what would be the acceptable and collaborative parameters for such a process. For example, we think it is helpful to tell supervisees we will *always* ask about their personal safety—because it needs to be a natural part of the ebb and flow of supervisory conversation. If it is mentioned for the first time in the context of a particular piece of therapeutic work, it can have the effect of unhelpfully raising anxiety rather than acknowledging that safety and threat always runs through the work.

Supervisors pay attention to the emotional wellbeing of their supervisees, and the many and various impacts this work has on them, both personally and professionally. There may be moments when the work triggers unexpected memories, resonance, and perhaps unprocessed trauma related responses that take everyone by surprise. We always ask new supervisees what there might be in their previous life experience that could be triggered unexpectedly, so if appropriate, we can zoom in, and illuminate the resonance. This can be sufficient. We will be straightforward about our willingness to be supportive in this way within the supervisory relationship, and we will offer appropriate advice and referral for further therapeutic work if needed. These 'boundaries' are also the responsibility of the supervisor when their personal issues impact on their supervisory work. Thus, we hold a commitment to *trying* to maintain a balance between getting overwhelmed (or frozen) on the one hand, or underwhelmed and potentially unresponsive, on the other—for both supervisors and supervisees!

In supervision, whether it is individual or group based supervision, and in our supervision of supervision, we develop a continuing conversation around the impact of our preferred ideas about emotional safety, emotional risk-taking and the development of trust on our work, from all perspectives involved in the work: therapists, their clients, supervisors, referrers and managers. So, for example, we might interrogate those theoretical ideas we are firmly wedded to, and ask what might be the implications for the above. We weave in consideration of those theoretical ideas and practices that we occasionally draw on, and importantly, those theoretical ideas and practices that are available to us, that we rarely draw on. This continuing conversation enables exploration of how our relationships with particular schools of thought may constrain or support emotional safety, emotional risk-taking and the development of trust in supervision and in practice. It keeps us alert to how we might want to adapt or experiment with our preferred theoretical ideas in order to develop our practice around safety and to further our understanding of ourselves in relation to these preferred ideas and their potential impact in the work.

Supervision with Practitioner Teams—Creating Conversations that Include Safety, Doubt and Progress

We offer supervision to teams of multidisciplinary practitioners on a regular basis. Often they will bring examples of their work where they find themselves stuck and unable to think creatively about the next steps in the work, or they might be divided in their views about these next steps. We find the following exercise and activities helpful in freeing up thinking so that possible solutions can emerge. The exercise and activities are based on the systemic principle of developing and illuminating a shared reflective understanding from the different perspectives of all participants—family, practitioners, managers, other professionals involved from other agencies, and so on. This consideration of the differences and similarities in the various perspectives promotes a context for calm reflection and consideration where safety, doubt and progress can be held in equal regard.

The exercise. We usually begin by asking supervisees to describe the work from the family members' point of view and then from their agency's point of view, and other professionals involved in working with the family. Often, we will map the family–professional system as we talk. We explore any other issues or descriptions of the family (and the team) that the team (and the family members) might want us to know about. We ask what our supervisees want from supervision in terms of goals for themselves, the client family and the other relevant perspectives. We explore shared and overlapping goals and how we might best understand a wish for different directions of travel in the work. We always ask about what the family members are doing right. This usually opens a conversation around corrective scripts, i.e. what the family members/parents are trying to differently and better for their children than was done for them (Byng-Hall 1995; Dallos and Vetere 2009). This allows us to construe some intentions positively because although the parents' corrective script may not have achieved a safer environment for the care of their children, we can offer an appreciation for trying to make it better. We ask about the history of domestic violence in this case and what action (if any?) has already been taken, and by whom, and to what end. We find it is always important to ask whether the supervisee/s and the team (and/or agency/other supervisors) agree about the level of risk and/or any action to be taken. The activity closes by considering what the family members and agency staff might say had they listened to our conversation.

The activities. Sometimes, in group supervision, our supervisees will present what feels to them like unresolvable and intractable dilemmas that usually involve a clear split over what to think, and what to do around safety and safe practice. In these circumstances we often use action based and embodied activities, such as sculpting (Vetere and Dallos 2013) and internalised other interviewing (Tomm et al. 1998). We also use these activities in supervision with supervisees to explore their experiences of compassion and relationships in teams with their colleagues, with management, and sometimes to explore temporal changes, in personnel, roles and relationships.

Sculpting with team members and in supervision groups can be carried out with objects, such as coins, buttons, stones, and little figures, and so on. Objects soon take on the representational characteristics of the people they personify and the action of moving objects around a table top provides a conjoint visual and cognitive focus. Reciprocal influences between relationships and dilemmas can be explored within a temporal frame of before, during and after, for example, certain decisions being made, disclosures of violence in a family, management changes, and so on. Debriefing after the activity can include consideration of why certain objects were chosen to represent each person in the sculpt. These choices can sometimes illustrate how particular people are held in mind in terms of what they represent for the 'sculptor/s'. Direct questions and circular questions can be used to both prompt and facilitate discussion during the sculpting activity. When sculpting with a supervision group, it possible to photograph each supervisee's sculpt and use these photographs of visual prompts for a discussion of what is similar and different, and what meanings such similarities and differences might hold for relationships and for possible future action.

The sculpting activity usually starts with an invitation to map current relationships and connections within the team, and/or the family–professional system, and so on. Exploration of trust and connection in relationships can be prompted by asking about emotional and practical support in the team, for example, who turns to whom for reassurance, advice, comfort and help with decisions before, during and after challenging moments or during a crisis? How is this support offered, sought and received? Current positioning and changes in positioning and responsibility in teams and family–professional systems can be explored with enquiry around how it might feel to be at the centre, on the edge, or between your colleagues, and so on? Or further, if you were to get closer to a team member, or more centrally involved in decision making, what would that be like? Conversely, how do you think your colleague might feel being more distant from you or less involved in decision making, and so on? The sculpting activity closes with shared reflection on the experience of 'helicoptering' or 'overviewing' team dynamics and dilemmas from a reflective and systemic perspective.

Internalised other interviewing is an activity designed to help and enhance an empathic appreciation of the experience of a significant other, for example, to explore, enhance and/or modify one person's inner experience of another person's inner experience. It was developed to explore 'stuckness' and impasse in couple and family relationships (Tomm et al. 1998). We have developed its use as an activity in both individual and group supervision, particularly when our supervisee brings forth a rupture in the therapeutic relationship and/or realises a loss of compassion for their client.

The supervisor assists the supervisee (usually the therapist) to identify their internal representation, or working model of their client and to try and imagine how their client might think, feel and act… Then the supervisor conducts an interview with their supervisee as if they were the client, i.e. with the supervisee's 'internal other'. The supervisor addresses the supervisee in the interview by the client's name, and explores the client's thoughts, feelings and action. Questions in the interview might include the following: How do you feel about working with your therapist? What is helpful, and not helpful? … and why? Does your therapist remind you of any members of your family, and/or attachment figures in your life? What is the effect of this resonance? What problems do you most/least want to focus on? How do you understand your worries and your difficulties? How do you think your relationships impact on these difficulties? What do you see as your strengths? Who do you turn to when you need support? Who can you trust? And so on.

Debriefing from this activity starts by deroling, and then reflecting on both the emotional and sensory experiences and the thoughts. We pay attention to areas of resonance in the interview and the unexpected and surprising moments in the interview. Usually this activity deepens the therapist's empathic appreciation of their client's experiences and circumstances, and helps clarify how to go on in the work.

In Conclusion

In our moments of meeting, as supervisors and supervisees, and as therapists with clients, our capacity for emotional sensitivity and attunement helps establish new attachment relationships and supports resilience in the face of stress and novelty. Conscious monitoring of our mutual regulatory processes of affect synchrony and of our implicit non-verbal communication assists with the co-creation of a growth enhancing context for all of us. This promotes interactive repair and healing in our relationships and helps us know how to be with family members.

As practitioners and supervisors we have a lifelong commitment to learning and personal and professional development (Vetere and Stratton 2016). As we gain experience and through a process of continuous reflection on our defining moments, our focus shifts from an emphasis on getting things right and following procedures to a lighter relationship with theory and practice. We are more comfortable with what we do not know and we are able to know that we can find out, and know how to go on, especially with the help and support of others.

References

Berger, H. (2001). Trauma and the therapist. In T. Spiers (Ed.), *Trauma: A practitioner's guide to counselling*. Hove: Brunner Routledge.

Bowlby, J. (1988) *A secure base: Clinical applications of attachment theory*. London: Routledge.

Byng Hall, J. (1995). *Re-writing family scripts: Improvisation and systems change*. New York: Guilford.

Crittenden, P. (2006). A dynamic-maturational model of attachment. *Australian and New Zealand Journal of Family Therapy, 27,* 105–115.

Dallos, R., & Vetere, A. (2009). *Attachment narratives and systemic therapy: Applications in a range of clinical settings*. London: Routledge.

Damasio, A. (2008). *Descartes' error: Emotion, reason and the human brain*. New York: Random House.

Figley, C. (2002). Compassion fatigue: Psychotherapists chronic lack of self care. *Journal of Clinical Psychology, 58,* 1433–1441.

Gottman, J. (2011). *The science of trust*. New York: Norton.

Mikulincer, M., & Goodman, G. (2006). *The dynamics of romantic love: Attachment, caregiving and s*ex. New York: Guilford.

Norcross, J., & Guy, J. (2007). *Learning to leave it at the office: A guide to therapist self care*. New York: Norton.

Skovholt, T. (2008). Two versions of erosion in the helping professions: Caring burnout and meaning burnout. *New Therapist, 52,* 28–29.

Skovholt, T., & Trotter-Mathison, M. (2011). *The resilient practitioner* (2nd ed.). New York: Routledge.

Tomm, K., Hoyt, M., & Madigan, S. (1998). Honoring our internalized others and the thics of caring: A conversation with Karl Tomm. In M. Hoyt (Ed.), *The handbook of constructive therapies*. pp. 198–218.

Vetere, A. (2012). Supervision and consultation practice with domestic violence. *Clinical Child Psychology and Psychiatry, 17,* 181–185.

Vetere, A. (2017). Systemic theory and narratives of attachment: Integration, formulation and development over time. In P. Stratton & M. Borcsa (Eds.), *Origins and originality in family therapy and systemic practice*. EFTA Book Series, Vol. I. Springer: New York.

Vetere, A., & Cooper, J. (2008). Supervision in domestic violence casework. In J. Hamel (Ed.), *Intimate partner and family abuse*. New York: Springer.

Vetere, A., & Dallos, R. (2013). Ouruse of action techniques in attachment narrative therapy. *Context, 126,* 17–19.

Vetere, A., & Stratton, P. (Eds.). (2016). *Interacting selves: Systemic solutions for personal and professional development in psychotherapy and counselling*. London: Routledge.

Wampold, B. (2011). Qualities and actions of effective therapists.In *Continuing education in psychology*. Washington, D.C: Education Directorate, American psychological Association.

Yalom, I. (2002). *The gift of therapy: An open letter to a new generation of therapists and their patients*. New York: Harper Collins.

Chapter 8
Supervision and Consultation with Practitioners Who Intervene with Families and Trauma

Introduction

Working with children and families who have been traumatised by violence and abuse is demanding and complex and supervision is critical for professionals working in the field. Herman (1997) makes the point that 'If a therapist finds herself isolated in her professional practice, she should discontinue working with traumatised patients until she has secured an adequate support system' (p. 153).

There is a gap in the literature on clinical supervision in the context of trauma (Virtue and Fouche 2010; West 2010) and most of the literature that is available has been written by clinicians with experience in the area. Vetere and Cooper (2008) were one of a very few to write about supervision of risky dangerous and traumatising work with couples who were violent towards each other. The other two authors of this book also highlighted the importance of collaborative supervision of professionals working in a home for adolescent girls with challenging behaviour (Abela and Sammut Scerri 2003).

In this chapter, we will start by highlighting the importance of a trusting supervisory alliance, which is based on safety. Developing a sound formulation, which is theoretically sound will be given prime importance and ways of supporting, helping and caring for clinicians will be discussed. Various dilemmas and ethical issues that clinicians who work in this field have to face will also be explored. The self-care of the supervisor will be prioritised.

It is assumed that supervisors who work in this complex and specialised field are trained in supervision, suitably qualified and up to date in the relevant theoretical frameworks and clinical applications. The supervisor's direct clinical experience with children, couples and families is also extremely valuable.

The original version of this chapter was revised: See the "Chapter Note" section at the end of this chapter for details. The erratum to this chapter is available at 10.1007/978-3-319-57789-0_10

C. Sammut Scerri et al., *Intervening After Violence*,
Focused Issues in Family Therapy, DOI 10.1007/978-3-319-57789-0_8

The Supervisory Alliance

Just as good practitioners seek to develop a good therapeutic relationship with their clients, so do supervisors with their supervisees. A trusting relationship with the supervisor is crucial for the work to be fruitful. This is even more so when working in the area of trauma. In a Delphi study carried out among supervisors working in the field of trauma, there was a consensus that supervisors need to know about their supervisees' personal history and whether this was affecting their clinical work (West 2010). This is because the stories that are heard by clinicians are bound to create resonance with their own traumatic experiences (Smith 2013). Supervisors need to be aware that such experiences are least talked about in supervision (Kavner and McNab 2005) as it takes a lot of courage and full trust in the supervisor on the part of the supervisee to want to bring personal, embarrassing and shameful stories to supervision.

Prouty (2014) mentions the importance of balancing hierarchy with collaboration in supervision. This augurs well for a good supervisory alliance. As authors of this book, the three of us hold a feminist postmodern collaborative style as supervisors (Abela and Sammut Scerri 2010). This fits very well given that feminism has influenced trauma therapy and social work practice (Virtue and Fouche 2010). Vetere (2012) makes the point that 'as supervisors, we hold responsibility for creating a safe space for thinking and reflection, within a trusting relationship where we can hold indecision, reflexivity and action in equal regard' (p. 183). Good supervisors are comfortable with authority and evaluation and shoulder the responsibility they are entrusted with. At the same time they 'wisely share doubts and errors; otherwise supervisees are less likely to disclose their fears and mistakes' (Neill et al. (2006), p. 15).

The different levels of competence of supervisees (See Stoltenberg et al. 1998) also need to be kept in mind when building the supervisory alliance. In this respect, collaborative relationships between supervisors and supervisees should not preclude the supervisor from offering advice and taking an expert role when needed.

The latter authors divide therapists into three levels. With therapists who are still new to the work, the supervisor needs to create a balance between building the competence of the therapist and being collaborative. Novice therapists are usually very hard working but also anxious and at times overwhelmed by the sheer complexity of the work. They are also very self-conscious about their work and this may interfere with their skills as they relate with the families they work with. It may also impinge on their capacity to think on their feet and on their ability to be creative. In this respect, the supervisor may do well to get in touch with the time when they themselves were beginners as it would help them to better connect with those supervisees who are still in the beginning of their careers. Novice therapists and related professionals need reassurance and supervisors who are available in the course of such delicate work.

Without specifically referring to novice therapists, Vetere (2012) points out that in her supervision and consultation around domestic violence work, she is ‘more direct and directive’ (p. 181) and considers helping supervisees identify contraindications for therapeutic work when violence creeps back into the relationship. In terms of work with children, Chard and Hansel (2006) also make the point that therapists start with limited skills. They suggest practical help including tips about ways of working that would include making use of play techniques and art and drawing. The use of therapeutic stories for children is also very helpful. Novice therapists working with children also need a helping hand with regards to the interplay between individual sessions and joint sessions with parents especially when the parents are separated or divorced, and with ways of how to involve other professionals (for example the social worker), other systems (such as the school system) and other important networks of support in the community. The supervisory relationship can be considered as an excellent opportunity for young practitioners to learn more about their work with this client population.

Busuttil (2016) also reports that the therapists she interviewed found it much more difficult to work with families whose stories resonated with theirs when they were still novice in their work as family therapists. Furthermore families who have experienced abuse already find it very hard to trust each other or the therapist because of the fact that they have already been betrayed. In the case of young therapists, they have the double challenge of also not being trusted by parents as easily as more experienced therapists are (Whitefield and Midgley 2015):

> A trainee psychologist was very upset when a grandmother who was taking care of an abandoned grandson had bluntly criticized her for not bringing about any change after the very first session. The trainee had spent about 15 minutes with the child alone to show him the play therapy room and to start to get to know him. A week later when they returned, the grandmother said to her: “I don’t know what you told him but he has barely eaten since we came here!” The trainee psychologist needed a lot of support from her group supervisor to be able to find ways how to win the grandmother’s trust. She claimed that this was an important learning experience for her.

Practitioners gain confidence in this area of work over time but may nevertheless vacillate between confidence and confusion especially when the work becomes complicated or the therapist experiences stuckness in her work. In such moments, therapists become uncertain and although they may not need their supervisor to be so readily available, they may still seek peer supervision until their next supervision session with their supervisor. More experienced practitioners may experience themselves to be more stable in their work and the supervisory relationship becomes increasingly collaborative although Courtois and Ford (2012) point out that experienced therapists who work in this area continue to need supervision by trauma—informed supervisors.

The Importance of Formulation

One of the building blocks of good therapeutic work with clients is the clinician's ability to develop a formulation which is theoretically sound and can 'summarise the clients' difficulties and the therapeutic context and show how the difficulties are connected using psychological theories and principles … attempt(ing) to explain why and how the difficulties developed in these ways, at this time, and in these situations, taking account of the complexity and multiplicity of family–professional network relationships' (Vetere 2012, p. 184).

Theoretical frameworks are deemed to be useful and provide explanations that are rooted in research about the dynamics at play. They keep practitioners on track when work with families becomes complicated.

Lowe (2016) shares her experience when working with 'Johnny' who had witnessed severe domestic violence perpetrated by his father onto his mother. The latter was consulting because the boy was becoming defiant and demanding and very difficult to manage to the extent that she was giving into his demands. Lowe explains how the work 'got under her skin' and she had taken it to supervision. At one point Lowe explains

> I had moved away from theoretical frameworks where I would have approached Johnny and his mother from a trauma and attachment understanding, and steered therapy towards achieving my own psychological needs to see this mother re-set the balance of power in her relationship (p. 62).

As already explained throughout the various chapters of this book, the preferred theoretical frameworks for understanding this area of work for us include attachment theory (Bowlby, 1969, 1973, 1988; Crittenden 2008) trauma theory (Briere 2002; Lanktree and Briere 2013; Courtois 2008; Van der Kolk 2015) and systems theory. As systemic thinkers, we give due importance to the socio-economic and cultural context in which families are embedded. Taking a resilience perspective in the face of adversity is also necessary as we must never forget that 'sometimes a traumatic experience is said to 'bring out the best' in people' (Smith 2013, p. 33). Walsh (2003) was among the first scholars to bring about this paradigm shift. More recently Papadopoulos (2007) has used the term 'adversity activated development' in light of the way refugees and their families continue to thrive in spite of the traumatic experiences that they go through. In this respect, the supervisor, who is working in this area, is expected to have a good understanding of the above theoretical frameworks when helping supervisees develop their own formulations. Whilst it is important to listen to the supervisees' preferred theoretical framework/s and help them understand how the theories that inform their thinking support them in their work with families, supervisors also need to be au courant with regard to the supervisees' level of training when working with traumatised clients.

Van der Kolk (2015) complains about how the lack of knowledge about trauma theory very often leads clinicians to misdiagnose children as ADHD and treat them with medication and/or behavioural therapy. He also explains how many clinicians ignore the fact that a very high proportion of patients who are diagnosed with a borderline personality disorder and admitted to a psychiatric hospital had been abused as children. Courtois and Ford (2012) also point out that most of the training received by therapists does not include training in trauma and they highlight the importance of using an integrative model to understanding this phenomenon. They highlight the current changes and new developments in the understanding of trauma with regard to adults. In the same vein, in their book dedicated to the treatment of children and adolescents, Ford and Courtois (2013) call for 'clinical creativity, guided by sound clinical theory, evidence–based assessment, wise clinical judgement and an evolving evidence base' (p. XII). In a Delphi study by West (2010), supervisors gave importance to assessing supervisees in terms of their experience and training in the field of trauma in the first supervision meeting. They felt that they needed to protect clients and supervisees as well as develop the latter's skills and practice.

The Value of Different Supervision Formats

Different supervision formats help clinicians in different ways in their work with trauma. Often the organisation or agency, which is offering therapeutic and welfare services for clients, makes group and individual supervision available. These two forms of supervision call for different skills on the part of the supervisors whereas there are different learning points to be made by supervisees.

When led by a warm and able supervisor, group supervision usually provides teams with the opportunity to come closer together and to share their knowledge and learn from each other in a very constructive way. A good supervisor will work to create a sense of safety in the group by validating the contribution of each and every member and by stressing how much the other members are missing out when members in the team keep silent for fear of being criticised. Such meetings can also be an opportunity for multi disciplinary teams to come together and extend each other's thinking. This way of working together is especially beneficial when working with families who would have survived trauma.

During group supervision for a small family therapy team working in the area of substance abuse, Angela had developed the idea of inviting the psychologist who would have been doing individual therapy with the symptom bearer prior to the start of family therapy work as well as the social worker who would have been following the client and the family before his entry into residential treatment. These supervision meetings would continue to be held quite regularly throughout the family therapy treatment. During such meetings stories around trauma and loss would unfold as is typical with clients who turn to substance and alcohol abuse. The different professionals-informed as they were, by overlapping but also different theoretical frameworks-used to enjoy these conversations thoroughly and find them extremely enriching, primarily because they would give them the opportunity to position themselves differently and gain manoeuverability in their work with the clients and their families.

Through the use of reflecting teams the various professionals would give feedback to each other on the work that was being carried out and the dilemmas with which they were being faced. When feeling stuck, the supervisees would then shift from problem saturated explanations that were derived from linear causation and which ended in pointing fingers and blaming "culprits" to systemic hypotheses that could help professionals better understand how best to go about helping couples, children and families now that the abuse had stopped.

This way of working augurs well for agencies catering for clients that have been traumatised. This is because monthly supervision by a qualified supervisor will not be enough to sustain professionals working in the organisation unless the experience itself does not generate a ripple effect whereby peer support is inherent in the day-to-day behaviour of the workers in the organisation. Of course not all organisations function in this ideal way as vicarious traumatisation and competition—rather than collaboration between professionals—can easily creep in, as we shall see further down. It is however often the case that the new ideas that are triggered during monthly group supervision are then followed up by the team. The following vignette originally published in French (Abela 2009, p. 173) illustrates an excerpt from a group supervision session with a multidisciplinary team working in a children's home. The shift from a problem-saturated conversation to a more systemic theoretical perspective dissolved the impasse the child psychotherapist had found herself in:

During the (supervision) session a child psychotherapist complained about the poor progress John[1] was making. The boy was going in and out of a psychiatric unit for children. According to the psychotherapist, the mother was unable to "contain" her son and yet she declined from availing herself of day care at the Home in spite of the fact that this was offered to her. The psychotherapist stated that she was rather shocked to hear from the mother during a case conference, that she was never offered such support. Following the case conference she double-checked with the social worker in charge who confirmed the invitation. This situation left her feeling very perplexed and somewhat indignant.

Katia, a family therapist, asked the group members for other stories that the various members knew about John and his mother.

The child psychotherapist remembered how after a multidisciplinary team meeting the mother had confided that she felt very ashamed of herself because of her inability to "contain" her son.

Patrick, the play therapist reminded the supervision group that John's father had left the marriage and was living with another woman. He was even planning to leave the Island with her.

(The supervision group) wondered whether John's upheavals were a way of calling his father back. After all, this was exactly what happened when John threw up a big tantrum. The father was asked to intervene.

Was the mother also yearning for her husband? Would John bring him back?
Together with the family therapist the child psychotherapist was interested in working around the boy saying goodbye to his father before he went abroad. The mother too would attend the family sessions.

[1]All names mentioned in this paper are fictitious.

The family therapy sessions proved to be very helpful. Father and son were able to bid farewell to each other before the father went abroad and the boy was increasingly able to relate calmly with his mother.

Systemic supervision has also introduced the concept of live supervision with the team and the supervisor watching from behind the one-way mirror. This is very different from having a supervisee bring in an account of the session be it during a one-to-one supervision or during a group supervision. Live supervision is very rich in that supervisors and supervisees gather to hypothesise together about a given family prior to the session. There is also the richness that comes not only from supervising the therapist in the room but also from the team behind the one-way mirror. In trauma work, the family therapist would need all the support she can get in order to offer the best help she can to the family. In this respect, supervision helps the team support the therapist in the room. The supervisor and the team are there to observe the therapeutic process during the session and to give feedback to the therapist and the family. Non-verbal communication is captured live. The team also provides the therapist with the opportunity to take a break, bring new information to the family and have the time to reposition herself with the family. In spite of all these advantages, Smith (2013) points out that live supervision in the presence of the team behind the one-way mirror may render the supervisee more anxious and vulnerable. This is especially so with novice therapists who lack the necessary confidence (Abela 2003) or when team members are critical towards or competitive with each other.

Safety issues within the group must always be addressed as a matter of priority as it is quite difficult—if not impossible—to work as a team without addressing these issues. Moreover, as two of us noted in one of our consultations with a therapeutic team in a residential home for adolescent girls with emotional and behavioural difficulties, 'as safety and trust between the different members of the group developed, their reflexivity regarding their own therapeutic practice with the adolescent girls increased.' (Abela and Sammut Scerri 2003, p. 41).

The use of video-recorded material, rather than live work, during supervision can capture precise segments of a therapeutic session. This can also provide an opportunity for some of the therapists working in a team to have more control over the material being presented. The supervision experience would hopefully help these supervisees to gain more confidence and to then feel that they can move on to live supervision.

Individual supervision is more conducive to a deeper and more personal relationship between the supervisor and supervisee. Although it is not excluded that the intersection between personal and professional issues is addressed during group supervision, individual supervision provides a more confidential setting.

Dilemmas that Arise During Supervision

As Keys (2009) points out 'Too much attention has been placed on what should be done in child welfare and not as much on how it should be done' (p. 243). There are a number of situations and dilemmas that clinicians need support with when working with family members who have experienced trauma.

In spite of the fact that many of those who live in adversity are poor and socially deprived (WHO and Calouste Gulbenkian Foundation 2014; Center on the Developing Child at Harvard University 2016), many practitioners tend to ignore the pressures these families are faced with (Falicov 1998). In spite of the recommendations put forward by the Council of Europe in their guidelines to professionals (see Daly 2007), service user involvement is not mainstreamed in professional training courses. This lack of sensitivity in the training may lead professionals to medicalise poverty, violence, racism and other threats in spite of their best efforts. This is especially so in situations of stress. When the sociocultural context of the families we see is so completely different from ours, we may find it hard to connect and may easily pathologise families (Walsh 2003). Novice therapists complain that their clients do not turn up in spite of the fact that they would have sent them a note regarding their meeting by post. They need to be reminded that many of these clients may not know how to read (Abela and Tabone 2008). They also expect their clients to behave in the same way they do and prepare to welcome them in the same way they would welcome their middle-class clients attending sessions in a private clinic. When teaching about class and culture in psychotherapy, Angela often cites her first encounter with a mother when she was still working as a clinical psychologist in schools. In this case, the head of school had sent for the mother as she had concerns regarding the neglect of her daughter:

> … I found myself completely thrown off … when (she) turned up for an appointment looking somewhat lost and holding a big Maltese loaf in her hand (which she could have easily put in a paper bag I thought) wearing a summer dress and a cardigan and a plastic flip-flop with a big orange dahlia in the middle of winter! (Abela 2009, p. 176)

The need for empathic attunement with our clients living in adversity has been highlighted and elaborated upon in various chapters throughout this book (see Chaps. 5 and 6). This human quality is extremely comforting for clients and contributes immensely towards their healing process. There may be various reasons why supervisees may find it difficult to empathise with their clients. Wilson and Lindy (1994) explain how this is manifested in the supervisees when they experience empathic strain and find it hard to remain in emotional contact with the client. Etherington notes that this kind of behaviour is a natural response to working with trauma and may lead to vicarious traumatisation. Processing vicarious trauma is an important component of supervision with clinicians working in the field of trauma (Virtue and Fouche 2010) and helps them regain empathic attunement.

Empathic attunement with clients is also dented because clinicians have difficulty making sense of their behaviour and lose their patience with them or else are anxious or afraid for various reasons. Etherington (2009) cites a study by Pope and

Tabachnick carried out in 1993 among 285 therapists working in the field of trauma. A high percentage of these therapists (89%) reported feeling angry with clients because of their lack of cooperation whereas over 90% feared for the well-being of their clients for some reason or other. Many clinicians (83%) were also afraid that they would be criticised by their colleagues.

During supervision, practitioners are helped to calm their anxieties and frustrations. Having a safe space where they can vent their own feelings and explore, with the help of the supervisor, therapeutic ways on how to intervene is very helpful. They need to be reminded that their emotional states in part reflect the dysregulation of their clients. In this respect supervision enhances empathy with clients.

Another related difficulty that clinicians present with when working in this area has to do with polarisation especially in the context of family work. Clinicians fall in the trap of being empathic with the child and expect either one or both parents to shoulder their responsibilities as parents. However, parents may struggle to empathise with their children for various reasons, including, their past traumatic history, poverty and stress, a poor network of support or difficult relationships with the family of origin and/or the biological father of the child. A systemic theoretical framework is an important point of reference for supervisees as are the ensuing therapeutic techniques some of which have been highlighted in Chap. 6. The supervisor needs to encourage a both/and positioning on the part of the practitioner. The supervisor's invitation to focus on what the mother needs for change to happen is very helpful. It can help the practitioners formulate a theory of change that can inform their work. At the same time revisiting and reassessing the extent of the risk involved for the child or victim is also important. The practitioner needs to prioritise safety at all times. Once that is ascertained, the practitioner is able to keep the needs of the parent/s and of the child (or victim in the case of a previous history of domestic violence) in mind rather than prioritise the needs of one of the family members over another.

Sometimes polarisation takes place at an agency level. Typically some of the workers might believe that the family is receiving too much help by a therapist whereas the therapist would think that the time invested in the family is needed and would bring about the desired change. The supervisor may point out that both sides have a point in the long term and reaching a compromise is extremely beneficial. Herman (1997) explains that conflict regarding the treatment of patients is typical of patients who are severely traumatised:

In institutional settings, the problem of staff splitting or intense conflict over the treatment of difficult patients frequently arises. Almost always the subject of the dispute turns out to have a history of trauma. The quarrel among colleagues reflects the unwitting re-enactment of the dialectic of trauma (p. 187).

Boundary keeping is considered to be an essential component of the therapeutic frame (Papadopoulos 1998). Smith (2013) elaborates on this by pointing out that clear boundaries are required to protect clients and practitioners from traumatisation or re-traumatisation. While working with 18 Bosnian medical evacuees,

Papadopoulos (1998) explains the danger of crossing boundaries when working therapeutically with clients who are subjected to trauma:

Throughout, I restrained myself from offering them any material gifts because I was fully aware that such action would have altered irrevocably the therapeutic connection; besides, no amount of presents would have eradicated the fundamental and multiple deprivation of their being. Tragically many other workers, overwhelmed by their spontaneous impulse to respond with human generosity and without the awareness of the importance of therapeutic boundaries, kept offering gifts to these men and kept transgressing professional boundaries by taking them out for weekends. Invariably, most of these relationships ended acrimoniously with tragic and at times even violent confrontations. (P. 470).

Trauma work triggers intense feelings and emotions and supervision is an important space where practitioners can process these feelings. As Dutta (2010) explains, the emotions experienced by therapists during sessions can be 'seen as a potential resource within the supervisory encounter' that would eventually lead the supervisee to 'the deconstruction of multiple possible meanings' (p. 105).

When working in the area of trauma, especially extreme situations of trauma, the needs of the clients are significant and the temptations to 'save' clients or to take responsibility for them are very common. Clients who are traumatised can be so much in need of love and protection and/or recognition that they would try in many ways to break the boundary and come closer to their therapist. Chard and Hansel (2006) explain how abused children or teenagers may become aggressive or seductive with the therapist. Supervisees need to be encouraged to process these attempts during supervision and to come to value the boundary that they create with their clients because of the space it creates for further reflection and creative ways of intervening.

Etherington (2009) also points out that when supervisors set boundaries by not being available at all times, or by not overworking, this serves as a form of modelling for therapists who come to understand that boundary keeping serves not only to protect clients but also to protect therapists in their work.

Of course boundary keeping does not translate into rigid ways of being with children and families. It is about the practitioners' ability to keep reflecting with their clients even in situations where they have to go out of their way to help them. Celebrating the birthday of a child who is in out of home care by bringing in cake and sweets during a session may be very therapeutic rather than a 'passage a l'acte'. Papadopoulos (1998) himself explains this need for creative adjustment. For example, he argued that it was more appropriate to work in an open setting rather than in a clinic when helping refugees. He would then find a quiet place where he would talk with those who were willing to open up. At the same time, by setting a regular time for visits, keeping a diary in hand and wearing a tie he tried to maintain a sense of boundary in his encounters with them.

Another common dilemma that practitioners have to contend with when working with traumatised clients is the fact that they have to *live with contradictions*. Clarissa Sammut Scerri has already discussed this phenomenon in more depth in Chap. 2 of this book when she explored the processes that adult survivors of domestic abuse go through. Her grounded theory research (Sammut Scerri 2015) explains how despite the fact that her female participants had experienced physical abuse at the hands of their father, they nevertheless wanted to have a connection with him. This was because her participants still had an attachment bond with him despite the abuse. Drawing from attachment theory (Bowlby 1969, 1973), she explains that 'the strength of attachment bonds does not predict the quality of the attachment relationships' (Sammut Scerri 2015, p. 247). This paradoxical relationship is often not completely clear to clients who consult for help. The need for connection with a parent who was also a perpetrator may at times be veiled. At other moments, the client may experience anger towards their attachment figure but may later long for reconnection or be drawn to a similar attachment figure in their adult life and continue in their role as victims. Others enter into abusive relationships and take the role of perpetrators themselves. Sammut Scerri makes the point that it is of paramount importance that practitioners

> remain a consistent and enduring object in the face of some of the clients' distressing and fragmented experiences. … (and that) therapists are able to recognise contain and integrate incongruent information recognising that someone can both love and hate another person (Lawrence 2014) whilst also managing their own intense emotions around violence. This is where supervision would be helpful to the therapists (p. 251).

This delicate work entails mindful therapists, who in the first instance, are aware and able to make sense of the contradictory nature of the clients' utterances and behaviour and who are alert to windows of opportunity where they can intervene in a creative and therapeutic manner. Having a supervisor who can support the work of the practitioner is very important. Participants appreciate practitioners who are compassionate and who go out of their way to help them (Sammut Scerri 2015). However, such an emotional investment cannot take place without the support of an equally invested supervisor.

There is other incongruent material that practitioners may have to help their clients process in the context of violence and abuse within the family. Sammut Scerri (2015) mentions participants who not only witnessed violence and were abused by their father but were also physically and emotionally abused by their mothers. Practitioners who adopt a feminist theoretical framework may understand abuse by men on women and children, but might minimise the feelings of their clients once the latter start expressing the loss and the hurt they endured from their mothers. The supervisor may help these clinicians by providing a systemic theoretical framework that can take into account and explain simultaneous and perhaps contradictory behaviour (Vetere 2006; Vetere and Cooper 2008).

Practitioners may also struggle to keep their head above the water as they empathise with clients as victims of childhood abuse who are now abusive towards their children and/or partner. Nevertheless, the need to bring to the attention of the clients the importance of taking responsibility for their abusive relationships is also important. This view is substantiated by a number of scholars in the field including Goldner et al. (1990), Goldner (1998, 1999); and others such as Dutton (2006), Hamel (2005), Hamel and Nicholls (2007), George and Stith (2014); and Lawrence (2014).

Clients may find it unbearable and shameful to face the part of themselves that is abusive and may find ways of instilling a sense of guilt in the practitioner when such issues are addressed. They are made to feel harsh, critical and insensitive to the extent that they start doubting themselves. The role of the supervisor is invaluable in these circumstances. It gives practitioners, the opportunity to reflect while maintaining compassion towards the client/s and to find creative ways of intervening that may help the client/s manage and process their aggression.

Caring for and Mentoring Practitioners Working in the Field

A lot has been written about the need to take care of practitioners when they are doing trauma work. Supervisees witness clients who are often dysregulated because of the repeated abuse they would have endured. Intense emotions including expressions of rage, pain and hurt have a direct impact on practitioners, with those who are less experienced being more prone to secondary traumatisation (McLean et al. 2003). Smith (2013) points out that:

Traumatic material can block receptivity by activating emotional deregulation in the practitioner through overloading with overwhelming negative emotional material (Mosley and Wievel 2011). This 'client-clinician emotional disregulation' can become stuck on hypersensitivity, characterised by increasing anxiety or dissociative emotionally cut-off interactions within therapy sessions (Mosley and Wiewel 2011, p. 149).

The self-regulation of the supervisee is of crucial importance for a good outcome in therapy. The WHO and Calouste Gulbenkian Foundation 2014 recognised such importance to the extent that they called for the training of professionals in self-regulation. There are various ways of how supervision can help professionals remain self-regulated, some of which I have already discussed further above such as the use of reflexivity and the application of a sound theoretical framework that would help in the understanding of the case. However, the personal care of supervisees is extremely important for supervisees to flourish and to become more secure and able to attend to the complex needs of their clients.

Trusting and Confiding in the Supervisor is Important for Supervisees to Flourish

The supervisors participating in West's (2010) Delphi study did not all agree that the supervisor had a right to know about the traumas endured by their supervisees. However, they all concluded that the supervisor should inquire 'into the supervisor's awareness of their own issues and how they monitor and manage these when they arise, utilizing their own internal supervisor' (p. 425) Busuttil (2016) reports that family therapists found supervision very helpful when working with families who were going through the same trauma they had gone through themselves. This is because such instances might raise the possibility of re-traumatisation on supervisees or may have implications for the client's therapy (West 2010). As already indicated further above, supervisees do not open up easily on their own stories of trauma with their supervisors (Kavner and McNabb 2005). Such a relationship may not be easily fostered in work settings, where the supervisor is also one's direct manager for fear that it may then reflect unfavourably on their appraisal. Ideally supervisees need to be given the freedom to choose their supervisor for their one to one supervision as long as the supervisor is suitably qualified to carry out such complex work. Having a say when choosing a supervisor is considered important for supervisees and helps them build a high level of trust with their supervisor (Virtue and Fouche 2010). Competent supervisors who are sufficiently trained in the area of work also inspire the trust of their supervisees.

How Can Supervisors Help Practitioners Act as a Secure Base?

Yusmarhaini and Carpenter (2015) point out that not all therapists (or any other practitioner for that matter) may have a secure attachment style. Nevertheless, they report that the therapist's attachment style influences the quality of the therapeutic alliance that family therapists build with the families. Those possessing a secure attachment succeed in building a closer attachment with the family. They also quote earlier research reporting similar results. In an exploratory study, Yusmarhaini and Carpenter (2015) also found that therapists with a secure attachment were better able to manage client hostility. The authors suggest that supervisors should take into account the therapist's and the family's attachment style and the interaction between the two in supervision. Supervisors too need to reflect on their attachment style if they are to act as a secure base for their supervisees.

In their chapter on personal and professional development in the context of trauma, violence, abuse and hardship, Hanks and Vetere (2016) believe that it is helpful for supervisees to learn about the supervision style and the role of the supervisor. They argue that the clarity of roles will help supervisees to feel safe and contained. The personal safety and well-being of the therapist is also prioritised as is the space for reflection. The authors believe that these conditions promote creativity and effective problem solving.

Supervising Practitioners for Resilience

Working with couples, children and families who are recuperating from the trauma of abuse is considered as being demanding and heavy work. Many of our supervisees who work in trauma related work tell us that they find that the work requires a lot of emotional energy, persistence, patience, good thinking and creativity. Various authors highlight the occupational hazards that this work entails. These include burnout, compassion fatigue and vicarious traumatisation. Hanks and Vetere (2016) note that the specificity of their work as supervisors and consultants in this area of work is about 'how we help practitioners stay present, thoughtful, compassionate and creative when working at the extremes of human experience.' (p. 65).

Compassion fatigue (Figley 2002) takes place when the professionals' capacity to be empathic decreases because of over exposure to pain and suffering which may in some cases resonate with the therapist's own stories of trauma and other adverse life events which the therapist may be going through. Addressing these issues in supervision is important by emphasising the importance of self-care and of staying connected with significant others and with colleagues at work.

Vicarious traumatisation is more common when working with trauma. It takes place when the trauma that is witnessed by practitioners affects them to the extent that they end up 'thinking constantly about the suffering of those they care for. Over time that can reach such a state that the carer becomes traumatised' (Figley 1995, p. 20). Smith (2013) stresses the importance of adequate supervision as a protection against secondary traumatisation. He also points out that even if many may not reach a full blown vicarious traumatisation, mental health professionals are reported to suffer from mild depression, exhaustion and disrupted relationships. Smith cites a number of authors who report that often enough practitioners are unable/ashamed to discuss that they are not coping with the work. When supervisors remind supervisees that they give importance to their safety and well-being (Hanks and Vetere 2016), this may give supervisees the courage to open up.

Supervisees who do not receive adequate support and who have to face intense and overwhelming emotional states may run the risk of burn out. Some of the symptoms include 'the gradual erosion of self care in the work place—tardiness, failure to complete tasks, taking more work or not working at all ….The Foresight Project on Mental Capital and Wellbeing raised the issue of 'presenteeism' at work where workers are physically present but not productively working. Their report suggests this could cost the UK 900 million sterling a year' (Smith 2013, p. 151)

The chances for burn out are exacerbated without the provision of good supervision. The lack of spaces for reflection that have the potential to generate helpful ideas for practitioners is apt to lead to feelings of hopelessness, failure and blame. Bad feelings—just like good ones—are contagious and burnout can contaminate whole teams.

Ultimately, it is the organisation as a whole that needs to take responsibility and to provide a caring and vibrant environment. The political and social context in which the organisation is operating has to be taken into account as well. Work overload, insufficient rewards, unfairness and breakdown in a department are some of the systemic ways of operating that bring about burn out in the organisation (Maslach and Leiter 2008). Hanks and Vetere (2016) rightly make the point that supervisors cannot ignore these processes. 'How do we conduct ourselves (as supervisors) when the organisation is visibly and intentionally hostile to the workforce, by, for instance, increasing workloads without additional resources, downgrading pay structures and/or disregarding workers' views?' (p. 76). This is indeed a pertinent question which they pose to supervisors. Smith (2013) points out that 'the inability to process intense emotional experiences can lead to authoritarian and punitive management and supervision styles and this increases the likelihood of vicarious traumatization.' (p. 153). We believe that while safeguarding confidentiality, supervisors working at various levels in the organisation cannot work in a fragmented manner on such serious issues such as pervasive burnout in the organisation. Supervisors need to be able to come together to reflect on how to keep the thinking going especially during difficult times. Positioning theory (Harre and Moghaddam 2003); Campbell and Groenback 2006) and a dialogical model for addressing conflict and making the voice of the workers heard may be considered as a very helpful way of intervening. (Campbell 2008; Abela et al. 2013).

Trauma work is not all about doom and gloom. Hernandez et al. (2010) offer an integrative and nuanced framework for understanding the effect that this work has on clinicians. This framework also includes positive effects that come out of trauma which can be grouped under a resilience framework. These phenomena include post-traumatic growth, altruism born of suffering and vicarious resilience. In the psychotherapeutic process, they serve to remind clients that in spite of the suffering they would have endured, they are still strong and able to lead a meaningful life.

Vicarious resilience is a process whereby therapists are positively effected by the resilience of survivors of trauma. Hernandez et al. (2010) argue that: 'The concept of vicarious resilience may strengthen the therapist's wellbeing by appreciating and incorporating what they learn from their clients' healing processes.' (p. 73). Altruism born of suffering is different from being resilient. It is about stepping into doing things for others because of the suffering one goes through whereas post-traumatic growth is the ability to derive new meaning in life following loss and suffering. It is about the revision of one's values and the assumptions that one makes about life.

Supervisors who are aware of these positive processes during the therapeutic encounter need to be able to pick these up and use them as opportunities to supervise practitioners for resilience. This does not imply that the potentially harmful effects when working with trauma are to be ignored. However, by integrating the richness and the inspiration that clients offer to their therapists, supervisors nurture the spirit of their supervisees and motivate them to persist in moments of difficulty.

Sources of Support for the Supervisor

Hanks and Vetere (2016) emphasise that it is equally important for supervisors to look after themselves. The supervision of supervision is one such opportunity. In a grounded theory study by Virtue and Fouche (2010), supervisors working in the field of trauma highlighted the need to be supported themselves. One supervisor explained how vital such support is when dealing with a difficult case:

> Well to know that my supervisor is aware of a particularly difficult case for example. And that I may even say to my supervisee look don't do anything until I have consulted my own supervisor about that. To feel that I am not alone in holding what might be quite difficult stuff. I am aware as I say (it) that (there's) a kind of chain (p. 71).

In the above study, this need for a '*chain of holding*' (p. 71) was also mentioned by the other supervisors. They also found agency policies and procedures helpful in guiding them. Supervisors also called for funding that would help them in keeping up to date with the growing body of knowledge on trauma. Easy access to colleagues was also important. In the case of supervisors external to the agencies where they supervise, it is also important to have easy communication and a good relationship, with the direct manager of the supervisee and other related professionals. Working collaboratively in teams, networking and liaison work are also opportunities for staying connected.

Hanks and Vetere (2016) also point out that friends and family are also considered as an important source of support, replenishment and feedback. The authors explain that this area of work can at times be a source of prolonged worry. They acknowledge the support of their loved ones during such moments and conclude by saying:

In our experience, our partners have been our 'stable fourths'! In the triangle between ourselves as supervisors, our supervisees and their clients, our partners have often helped us stabilise these working triangles with their quiet commitment and understanding. In the creation and maintenance of stable triangles of interaction, we are able to think reflexively and clearly, to actualise support and to make our best decisions (Hanks and Vetere, p. 81).

The Role of the Supervisor Regarding Ethical Issues

Ethical issues must be prioritised at all times in our work. This is understandable given the very big responsibility that we carry when we are entrusted with helping vulnerable people heal from abuse and trauma. There is not much research in this area and according to West (2010) it requires further investigation. Supervisors have an important role to play regarding ethical behaviour and are ultimately held responsible to protect clients from poor practice.

More over as Clark and Croney (2006) point out:

> Supervision is the place where ethical choices must be recognized, evaluated and modeled … no ethics code or course can replace the consistent presence and modeling of a supervisor who actively helps the supervisee to integrate the principles of ethical practice with the supervisee's pre-existing moral framework (Handelsman et al. 2005, p. 52).

In this respect, a supervisor in this particular area needs to have the moral authority gained from knowledge and experience in the field of child, couple and family psychotherapy with regard to those who have been traumatised by abuse. Training in supervision also provides the supervisor with skills and knowledge that may better equip her to offer a containing supervisory framework.

Supervisees look up to supervisors who are ethically sound themselves. Clark and Croney (2006) point out that it is difficult for supervisees to build a good supervisory alliance with a supervisor who violates ethical principles. They cite a related survey carried out among 151 therapists by Ladany, Lehrman-Waterman, Molinaro and Walgast in 1999, which shows that supervisors have to be more aware of their ethical principles. More than half of the therapists (51%) cited at least one ethical violation with the three most cited being inadequate performance evaluations, confidentiality issues in supervision and theoretical clinical inflexibility. Supervisors have an ethical responsibility to be able to process their own personal issues, be coherent and to manage the supervisory relationship. Should heavily laden disagreement arise between the supervisee and the supervisor, the latter is expected to be able to manage the relationship in a constructive manner.

In extreme situations, boundary keeping may even be a cause for concern when supervisors are morally obliged to make a formal complaint especially when supervisees persist in their behaviour. In extreme situations, the supervisor may actually counsel supervisees to change their workplace or even move to another profession. Such drastic action may prove stressful for supervisors who would also need to seek support for themselves.

In Chap. 6, reference is made to parents who may stop being physically abusive but would still be emotionally abusive towards their child. Reporting child abuse or neglect necessitates concerted effort and the role of the supervisor can be extremely helpful for the supervisee. The following case from the literature illustrates the kind of supervisory work a case might entail (Clark and Croney 2006, pp. 61–62).

> After many weeks of work, 13-year old John had developed a positive alliance with his clinician. John struggled with symptoms of post traumatic stress disorder (PTSD), the sequelae of many years of sexual abuse. John disclosed that he had been having compulsive sex and using non prescribed benzodiazepines every day. Fearful of being kicked out of his foster home and new school, he begged the clinician not to tell anyone. This outcome he warned, would make life not worth living. In supervision, the clinician appeared overwhelmed with the possible consequences of John's activities but also felt guilty about disclosing them to authorities and was fearful that disclosing them to the supervisor would be an admission to failure. After empathically exploring the clinician's emotional responses and identifying the situation as a typical dilemma facing those who work with high-risk clients, the supervisor explored what clinical approaches had been taken. On determining that John has persisted in his behaviours despite standard interventions, the supervisor

examined the possibility that John was so out of control, that his disclosures were a way to signal his desperation and his terror that therapy was not working.

After the supervisor reframed the situation as a complex case requiring multiple treatment providers and possibly requiring hospitalisation to protect John, the clinician became more comfortable with objectively reviewing evidence-based approaches to comorbid PTSD and addictive behaviours. He saw John for an emergency session, and with John present, he contacted the foster care worker and foster parents. A behavioural contract was established that would reward John by maintaining his current placement if he immediately participated in inpatient treatment. John completed his inpatient treatment and, after discharge resumed outpatient work where he and the clinician were able to use the strengthened therapeutic alliance and behavioural contracting to maintain his treatment gains.

Given the above risk factors, confidentiality issues may arise when working with such sensitive cases. Supervisees would need both emotional support as well as practical support in preparing the data. They would need to be helped on how to keep their files. Conversations about data protection and on which information is to be shared need to take place. In extreme circumstances a case may end up in court. Support by the supervisor and other forensic experts may be critical at this stage.

Another area that is of special ethical concern in supervision relates to situations, where clients who have been traumatised and abused are neglected or treated inappropriately by the agency staff. Very often this is a reflection of the way this client group would have been treated throughout their lives but is also a symptom of burnout on the part of the professional. Other reasons may be related to cuts in expenditure, which may lead to bigger caseloads that may become unmanageable. Appointments are then missed either by the client or by the professional and are not rescheduled. It is always helpful to ask supervisees to present on clients that they have not talked about for a long time. Being ethical is also about advocating for the well-being of the client in an agency. Supervisors may have an influential role to play not only in protecting clients but also professionals when they are burnt out. One of us (Angela) remembers how concerned she became when the workplace where she worked as a supervisor, had an alarming turnover rate of caring professionals. She felt the need to set a meeting with management to discuss her concern.

Finally termination when working on these issues may also be a delicate process. As West (2010) points out a short time-focused session policy is unethical. Very often such work is long term. At the same time, the health and social services are not very likely to offer sessions ad infinitum in spite of the fact that most people continue to process and reframe the adverse experiences they would have lived throughout their lives. Supervisors need to help supervisees with termination and closure by helping them develop increasingly collaborative relationships with their clients such that both clinician and client/s can construct criteria that can help them ascertain termination.

Conclusion

The supervisor's qualities of warmth, security, compassion, ability to support the supervisee, the ability to process vicarious trauma, curiosity and openness (Neill et al. 2006; Virtue and Fouche 2010), that allow for the creation of a safe haven for supervisees are considered as important characteristics of the supervisor in the supervisory relationship. Supervisors also need to feel supported themselves. They want to be au courant with the latest knowledge on the treatment of trauma, seek supervision of supervision, inform themselves about statutory and regulatory guidelines and create collaborative relationships with colleagues that provide opportunities for discussion and feedback.

The notion of 'multiple holding' captures the importance of the various sources of support that supervisors and supervisees look for. This core concept that emerged from a grounded theory study by Virtue and Fouche (2010) on what is needed to provide support for professionals working in the area of trauma and abuse 'is a term for the processes practitioners use to enable them to remain working in the field' (p. 64) and is not only linked to supervision, knowledge and skills but also to outside resources such as collegiality, personal therapy, spirituality and ongoing training.

It is this 'chain of holding' that keeps professionals going. As Smith (2013) concludes, trauma work needs to honour the connection between people. It is this connection that helps practitioners think about trauma work creatively. The children, their families, the couples and the clients in turn remind us that in suffering and loss there is also growth and altruism that is borne out of suffering.

References

Abela, A. (2003). *Who's knocking at the door? Experiences of trainees and families when supervisors knock during live supervision* (Unpublished study for Supervisor's Course Tavistock Clinic), Tavistock Institute, London.

Abela, A. (2009). Travailler en collaboration avec les enfants et les familles en risqué d'exclusion sociale. In C. Paisant (Ed.), *Familles et Professionnels de l'Action Sociale* (pp. 167–179). Lyon: Editions Chronique Sociale.

Abela, A., & Sammut Scerri, C. (2003). Collaborative enquiry versus didactic training with organisations: A case study. *Human Systems, 14*(1), 41–54.

Abela, A., & Sammut Scerri, C. (2010). Managing multiple relationships in supervision. In C. Burck & G. Daniel (Eds.), *Mirrors and reflections: Processes of systemic supervision* (pp. 289–308). London: Karnac.

Abela, A., & Tabone, C. (2008). Processes of poverty and social exclusion in poor families. In D. R. Crane & T. B. Heaton (Eds.), *Handbook of families & poverty* (pp. 144–160). Los Angeles: Sage.

Abela, A., Zahra de Domenico, R., Formosa Ventura, R., & Zammit, J. (2013). The ultimate ethical position is to keep talking: dealing with difference in teams, in supervision, and in therapy. In C. Burck, S. Barratt, & E. Kavner (Eds.), *Positions and polarities in contemporary systemic practice: The legacy of David Campbell* (pp. 215–226). London: Karnac.

Bowlby, J. (1969). *Attachment and loss, Vol 1: Attachment*. New York, NY: Basic Books.

Bowlby, J. (1973). *Attachment and loss, Vol 2: Separation: Anxiety and anger*. New York, NY: Basic Books.

Bowlby, J. (1988). *A secure base: Parent-child attachment and healthy human development*. New York: Basic Books.

Briere, J. (2002). Treating adult survivors of severe childhood abuse and neglect: Further development of an integrative model. In J. E. B. Myers, L. Berliner, J. Briere, C. T. Hendrix, T. Reid, & C. Jenny (Eds.), *The APSAC handbook on child maltreatment* (2nd ed., pp. 175–191). USA: Sage.

Busuttil, C. (2016). *The school of life: Exploring the Relationship between family therapists' own parenting experience and their clinical practice*. Unpublished Master Dissertation, University of Malta, Malta.

Campbell, C., & Groenbaek, M. (2006). *Taking positions in the organization*. London: Karnac Books.

Campbell, D. (2008). Locating conflict in team consultations. In D. Campbell & C. Huffington (Eds.), *Organisations connected: A handbook of systemic consultation* (pp. 79–98). London: Karnac Books.

Center on the Developing Child at Harvard University. (2016). From best practices to breakthrough impacts: A science-based approach to building a more promising future for young children and families. Retrieved from: http://www.developingchild.harvard.edu.

Chard, K. M. & Hansel, J. E. (2006). Supervising therapists working with traumatised children. In T. Kerby Neil (Ed.), *Helping others help children: Clinical supervision of child psychotherapy* (pp. 193–207). Washington, DC: American Psychological Association.

Clark, J. J. & Croney, E. L. (2006). Ethics and accountability in supervision of child psychotherapy. In T. Kerby Neil (Ed.), *Helping others help children: Clinical supervision of child psychotherapy* (pp. 51–71). Washington, DC: American Psychological Association.

Courtois, C. A. (2008). Complex trauma, complex reactions: Assessment and treatment. *Psychological Trauma: Theory, Research, Practice, and Policy, S*(1), 86–100. doi:10.1037/1942-9681.S.1.86.

Courtois, C. A., & Ford, J. D. (2012). *Treatment of complex trauma: A sequenced, relationship-based approach*. NY, New York: Guilford Press.

Crittenden, P. M. (2008). *Raising parents: Attachment, parenting, and child safety*. Abingdon, UK: Routledge/Willan.

Daly, M. (Ed.). (2007). *Parenting in Contemporary Europe: A Positive Approach*. Strasbourg France: Editions du Conseil de l'Europe.

Dutta, S. (2010). Exploring emotions: A critical incident for a supervisor. In C. Burck & G. Daniel (Eds.), *Mirrors and reflections: Processes of systemic supervision* (pp. 103–120). London: Karnak.

Dutton, D. G. (2006). *Rethinking domestic violence*. Vancouver, Canada: UBC Press.

Etherington, K. (2009). Supervising Helpers Who Work with the Trauma of Sexual Abuse. *British Journal of Guidance and Counselling, 37*(2), 179–194. doi:10.1080/03069880902728622.

Falicov, C. J. (1998). *Latino families in therapy: A guide to multicultural practice*. New York: Guilford Press.

Figley, C. R. (1995). *Compassion Fatigue: Coping with secondary traumatic stress disorder in those who treat the traumatized*. New York: Brunner/Mazel.

Figley, C. R. (2002). Compassion fatigue: Psychotherapists' chronic lack of self care. *Journal of Clinical Psychology, 58*(11), 1433–1441. doi:10.1002/jclp.10090.

Ford, J. D., & Courtois, C. A. (Eds.). (2013). *Treating complex traumatic stress disorders in children and adolescents: Scientific foundations and therapeutic models*. New York, USA: Guilford Press.

George, J., & Stith, S. M. (2014). An updated feminist view of intimate partner violence. *Family Process, 53*(2), 179–193. doi:10.1111/famp.12073.

Goldner, V. (1998). The treatment of violence and victimization in intimate relationships. *Family Process, 37*(3), 263–286. doi:10.1111/j/1545-5300.1998.00263.x.

Goldner, V. (1999). Morality and multiplicity: Perspectives on the treatment of violence in intimate life. *Journal of Marital & Family Therapy, 25*(3), 325–336. doi:10.1111/j.1752-0606.1999.tb00251.x.

Goldner, V., Penn, P., Sheinberg, M., & Walker, G. (1990). Love and Violence: Gender paradoxes in volatile attachments. *Family Process, 29*(4), 343–364. doi:10.1111/j.1752-0606.1999.tb00251.x.

Hamel, J. (2005). *Gender inclusive treatment of intimate partner abuse: A comprehensive approach*. New York: Springer.

Hamel, J., & Nicholls, T. L. (Eds.). (2007). *Family interventions in domestic violence: A handbook of gender inclusive theory and treatment*. New York: Springer.

Hanks, H., & Vetere, A. (2016). Working at the Extremes: the impact on us of doing the work. In A. Vetere & P. Stratton (Eds.), *Interacting selves: Systemic solutions for personal and professional development in counselling and psychotherapy* (pp. 65–84). London and New York: Routledge.

Handelsman, M. M., Gottlieb, M. C., & Knapp, S. (2005). Training ethical psychologists: an acculturation model. *Professional Psychology: Research and Practice, 36*(1), 59–65. doi:10.1037/0735-7028.36.1.59.

Harre, R., & Moghaddam, F. (Eds.). (2003). *The self and others: Positioning individuals and groups in personal, political, and cultural contexts*. Westport, CT: Praeger Publishers.

Herman, J. L. (1997). *Trauma and recovery. The aftermath of violence from domestic abuse to political terror* (2nd ed.). New York, NY: Basic books.

Hernandez, P., Enstorm, D., & Gangsei, D. (2010). Exploring the impact of trauma of therapists: Vicarious resilience and related concepts in training. *Journal of Systemic Therapies, 29*(1), 67–83.

Kavner, E., & McNab, S. (2005). Therapist experience of shame. In C. Flaskas, B. Mason, & A. Perlesz (Eds.), *The space between: Experience, context and process in the therapeutic relationship* (pp. 141–156). London: Karnac.

Keys, M. (2009). Determining the skills for child protection practice: From quandary to quagmire? *Child Abuse Review, 18*(5), 297–315. doi:10.1002/car.1088.

Lanktree, C., & Briere, J. (2013). Integrative treatment of complex trauma. In J. D. Ford & C. A. Courtois (Eds.), *Treating complex traumatic stress disorders in children and adolescents: Scientific foundations and the rapeutic models* (pp. 143–161). New York: Guilford Press.

Lawrence, J. A. (2014). Managing dissonance: Implications for therapeutic practice with partner violence. *Partner Abuse, 5*(2), 119–151. doi:10.1891/1946-6560.5.2.119.

Lowe, C. (2016). The professional's influence within the client system: Exploring counter-transference and adult attachment within the therapeutic relationships with children experiencing abuse and their caregivers. *Journal of Social Work Practice, 30*(1), 59–68. doi:10.1080/02650533.2015.1035236.

Maslach, C., & Leiter, M. P. (2008). Early predictors of job burnout and engagement. *Journal of Applied Psychology, 93*(3), 489–512. doi:10.1037/0021-9010.93.3.498.

McLean, S., Wade, T., & Encel, J. S. (2003). The contribution of therapist beliefs to psychological distress in therapists: An investigation of vicarious traumatization, burnout and symptoms of avoidance and intrusion. *Behavioural and Cognitive Psychotherapy, 31*(4), 417–428. doi:10.1017/S135246580300403X.

Mosley, T., & Wiewel, B. (2011). Trauma focused clinical supervision. *UCLA Integrated Substance Abuse Programs.*

Neill, T. K., Holloway, E. L., & Kaak, H. O. (2006). A systems approach to supervision of child psychotherapy. In T. Kerby Neil (Ed.), *Helping others help children: Clinical supervision of child psychotherapy* (pp. 7–33). Washington, DC, US: American Psychological Association.

Papadopoulos, R. K. (1998). Destructiveness, atrocities and healing: epistemological and clinical reflections. *Journal of Analytical Psychology, 43*(4), 455–477. doi:10.1111/1465-5922.00047.

Papadopoulos, R. K. (2007). Refugees, trauma and adversity-activated development. *European Journal of Psychotherapy and Counselling, 9*(3), 301–312. doi:10.1080/13642530701496930.

Prouty, A. M. (2014). Incorporating feminist practices in systemic supervision. In C. L. Storm & T.C Todd (Eds), *The systemic supervisor electronic resources.*London: Wiley-Blackwell.
Sammut Scerri, C. (2015). *Living with contradictions of love and violence: A grounded theory study of women's understanding of their childhood experiences of domestic violence.* Unpublished doctoral dissertation, University of Surrey, UK.
Smith, G. (2013). *Working with trauma: systemic approaches.* Palgrave, Macmillan: Basingstoke.
Stoltenberg, C. D., McNeill, B., & Delworth, U. (1998). *IDM supervision: An integrative developmental for supervising counselors and therapists.* San Fransico: Jossey-Bass.
Van der Kolk, B. (2015). *The body keeps the score: Brain, mind, and body in the healing of trauma.* Great Britain: Penguin Books.
Vetere, A. (2006). Commentary—The role of formulation in psychotherapy practice. *Journal of family Therapy, 28*(4), 388–391. doi:10.1111/j.1467-6427.2006.00359.x.
Vetere, A. (2012). Supervision and consultation practice with domestic violence. *Clinical child psychology and psychiatry, 17*(2), 181–185. doi:10.1177/1359104511433563.
Vetere, A., & Cooper, J. (2008). Supervision and family safety: Working with domestic violence. In J. Hamel (Ed.), *Intimate partner and family abuse: A casebook of gender-inclusive therapy* (pp. 347–359). New York: Springer.
Virtue, C., & Fouche, C. (2010). Multiple holding: A model for supervision in the context of trauma and abuse. *Aotearoa New Zealand Social Work, 21*(4), 64–72.
Walsh, F. (2003). Clinical views of family normality, health and dysfunction. In F. Walsh (Ed.), *Normal Family Processes* (3rd ed., pp. 27–57). New York: Guilford Press.
West, A. (2010). Supervising counselors and psychotherapists who work with trauma: a Delphi study. *British Journal of Guidance and Counselling, 38*(4), 409–430. doi:10.1080/03069885.2010.503696.
Whitefield, C., & Midgley, N. (2015). "And when you were a child?": how therapists working with parents alongside individual child psychotherapy bring the past into their work. *Journal of Child Psychotherapy, 41*(3), 272–292. doi:10.1080/0075417X.2015.1092678.
Wilson, J. P., & Lindy, J. D. (1994). Empathic Strain and countertransference. In J. P. Wilson & J. D. Lindy (Eds.), *Countertransference in the treatment of PTSD* (pp. 5–30). New York, US: Guilford Press.
World Health Organisation & the Calouste Gulbenkian Foundation. (2014). *Social Determinants of Mental Health* (NLM classification: WM 101). Geneva: World Health Organisation. Retrieved from: http://www.who.int/mental_health/publications/gulbenkian_paper_social_determinants_of_mental_health/en/.
Yusmarhaini & Carpenter. (2015). Family therapists adult attachment styles and the therapeutic alliance. *Journal of Family Therapy, 38*(1), 59–81. doi:10.1111/1467-6427.12079.

Chapter 9
Prevention and Early Intervention with Violence and Abuse in Families

Introduction

The damage caused by intimate partner violence and child abuse can be quite significant and remains a risk factor from one generation to the next. Researchers estimate that child abuse may be considered as the gravest and most costly public health issue in the United States. Van der Kolk (2015) makes the point that: 'the overall costs exceed those of cancer or heart disease and eradicating child abuse in America would reduce the overall rate of depression by more than half, alcoholism by two thirds, and suicide, drug use and domestic violence by three quarters. It would also have a dramatic effect on workplace performance and vastly decrease the need for incarceration' (p. 148).

Similarly, the costs of intimate partner violence have been repeatedly stated. The WHO reports that globally as many as 35% of murders of women are committed by an intimate partner (WHO 2016). The costs include medical and mental healthcare expenses and the effects on productivity in the workplace (Campbell 2002; Krug et al. 2002; Reeves and O'Leary-Kelly 2007). Moreover, when the victims and perpetrators are also parents, the effect on the children can be long lasting.

Quite frequently, a family member or members can be dangerous and a threat to the well-being of others who are more vulnerable. One in four children in the United States is abused, more often than not, in their own homes (Costello et al. 2002; Van der Kolk 2015). The statistics are higher in Europe (WHO 2013). Moreover, 35% of women around the world experience physical and/or sexual abuse from either a current or a previous partner (WHO 2016). Although male violence results in more injury overall than female violence (Lawrence 2014), men too are victims of abuse, and both men and women are victims of severe violence. Desmarais et al. (2012a, b) conducted a review of studies and found that approximately one in four women and one in five men reported that they were victims of

The original version of this chapter was revised: See the "Chapter Note" section at the end of this chapter for details. The erratum to this chapter is available at 10.1007/978-3-319-57789-0_10

C. Sammut Scerri et al., *Intervening After Violence*,
Focused Issues in Family Therapy, DOI 10.1007/978-3-319-57789-0_9

physical violence by their intimate partner. In a significant number of families, domestic violence and child abuse overlap (Appel and Holden 1998; Edleson 1999; Jouriles et al. 2008; Sammut Scerri 2015).

This chapter is about the prevention of intimate partner violence and child abuse that take place inside the home. It starts by providing a theoretical framework for understanding the processes at play when there is abuse in the family. The current legal frameworks that are in place and the strategic policies—including examples of good practice and evidence-based policies aimed to prevent violence and abuse between family members—are then reviewed.

The Need for Developing a Theoretical Framework for Understanding Abuse

It is impossible to come forward with primary preventive interventions to prevent or stop abuse if one does not have a clear understanding of the reasons why violence happens in families. In Chap. 1 of this book, we make explicit our understanding of violence and abuse within the family. It is the same as the one used by the Council of Europe (2011), also known as the Istanbul Convention, which includes 'All acts of violence, sexual, psychological or economic violence that occur within the family or domestic unit or between former or current spouses or partners, whether or not the perpetrator shares or has shared the same residence with the victim'. We also take into account the Council of Europe definition of 1986: 'any act or omission committed within the framework of the family, by one of its members that undermines the life, the bodily or psychological integrity or the liberty of another person of the same family or that seriously harms the development of his or her personality' (Recommendation No. R (85) 4).

In this respect, it incorporates the views of many feminist scholars who see domestic violence against women as a reflection of patriarchy (Jewkes 2002), where the prevalent ideology is one of male superiority and the ideas of manhood are linked to the control of women, even through violent means. From this perspective, women are perceived to have low social value and less power than men.

This feminist perspective does not preclude us from acknowledging other scholars, such as Dutton (2006), Hamel (2005), Hamel and Nicholls (2007), George and Stith (2014), and Lawrence (2014), who make the point that violence can also take place from women towards men or between persons of the same sex, and is not always from men to women.

Moreover, intimate partner violence can also be situational (Johnson 2008) rather than perpetrated exclusively by one of the partners on the other. This is not the case for sexual assault, which is almost always perpetrated by men. When there is gender symmetry in abuse, an overarching systemic theoretical framework for understanding intimate partner violence is very pertinent (See Chaps. 3 and 4).

In Chap. 6 of this book, we have already elaborated upon the processes at play when children are abused in their own homes. Very often, it is the parents themselves who abuse their children. However, violence can also take place between siblings or by children towards their parents. Research and clinical practice concur that violence by parents towards their children is very often a reflection of existing trauma.

Nevertheless, many parents who are abused can be very resilient and are able to reflect upon their experience and develop a coherent story of why their parents abused them (Main et al. 1985). Their developed sense of compassion makes them therapeutic rather than the ones to perpetuate abuse. As parents, they can be high in reflective function (Steele and Steele 2008) and their children are securely attached and grow to form secure romantic relationships. In this respect, attachment theory and the body of knowledge we have about resilience offer rich theoretical frameworks for policymakers, who are interested in family relationships.

Other parents are, in turn, abusive towards their children (Herzog et al. 1992; Lyons-Ruth and Block 1996). From an emotional regulation perspective, modern attachment research suggests that the transmission of violence from one generation to another is brought about because of the dysregulation that is experienced in the face of stress, abuse and neglect. A trauma-informed and expanded family systems approach to understanding violence and abuse provides important insights to this multi-layered phenomenon (Perry 1997; Siegel 2013).

The systemic theoretical framework also helps us understand other forms of violence in the family. Haskins (2003) points out that sibling incest and assault are frequent and form 'part of a family interdependent network' (p. 328). Similarly, child-to-parent violence is more likely to occur when there is domestic violence between the parents, and boys are more likely to be violent towards their mother if she was victimised by the father. On the other hand, parenting styles that are punitive and lacking in warmth and emotional support, as well as permissibility, and a lack of limits within the family are also considered to be risk factors (Ibabe et al. 2013; Calvete et al. 2013).

Contextual pressures also need to be taken into account. Poverty is considered to be a key mediating factor for the occurrence of domestic violence. Jewkes (2002) explains that whereas domestic violence happens across different socioeconomic groups; it is more frequent and severe in the context of poverty. This is the case across diverse countries around the world. A plausible explanation is that poverty creates stress. Moreover, men who perceive themselves to be in charge may experience a crisis in their masculinity when they find themselves unable to provide for the family. Heavy alcohol consumption is also considered to be an influencing factor that exacerbates violence in the family. Child abuse is also more common when the family is living in poverty (See Chap. 6 for a more detailed explanation in this regard).

Developing a Preventive Strategy to Eradicate Abuse

The long-term deleterious effects of domestic violence have become a widespread concern. Ending violence was considered as one of the top five priorities by five million citizens who participated in United Nations-led consultations (WHO 2014).

On the basis of a number of systematic reviews about prevention, The Global Status Report on Violence Prevention led by the World Health Organisation (2014), together with the United Nations Development Programme and the United Nations Office on Drugs and Crime, identified seven strategies that are considered to be evidence-based and that can prevent violence. They are captured in the textbox below:developing safe, stable and nurturing relationships between children and their parents and caregivers;

developing life skills in children and adolescents;
reducing the availability and harmful use of alcohol;
reducing access to guns and knives;
promoting gender equality to prevent violence against women;
changing cultural and social norms that support violence.
victim identification, care and support programmes;
the development of safe, stable and nurturing relationships

Interventions include the setting up of a legal framework to combat and eradicate abuse, education in the community, teaching which forms part of the school curriculum, campaigns in the media and policy development.

This leads us to delve into some of these strategies, highlighting examples of good practice and policy interventions that are evidence-based. As we shall see, in spite of the ever-growing evidence base, and in tune with the findings of the survey carried out by the World Health Organisation and the other two collaborating partners (WHO 2014), there is still insufficient investment in the prevention of violence and abuse.

Giving Families Their Social Right to Live in Dignity

It is of no use trying to help and support families to live respectfully without alleviating the standard of living of those living in misery and without adequate income. Partner violence can be reduced if poverty is kept in check, the level of education is increased and equality between the sexes is promoted (Stith et al. 2013).

Many researchers in the field often make reference to families at risk and suggest interventions to prevent violence and abuse but fail to highlight the importance of interventions that fight socio-economic or structural barriers such as poverty, gender inequality and racism. By failing to do so, they may inadvertently medicalise these issues (Center on the Developing Child at Harvard University 2016). The WHO report (2013) notes that we have very few studies on how reducing poverty can prevent child maltreatment; the ones that exist focus on the evaluation of welfare reforms and have produced conflicting results so far (Klevens and Whitaker 2007).

Nevertheless, we do know how poverty can be reduced. Families need jobs that pay. Ridge (2009) in the UK and Povich et al. (2015) in the US both make the point that employment is limited for those with a low level of education and does not lift them out of poverty. Good accommodation and/or income support for those on one salary or for vulnerable families where the breadwinner/s cannot hold a job or may need to work on a part-time basis are necessary. Ongoing adult education and job training may also open avenues to many who might have left school early due to adverse circumstances in their lives, including poverty and trauma that might have put them at a great disadvantage. In this respect, the European Union has put a number of issues on its agenda that have ecological importance in terms of curbing violence and abuse. These include gender equality, immigration, the reconciliation of work and family, lifelong learning, the Europe 2020 reduction in early school leaving, and the resolution to decrease poverty and social exclusion in the EU. Unfortunately, the fight against poverty continues (Abela and Renoux 2014). Many children and families, even in highly developed countries, fare very badly in this regard (Unicef Innocenti Research Centre 2012; Amato et al. 2015). Stith et al. (2013) make the point that the human rights of all people need to be respected if we aspire to a world free of violence. This also holds in the case of women when they are treated unequally when compared to men.

Providing the Legal Framework to Counteract Abuse

The wide recognition of the ill effects of abuse and the increasing awareness about its frequency within the family prompted several States across the world to intervene. As Hartman (2003) points out, 'Slowly over the years, the State has put limits on family inviolability, particularly in regard to the protection of children' (p. 639). The United Nations Convention on the Rights of the Child (UNCRC), which came into force in 1990, was an important landmark in this respect. The treaty, ratified by 195 countries, is the most widely ratified treaty in history and protects the civil, political, economic, social, health and cultural rights of children.

In 1993, the United Nations General Assembly issued a Declaration on the Elimination of Violence against Women. To date, at least 119 countries have passed laws on domestic violence. Moreover, 125 have laws on sexual harassment and 52 have laws on marital rape.

Legal frameworks are an important deterrent when addressing abuse from a public health perspective. Such laws highlight the social injustice of domestic violence against vulnerable family members, primarily women and children.

However, legislation is not enough to bring about a cultural change in behaviour. Very often, the State might not have the infrastructure to implement such laws. The police or the child protection services may not be sufficiently trained to see that the legislation is working effectively. In this respect, The Global Status Report on Violence Prevention (WHO 2014) emphasised that laws need to be promulgated and rigorously applied. In a survey they carried out, it emerged that only 57% of the countries who endorsed corporal punishment enforced laws fully. Moreover, only 44% out of the 87% who had laws on sexual harassment and domestic violence practised full enforcement. They call for the strengthening of resources. A change in culture also needs to be supported by policy development that promotes positive relationships between partners, and positive parenting towards the children.

Informal and Formal Support to Counteract Violence and Abuse

Families do better when they are supported by their next of kin and have friends or neighbours to turn to, especially in moments of distress. Formal support is also extremely important. The Council of Europe recommendation on the *Policy to Support Positive Parenting* (Council of Europe 2006) highlighted the importance of both informal and formal support for families, with a special emphasis on those who are at risk.

Van Wyk et al. (2003) found that women who enjoy a good level of social support are less likely to be victimised. Spouses who have no one to turn to other than their husband or partner are more at risk of intimate partner violence (Stets 1991). Van Wyk et al. (2003) also point out that if one lives in a deprived neighbourhood where there is high unemployment, violence and drug problems, isolation is further exacerbated. The WHO European Report on child maltreatment also considers strong social networks and a high level of social capital as being very effective to reduce child maltreatment (WHO 2013).

The way in which extended family members, neighbours and friends respond when families are going through a difficult time will make a big difference in terms of the well-being of the family. Victims of intimate partner violence find positive empathic reactions to be very helpful and psychologically beneficial (Slaska and Edwards 2013). Australian women that were interviewed also found informal support invaluable. They found the respectful and empathic contact with family and friends helpful and also appreciated practical support, including financial help, housing and child care (Taket et al. 2014). On the contrary, critical and/or blameful feedback was considered to be very unhelpful by victims. Sometimes, relatives and friends might need support themselves, especially when their loved ones are in danger. Some relatives and friends, especially those who are very close to the victim, may freeze in the face of the trauma and feel traumatised and/or in danger themselves. Others may become very critical. In a systematic review on how domestic violence impacted on informal supporters, it transpired that at present there is little support available for them. (Gregory et al. 2016). The same principles apply when helping distressed parents who are struggling to bring up their children. Psychological and practical support by family and friends are greatly appreciated.

Formal support is also indispensable for families to thrive in their communities. Formal support includes relationships with professionals, and support from school, associations, NGOs and/or the local parish.

The two most effective components of five different community prevention programmes in the United States aiming at preventing child abuse were the social capital development of families in the community and the coordination of services offered by different entities (Daro and Dodge 2009). Family Resource Centres planted in the community are ideal places where this can happen. They can serve as cultural centres where families can meet and get to know each other, as well as one-stop shops where families can be helped to reach the service they need. Strong links between the family and the school are also important.

In this respect, communities need to embrace a cohesive strategy and be well-resourced. The Center on the Developing Child at Harvard University (2016) advocates for science-informed innovation at the neighbourhood systems level for this to happen. Working at the community level, rather than targeting high-risk families, may prove to be more costly, and one may need to evaluate the trade-offs before considering whether to go for more personal services for children and families at risk, as opposed to more community intervention (Daro and Dodge 2009). We believe that specialised services will continue to be needed to prevent as well as offer help to families who have been traumatised by abuse; however, intervening at the community level is also very helpful. This is because community work builds the families' resilience and empowers its members to tap into a variety of resources rather than become too dependent on professional services (Rodrigo et al. 2016).

Heightening Awareness of the Dangers of Violence and Abuse Through the Media

Media campaigns are meant to educate the public on positive parenting and the adoption of constructive styles of conflict. They help to change social norms regarding intimate partner violence and child abuse. They also encourage the public to seek help and to report maltreatment where necessary, so that the necessary legal action is taken. The WHO report (2013) on the prevention of child maltreatment notes that 'mass media programmes have been found to have at least modest benefits in addressing a wide range of health-related attitudes and behaviours, can encourage discussion and debate and drive other prevention work' (pp. 62–63). Awareness campaigns in the eighties and nineties registered reductions in verbal and corporal punishment; nevertheless, the number of parents who reported hitting their children or injuring them remained the same (Daro and Gelles 1992; Daro and McCurdy 2007). This finding is in tune with the conclusions of Harvey et al. (2007) when writing about campaigns addressing intimate partner violence, which concluded that campaigns alone are not enough to bring about change and need to be complemented with other strategies. Evidence-based programmes in relationship education and parental education are some examples of more targeted interventions.

The WHO study on the prevention of child maltreatment (2013) also mentions television series like 'Families' in Australia or 'Driving Mum and Dad Mad' in the UK as another way of improving parental competence. Evaluation studies concluded that those who followed the first series improved their competence as parents, and their children were better behaved, whereas those who followed the UK series were better able to manage their anger, felt less depressed and more in charge, and the behaviour of their children improved. Moreover, in the UK series, parents were also offered personalised Internet-based support to complement the watching of the episodes.

Reducing Alcohol

Alcohol misuse can exacerbate intimate partner violence and sexual violence. Many children are also maltreated when the parents are under the influence of alcohol or drug misuse (Harvey et al. 2007; WHO 2013).

Three main approaches are normally taken to reduce the intake of alcohol. These include the regulation of price, the introduction of tax on the product, and the regulation of the availability of alcoholic drinks and the context in which drinking is permitted.

Economic modelling studies have estimated that the reduction of alcohol intake is possible. Markowitz and Grossman (1998) have calculated that by increasing the price of beer by 10%, the likelihood of violence towards children would decrease by 2.3%, whereas violence in general would decrease by another 1.2%. They also estimated that by closing one alcohol outlet for every 1000 persons in the population, child abuse could possibly decrease by 4%. A series of studies in different parts of the world have shown that examples of such regulations have actually resulted in the reduction of accidents and violence, and better outcomes for children. One of the most impressive was the intensive anti-alcohol campaign in the former Soviet Union in 1985. The policy was very comprehensive and included a decrease in alcohol production, the reduction of alcohol outlets, an increase in the price on alcohol, the prohibition of alcohol in official functions, and increasing the age limit for those buying alcohol to 21. The new policy actions were enforced with heavy penalties. This led to a 33% reduction in violent deaths. Children also enjoyed better health conditions in that period (Balan-Cohen 2008).

The Prevention of Partner Abuse

Other ways of implementing the primary prevention of abuse between partners include screening and relationship education.

Screening

The partner abuse state of knowledge (PASK) findings for prevention, treatment and policy highlight the importance of screening with regard to intimate partner violence (Stith et al. 2013). The authors cite a growing body of research on this topic and provide a number of important reasons for making use of well-thought-out assessments and measures that are validated. Whilst they acknowledge that the tools available vary in their predictive accuracy (See Nicholls et al. 2013) and therefore one has to be well informed when making use of a particular instrument, by so doing one can have the advantage of accuracy, validity and replicability. Other advantages of certain tools include the possibility of assessing recidivism and other risk factors. They help to develop safety plans and interventions, and by so doing reduce the incidence and severity of partner violence (See Chap. 4).

Screening may also have both a preventative and an interventive role. One of the policy actions of a national strategic policy on positive parenting in Malta (Abela and Lanfranco 2016) which was published by the Maltese Ministry for the Family and Social Solidarity was about the routine screening of expectant mothers by midwives at the Antenatal Outpatient Services, regarding the mental health of the mother and any adverse situations in the home (such as domestic violence). Those in need of specialised support would then be referred to the appropriate service. Screening could also take place to identify child maltreatment. The *Safe Environment for Every Kid* (SEEK) programme in the United States identifies at-risk families through the use of a questionnaire which parents are asked to fill in the waiting room of an in-service or in a primary service in the community. The questionnaire includes very personal questions about depression, stress, intimate partner violence, alcohol intake and drug use, and the use of harsh discipline. Any risk factors are then discussed with a health professional and the parent or parents are referred for help, if appropriate. The programme brought about a reduction in child maltreatment (Dubowitz et al. 2009).

The use of validated measures when screening for violence should not be considered as the only way of screening for violence. Including reports from both partners and interviewing victims have the potential for more predictive power than other forms of assessment (Nicholls et al. 2013). Other important tips included the need to ask for specific acts rather than keeping to general questions, and to assess for both partner violence as well as child abuse when either is reported. The latter suggestion makes sense in light of the overlap that exists between the two forms of abuse. Last but not least, given the implications in terms of intervention, the direction of the abuse also needs to be noted. In tune with other researchers already cited in our theoretical framework, Langhinrichsen-Rohling et al. (2012) reported both bi-directional and uni-directional violence when conducting a comprehensive review consisting of 48 studies of intimate partner violence.

Relationship Education

Recent studies such as the one in Australia (Halford et al. 2010) reveal that 20% of newlywed couples reported at least one incident of relationship violence in the past year. Similar rates were reported in the United States (See Leonard and Schencak 1996). Traditional approaches to relationship education focus on conflict management skills and constructive communication. A meta-analysis, which was carried out by Jakubowski, Milne, Brunner and Miller in 2004, concluded that the Prevention and Relationship Enhancement Program (PREP) has the strongest evidence regarding its effectiveness.

In spite of the strong evidence for the effectiveness of relationship education, only 30% of marrying couples attend when such courses are offered in countries such as Australia and the United States (Halford et al. 2006; Stanley et al. 2006). In the UK, only one in 12 engaged couples go for preparation lessons before marriage, and most of this happens through churches (Callan 2009). In their literature review, Petch et al. (2012) point out that relationship education first started to be offered by the church and, to this day, religious organisations continue to be very active in the area. Nevertheless, a number of governments promote relationship education in varying degrees (See Halford and Simons 2005 for Australia, Helskog 2009 for Norway and Coffin 2009 for the United States).

Although traditional approaches to relationship education are also effective in reducing aggressive behaviour (Markman et al. 1993), a number of studies show that more focused training could reach those populations who are at risk in a more effective way.

Bradford et al. (2011) suggest introducing a protocol that relationship educators need to follow to be able to offer support to couples who resort to abusive behaviour. The study highlights the importance of the proper screening of couples who are abusive towards each other when offering relationship education, as well as the training for relationship educators in dealing with couples where there is partner abuse.

The team at the University of Denver also developed a preventive programme focusing on individuals (rather than couples). The programme explores intimate partner violence and how to leave such relationships safely. They argue that such interventions may be more difficult to explore in the context of a couple relationship. The programme also helps those attending to clarify issues in their relationships, including those related to co-parenting and/or how to choose partners wisely (Stanley et al. 2005). This programme was evaluated with individuals with a low income and other at-risk participants. A significant reduction in physical and emotional abuse at 6 months following the programme as well as a significant difference in the reduction of emotional abuse between the abovementioned population and those with a university level of education was noted (Antle et al. 2011).

Recruiting couples for relationship education during the transition to parenthood was considered better in terms of reaching new parents who are at risk for future relationship problems (Petch et al. 2012). Although minority couples were under-represented, 80% of those who opted for the course had not previously enrolled for relationship education and 30% of them had three or more risk factors, including inter-partner violence, high distress and an unplanned pregnancy, a low level of education and low income. The authors attribute the high uptake to the fact that normally, relationship education is only offered to those who are preparing to get married. Cohabiting couples, who are on the increase (See Noack et al. 2014), could now be reached. Another important factor had to do with the stage in the family life cycle that the couples were in. Becoming parents made couples more open to invest in their relationship. It is anticipated that technology will be increasingly used in delivering relationship education and parental education services (Mansfield 2009; Long 2016).

Interventions with Adolescents

Stith et al. (2013) point out that programmes targeting adolescents have proved to be more effective than those targeting young people in terms of prevention. Usually, the interventions are of an educational nature. Safe Dates is one such evidence-based programme (Foshee et al. 1996, 1998, 2000, 2004) where eighth and ninth graders in the United States were provided with a creative adolescent dating violence prevention programme. Another programme targeting adolescents, which was also effective and was more focused on relationships, is the LoveU2 for high-school students (Adler-Baeder et al. 2007).

Murphy (2013) too gives importance to targeting young people, given that abusive behaviour is common between young couples. She argues that inter-partner dynamics play a critical role in how abusive behaviour escalates. Murphy develops a dyadic slippery-slope model outlining warning signs behaviour that has the potential to escalate into abuse. She believes that teaching young people how to reduce accommodating and aggressive responses to warning signs behaviour is crucial if partner abuse is to be prevented. The evidence for this programme still needs to be established.

Preventing Child Maltreatment

In this section, preventive interventions focusing on child maltreatment that takes place within the family will be reviewed with a special emphasis on evidence-based interventions.

Educating Children in Schools

Many schools offer programmes in the classroom aiming to teach children about abuse and to provide them with skills on how they can keep themselves safe and who to confide in when abuse takes place. Evidence-based preventive education programmes with this cohort are very limited. Most of the education that takes place is about awareness, and its impact is not evaluated properly in the sense that it is the children's knowledge on the subject rather than the outcomes in terms of child abuse that are evaluated (Mikton and Butchart 2009; Topping and Barron 2009; MacMillan et al. 2009). In this respect, more research on the effectiveness of preventive programmes with school children is recommended.

Parenting Education

Parenting education started to be perceived as a very effective way to address many prevailing social problems in the seventies, but it was not until the twenty-first century that parenting programmes started to be reviewed for their effectiveness. The reviews showed that the programmes were linked to lower rates of child abuse and better outcomes for children in terms of child development. Moreover, the communication between children and their parents improved and the latter were better able to discipline their children (Ponzetti 2016).

Once ecologically important policies were in place, namely those related to employment and other related family-friendly measures, housing, education and health, many countries started to introduce parenting policies. The United Nations Convention on the Rights of the Child (1990), and the growing body of research on the cost effectiveness of early prevention and intervention, contributed towards this shift. Other factors adding impetus were the increasing trend to empower citizens in the formation of policy and the motivation of the parents themselves who were eager to learn more about the upbringing of their children rather than rely on traditional models (Hermanns 2014). The European Union was also giving importance to family support, good quality alternative child care and evidence-based policies. The Council of Europe supported the initiative through its policy to support positive parenting (Council of Europe 2006). The needs of parents and children at risk of social exclusion were highlighted (Abela and Berlioz 2007; Daly 2007).

Many countries across Europe have now introduced parenting policies. Most of these policies include parenting programmes that have been imported from Australia, Canada and the United States. The Nordic countries and the UK have adopted more universal parenting policies that have different components to them, such as the Parent Management Training-Oregon model and the Multi-systemic Therapy Programme in Norway. Norway has also launched an interministerial policy which is specifically targeted to fight child abuse (Norwegian Ministry of Children, Equality and Social Inclusion, 2014–2017). In the UK, *Sure Start* children's centres were launched in 1999 to fight poverty among children. These services are very similar to Head Start in the United States and Australia and provide a number of services for parents and children under four, including health services, child care, pre-school education, parenting programmes and support for parents to continue with their education or find work. This is a very good example of a one-stop shop service where the services provided cut across various government departments and entities, and is an example of good practice which possesses the two key features of effective community prevention programmes according to Daro and Dodge in 2009. In spite of the significant improvements in the children (Melhuish et al. 2008), austerity measures in the UK have led to an overall cut of 20% of Children's Services between 2012/2013 and 2014/2015 (British Medical Association, September 2016).

Other countries, like Italy, Portugal, Spain, Poland, Bulgaria, Hungary, Lithuania and Latvia, aim specifically to reduce maltreatment. According to Molinuevo (2013), the focus in the latter countries is slowly changing to include more general concerns on parenting by supporting parents through education and other support services offered to the population at large. Such services are offered in the community and include families at risk as well as other families who may need minor support. This approach is more inclusive, focuses more on prevention, and is less stigmatising towards families.

There are a number of parenting programmes that have passed through the tests imposed by randomised control trials. Although the studies do not specifically measure child abuse outcomes (Mikton and Butchard 2009; MacMillan et al. 2009), systematic reviews show that risk factors for child abuse decrease and parents and children enjoy a better relationship. There is quite a number of evidence-based parenting programmes on offer that show these results (Ponzetti 2016), and we will make reference to three of these programmes hereunder because of their wide dissemination in different parts of the world.

Triple-P, which is an Australian parenting programme, reported a significant decrease in terms of child maltreatment injuries and out-of-home placements compared with treatment as usual in the United States (Prinz et al. 2009). However, the study was later questioned because the study for effectiveness lacked the stringent requirements of a randomised control trial (Wilson et al. 2012). Triple-P has been imported in different European countries. When the programme was evaluated in Switzerland (Bodenmann et al. 2008), the results showed that mothers were less stressed, had better self-esteem and were more competent as parents. However, fathers did not register much improvement. This is because the programme is more focused on parent–child interactions with one of the parents. The motherhood mandate organises mothers to feel that they are the ones to attend such courses. Research on parenting programmes shows that when both parents attend, better outcomes ensue (Knox et al. 2011; May et al. 2013). A previous meta-analytic study by Lundahl et al. (2008) also came up with similar findings.

The Incredible Years Programme is also an evidence-based parental programme which uses social learning, modelling and self-efficacy theory (Bandura 1977) as a theoretical framework. The programme is widely used internationally and has been endorsed by the Office for Juvenile Justice and Delinquency Prevention as a model evidence-based programme for the prevention of violence and for treating behaviour disorders (Webster-Stratton and Mihalic 2001). It has also been evaluated by independent investigators. It originally targeted children with oppositional behaviour, but is now also used preventively with other populations (Webster-Stratton 2016). The programme was found to reduce parental stress and depression when delivered in Wales (Hutchings et al. 2007) and has also improved maternal well-being in Sweden (Axberg et al. 2007). It has also been found to reduce harsh discipline and harsh conduct problems (Gross et al. 2003). In spite of the fact that both parents are invited to attend, the programme is often followed by only one of the parents and it is usually the mother who attends. This is possible because the programme focuses on child–parent interactions rather than co-parenting. It also includes group sessions for teachers and children.

Cowan and Cowan (2008) argue that in terms of policy, more importance should be given to the quality of the relationship between the parents, with their children and with others forming part of their informal or formal network of support, irrespective of whether parents are living together or separated. This is because research shows that children and parents increase their sense of well-being when their relationships are doing well, and children develop fewer troubling behaviour problems.

The Supporting Father Involvement parenting programme, or the Parents as Partners programme as it is known in the UK, has a systemic theoretical framework. It gives importance to secure attachment as being a source of comfort for children and couples. In this parenting programme, the co-parent relationship is highlighted as is the relationship between the parents as a couple and with the children. Bi-directional relationships between the couple and between the parents and the children are taken into account. The programme was also funded by the California Department of Social Service, the Office of Child Abuse, for low-income families from various cultural backgrounds. Many of these families had a history of domestic violence, child physical abuse, child sexual abuse, or emotional abuse and neglect, and the programme worked equally well for those higher risk families.

The programme began in 2009 in five counties in California with 60 new families per site. Pruett et al. (2016) point out that their assumption was that the programme would 'reduce symptoms of distress in the participants, affect the quality of the relationship as a couple and as co-parents, improve each of their relationships with the child and with the families of origin, and help them to use social supports more effectively to cope with life stress and by so doing would have a positive preventive effect on child abuse and neglect and promote healthy family development' (p. 178). The programme was evaluated with a longitudinal randomised clinical trial research methodology (Cowan et al. 2014). Results showed that the programme increased fathers' involvement in the care of their children, showed reductions in anxiety symptoms, especially in fathers, and showed a reduction in parenting stress for mothers. There was also a decline in couples' use of violent problem-solving strategies and less harsh physical punishment of the children. The children were also less aggressive overall. Besides its efficacy with children and families with a history of violence and abuse, this parental programme is also being used effectively in a preventive way with parents who are in the early stages of a difficulty or for those who wish to look after their marriage. Other projects regarding this programme are underway in Alberta, Canada and in the UK.

Home-Visiting Programmes

Home-visiting programmes are adopted once a problem has begun. The Nurse–Family Partnership (NFP) home visitation programme is an evidence-based programme usually offered to low-income pregnant mothers who are screened for a number of adverse circumstances in their lives, including domestic violence and the risk of child maltreatment. Specially trained nurses or other health professionals pay 10 home visits during pregnancy and another 20 up until the child's second birthday, providing health advice, education about the development of the child, and life coaching on how they can improve their family circumstances. An evaluation of the programme revealed a decrease in injury in early childhood (Olds et al. 1986). Fifteen years later, mothers were 48% less likely to abuse or neglect their children (Olds et al. 1997). Nevertheless, child abuse was still prevalent in families where domestic violence was high (Eckenrode et al. 2000). A further evaluation of this programme showed that domestic violence had decreased by the end of the visitation programme (Olds et al. 2004). Mothers following this programme also reduced their use of welfare services and their criminal behaviour (Olds et al. 1997), and children improved their academic achievement. Girls in particular were less prone to serious criminal behaviour (Kitzman et al. 2010). Cost–benefit analyses suggest that the programme generates savings of $2.88 for every one dollar spent. In the case of high-risk families, the savings go up to $5.70 (Kilburn and Karoly 2008). The NFP programme has been imported to the UK and the Netherlands.

There are other home-visiting programmes that are evidence-based, such as the *Early Start Programme* in New Zealand. The Attachment and Biobehavioural Catch-up (ABC) home-based programme is a nurturing programme. According to Bavolek (2016), there are 50 such programmes. They are designed for the prevention and treatment of child abuse and neglect and are directed towards children who are in care and may be severely traumatised and need a lot of attention. The ABC programme was developed by Mary Dozier for caregivers of infants between 6 and 24 months and includes high-risk birth parents and foster carers, including those carers who are next of kin. This short but intensive programme provides nurturance to children who have been severely traumatised and need carers who are attuned to the children. The programme gives importance to mutually responsive interaction in which caregivers follow the children's needs.

Out-of-Home Care as a Last Resort

Some children may need an out-of-home placement to be protected from the dangers at home. This is a very difficult decision that social care practitioners have to take in the best interest of the child. The WHO Report on the Prevention of Child Maltreatment (2013) notes the main conclusions, which were reached following a systematic review on the outcomes for children in out-of-home care compared with children who are taken care of in their own parents' home. The results were not conclusive and more research needs to be carried out, especially in situations where professionals remain uncertain on what would be in the best interest of the child. On the other hand, social workers should not hesitate to take swift action when the situation is more straightforward and there is agreement on the best way forward. In terms of out-of-home placements, kinship care seems to yield better outcomes in terms of the mental health of the child and the stability of the placement (Winokur et al. 2009). Of course, the placement is not the only intervention needed. However, it is not the aim of this chapter to write about psychological therapies. We have amply discussed this topic in the various chapters of this book (See Chaps. 3 and 6). Suffice it to mention here, the therapeutic value of reunification, where this is possible, and the need for therapeutic work with the family and the child before reunification takes place.

Conclusion

The global status report on violence prevention points out that the prevention of violence features high in the post-2015 development agenda. The target is that by 2030, violence-related deaths will be halved, whereas violence against children, women and girls will be eliminated (WHO 2014).

Our knowledge and research on the prevention of partner abuse and child maltreatment is marking a trail on where we need to be going. This is extremely valuable and researchers need to continue to address the various research gaps that exist in the area (Stith et al. 2013; WHO 2013; Baker et al. 2012). At the same time, the existing body of knowledge that we have informs us that intervening early with at-risk families and in a child's life by improving parenting practices and relationships in the home will yield the best outcomes for children. Similarly, earlier interventions with adolescents and younger people are more effective with regard to intimate partner violence. Moreover, combining interventions to combat violence and abuse when providing universal services such as antenatal care services is an effective way of intervening to reach at-risk populations. We also need to be addressing inequalities when addressing policies related to violence prevention and child abuse.

At the end of the day, a great deal depends on political will. A number of governments tend to neglect prevention work, especially during periods of austerity. The survey carried out by WHO in 2014 found that countries were not sufficiently investing in prevention. At present there is a huge imbalance between the money invested in child protection and the money invested in child prevention (WHO 2013). We hope that the recent interest and growing knowledge in cost–benefit analyses when rolling out policy interventions may increasingly alert governments in different countries across the world to the fact that prevention is indeed cost effective.

References

Abela, A., & Berlioz, G. (2007). Support for parenting children at risk of social exclusion. In M. Daly (Ed.), *Parenting in contemporary Europe: A positive approach* (pp. 87–101). Strasbourg: Editions du Conseil de l'Europe.

Abela, A., & Lanfranco, I. (2016). *Positive parenting: National strategic policy 2016–2024*. Ministry for the Family and Social Solidarity, Government of Malta. Retrieved from https://mfss.gov.mt/en/Pages/Policies.aspx.

Abela, A., & Renoux, M. C. (2014). Families living on the margin in affluent societies. In A. Abela & J. Walker (Eds.), *Contemporary issues in family studies: Global perspectives on partnerships, parenting and support in a changing world* (pp. 302–316). Chichister: Wiley-Blackwell.

Adler-Baeder, F., Kerpelman, J. L., Schramm, D. G., Higginbotham, B., & Paulk, A. (2007). The impact of relationship education on adolescents of diverse backgrounds. *Family Relations, 56* (3), 291–303. doi:10.1111/j.1741-3729.2007.00460.x.

Amato, P. R., Booth, A., McHale, S. M., & Van Hook, J. (2015). *Families in an era of increasing inequality, diverging destinies*. Cham: Springer.

Antle, B. F., Karam, E., Christensen, D. N., Barbee, A. P., & Sar, B. K. (2011). An evaluation of healthy relationship education to reduce intimate partner violence. *Journal of Family Social Work, 14*(5), 387–406. doi:10.1080/10522158.2011.616482.

Appel, A. E., & Holden, G. W. (1998). The co-occurrence of spouse and physical child abuse: A review and appraisal. *Journal of Family Psychology, 12*(4), 578–599. doi:10.1037/0893-3200.12.4.578.

Axberg, U., Hansson, K., & Broberg, A. G. (2007). Evaluation of the incredible years series—An open study of its effects when first introduced in Sweden. *Nordic Journal of Psychiatry, 61*(2), 143–151. doi:10.1080/08039480701226120.

Baker, A., Schneiderman, M., Brassard, M. R., & Donelly, L. J. (2012). Do evidence-based parenting programs for high-risk or maltreating parents include content about psychological maltreatment?: A programme review. *Child Welfare, 91*(2), 7–37.

Balan-Cohen, A. (2008). *Sobering up: The impact of the 1985–1988 Russian anti-alcohol campaign on child health*. Boston, MA: Tufts University.

Bandura, A. (1977). Self-efficacy: Toward a unifying theory of behavioral change. *Psychological Review, 84*(2), 191. doi:10.1037/0033-295X.84.2.191.

Bavolek, S. (2016). Nurturing parenting programs for the prevention of child maltreatment. In J. J. Ponzetti (Ed.), *Evidence-based parenting education. A global perspective* (pp. 206–225). New York: Routledge.

Bodenmann, G., Cina, A., Ledermann, T., & Sanders, M. R. (2008). The efficacy of the Triple P-Positive Parenting Program in improving parenting and child behavior: A comparison with two other treatment conditions. *Behaviour Research and Therapy, 46*(4), 411–427. doi:10.1016/j.brat.2008.01.001.

Bradford, K., Skogrand, L., & Higginbotham, B. J. (2011). Intimate partner violence in a statewide couple and relationship education initiative. *Journal of couple and relationship therapy: Innovations in clinical and educational interventions, 10*(2), 169–184. doi:10.1080/15332691.2011.562468.

British Medical Association. (2016). *Cutting away at our children's futures: how austerity is affecting the health of children, young people and families.* Retrieved from https://www.bma.org.uk/collective-voice/policy-and-research/public-and-population-health/child-health/cutting-away-at-our-childrens-future.

Callan, S. (2009). Preface. In H. Benson, & S. Callan (Eds.), *What works in relationship education? Lessons from academics and service deliverers in the United States and Europe* (pp. 7–10). Retrieved from www.relationshipeducation.info.

Calvete, E., Orue, I., & Gámez-Guadix, M. (2013). Child-to-parent violence: Emotional and behavioral predictors. *Journal of Interpersonal Violence, 28*(4), 755–772. doi:10.1177/0886260512455869.

Campbell, J. (2002). Health consequences of intimate partner violence. *The Lancet, 359,* 1331–1336. doi:10.1016/S0140-6736(02)08336-8.

Center on the Developing Child at Harvard University. (2016). *From best practices to breakthrough impacts: A science-based approach to building a more promising future for young children and families.* Retrieved from http://www.developingchild.harvard.edu.

Coffin, B. (2009). Marriage.gov: A promising public policy. In H. Benson, & S. Callan (Eds.), *What works in relationship education? Lessons from academics and service deliverers in the United States and Europe* (pp. 121–136). Retrieved from www.relationshipeducation.info.

Costello, E. J., Erlanki, A., Fairbank, J. A., & Angold, A. (2002). The prevalence of potentially traumatic events in childhood and adolescence. *Journal of Traumatic Stress, 15*(2), 99–112. doi:10.1023/A:1014851823163.

Council of Europe. (2006). *Policy to support positive parenting.* Retrieved from https://rm.coe.int/CoERMPublicCommonSearchServices/DisplayDCTMContent?documentId=090000168046d340.

Council of Europe. (2011). *Council of Europe convention on preventing and combating violence against women and domestic violence*: Istanbul, 11 V. Retrieved from https://rm.coe.int/CoERMPublicCommonSearchServices/DisplayDCTMContent?documentId=09000016804603lc.

Cowan, P., & Cowan, C. (2008). Diverging family policies to promote children's well-being in the UK and US: Some relevant data from family research and intervention studies. *Journal of Children's Services, 3*(4), 4–16. doi:10.1108/17466660200800022.

Cowan, P. A., Cowan, C. P., Pruett, M. K., Pruett, K., & Gillette, P. (2014). Evaluating a couples group to enhance father involvement in low-income families using a benchmark comparison. *Family Relations, 63*(3), 356–370. doi:10.1111/fare.12072.

Daly, M. (Ed.). (2007). *Parenting in contemporary Europe: A positive approach.* Strasbourg: Editions du Conseil de l'Europe.

Daro, D., & Dodge, K. A. (2009). Creating community responsibility for child protection: Possibilities and challenges. *Future of Children, 19*(2), 67–93.

Daro, D., & Gelles, R. J. (1992). Public attitudes and behaviors with respect to child abuse prevention. *Journal of Interpersonal Violence, 7*(4), 517–531. doi:10.1177/088626092007004007.

Daro, D., & McCurdy, K. (2007). Interventions to prevent child maltreatment. In E. N. Haas, L. Doll, S. Bonzo, D. Sleet, & J. Mercy (Eds.), *Handbook of injury and violence prevention* (pp. 137–156). New York: Springer Science & Business Media.

Desmarais, S. L., Reeves, K. A., Nicholls, T. L., Telford, R., & Fiebert, M. S. (2012a). Prevalence of physical violence in intimate relationships—part 1: Rates of male and female victimization. *Partner Abuse, 3*(2), 140–169. doi:10.1891/1946-6560.3.2.140.

Desmarais, S. L., Reeves, K. A., Nicholls, T. L., Telford, R., & Fiebert, M. S. (2012b). Prevalence of physical violence in intimate relationships—part 2: Rates of male and female perpetration. *Partner Abuse, 3*(2), 170–198. doi:10.1891/1946-6560.3.2.170.

Dubowitz, H., Feigelman, S., Lane, W., & Kim, J. (2009). Pediatric primary care to help prevent child maltreatment: The Safe Environment for Every Kid (SEEK) model. *Pediatrics, 123*(3), 858–864. doi:10.1542/peds.2008-1376.

Dutton, D. G. (2006). *Rethinking domestic violence*. Vancouver, Canada: UBC Press.

Eckenrode, J., Ganzel, B., Henderson Jr, C. R., Smith, E., Olds, D. L., Powers, J.,… & Sidora, K. (2000). Preventing child abuse and neglect with a program of nurse home visitation: The limiting effects of domestic violence. *JAMA, 284*(11), 1385–1391. doi:10.1001/jama.284.11.1385.

Edleson, J. L. (1999). Children's witnessing of adult domestic violence. *Journal of Interpersonal Violence, 14*(8), 839–870. doi:10.1177/088626099014008004t.

Foshee, V. A., Bauman, K. E., Arriaga, X. B., Helms, R. W., Koch, G. G., & Linder, G. F. (1998). An evaluation of safe dates, an adolescent dating violence prevention program. *American Journal of Public Health, 88*(1), 45–50. doi:10.2105/AJPH.88.1.45.

Foshee, V. A., Bauman, K. E., Ennett, S. T., Linder, G. F., Benefield, T., & Suchindran, C. (2004). Assessing the long-term effects of the safe dates program and a booster in preventing and reducing adolescent dating violence victimization and perpetration. *American Journal of Public Health, 94*(4), 619–624. doi:10.2105/AJPH.94.4.619.

Foshee, V. A., Bauman, K. E., Greene, W. F., Koch, G. G., Linder, G. F., & MacDougall, J. E. (2000). The safe dates program: 1-year follow-up results. *American Journal of Public Health, 90*(10), 1619–1622.

Foshee, V. A., Linder, G. F., Bauman, K. E., Langwick, S. A., Arriaga, X. B., & Bangdiwala, S. (1996). The safe date project: Theoretical basis, evaluation design, and selected baseline findings. *American Journal of Prevention Medicine, 12*(5), 39–47.

George, J., & Stith, S. M. (2014). An updated feminist view of intimate partner violence. *Family Process, 53*(2), 179–193. doi:10.1111/famp.12073.

Gregory, A. C., Williamson,E., & Feder,G. S. (2016). The impact on informal supporters of domestic violence survivors: A systematic literature review. *Trauma, Violence & Abuse,* 1–19. doi:10.1177/1524838016641919.

Gross, D., Fogg, L., Webster-Stratton, C., Garvey, C., Julion, W., & Grady, J. (2003). Parent training of toddlers in day care in low-income urban communities. *Journal of Consulting and Clinical Psychology, 71*(2), 261–278. doi:10.1037/0022-006X.71.2.261.

Halford, W. K., Farrugia, C., Lizzio, A., & Wilson, K. (2010). Relationship aggression, violence and self-regulation in Australian newlywed couples. *Australian Journal of Psychology, 62*(2), 82–92. doi:10.1081/00049530902804169.

Halford, W. K., O'Donnell, C., Lizzio, A., & Wilson, K. L. (2006). Do couples at high risk of relationship problems attend premarriage education? *Journal of Family Psychology, 20*(1), 160–163. doi:10.1037/0893-3200.20.1.160.

Halford, W. K., & Simons, M. (2005). Couple relationship education in Australia. *Family Process, 44*(2), 147–159. doi:10.1111/j.1545-5300.2005.00050.x.

Hamel, J. (2005). *Gender inclusive treatment of intimate partner abuse: A comprehensive approach*. New York, NY: Springer.

Hamel, J., & Nicholls, T. L. (Eds.). (2007). *Family interventions in domestic violence. A handbook of gender-inclusive theory and attachment*. New York: Springer.

Hartman, A. (2003). Family policy: Dilemmas, controversies and opportunities. In F. Walsh (Ed.), *Normal family processes: Growing diversity and complexity* (3rd ed., pp. 635–662). London, UK: The Guilford Press.

Harvey, A., Garcia-Moreno, C., & Butchart, A. (2007). *Primary prevention of intimate-partner violence and sexual violence: Background paper for WHO expert meeting May 2–3, 2007*. Geneva: World Health Organization, Department of Violence and Injuy Prevention and Disability.

Haskins, C. (2003). Treating sibling incest using a family systems approach. *Journal of Mental Health Counseling, 25*(4), 337–350. doi:10.17744/mehc.25.4.r0vm1whayctmlmww.

Helskog, H. G. (2009). The Norwegian state: A relationship educator. In H. Benson, & S. Callan (Eds.), *What works in relationship education? Lessons from academics and service deliverers in the United States and Europe* (pp. 137–148). Retrieved from www.relationshipeducation.info.

Hermanns, J. (2014). Parenting support in Europe: What it brings and what it can take away. In R. Fukkink, C. Vink, & N. Bosscher (Eds.), *Think parents! Putting parents at the heart of parenting support* (pp. 11–25). Amsterdam: SWP.

Herzog, E. P., Gara, M. A., & Rosenberg, S. (1992). The abused child as parent: Perception of self and other. *Infant Mental Health, 13*(1), 83–98. doi:10.1002/1097-0355(199221)13:1<83:AID-IMHJ2280130111>3.0.CO;2-6.

Hutchings, J., Bywater, T., Daley, D., Gardner, F., Whitaker, C.,… Edwards, R. T. (2007). Parenting intervention in Sure Start services for children at risk of developing conduct disorder: Pragmatic randomised controlled trial. *Bmj, 334*(7595), 678–682. doi:10.1136/bmj.39126.620799.55.

Ibabe, I., Jaureguizar, J., & Bentler, P. M. (2013). Risk factors for child-to-parent violence. *Journal of Family Violence, 28*(5), 523–534. doi:10.1007/s10896-013-9512-2.

Jakubowski, S. F., Milne, E. P., Brunner, H., & Miller, R. B. (2004). A review of empirically supported marital enrichment programs. *Family Relations, 53*(5), 528–536. doi:10.1111/j.0197-6664.2004.00062.x.

Jewkes, R. (2002). Intimate partner violence: Causes and prevention. *The Lancet, 359*(9315), 1423–1429. doi:10.1016/S0140-6736(02)08357-5.

Johnson, M. P. (2008). *A typology of domestic violence: Intimate terrorism, violent resistance, and situational couple violence*. Boston, MA: Northeastern University Press.

Jouriles, E. N., McDonald, R., Smith Slep, A. M., Heyman, R. E., & Garrido, E. (2008). Child abuse in the context of domestic violence: Prevalence, explanations, and practice implications. *Violence and Victims, 23*(2), 221–235. doi:10.1891/0886-6708.23.2.221.

Kitzman, H. J., Olds, D. L., Cole, R. E., Hanks, C. A., Anson, E. A., Arcoleo, K. J., et al. (2010). Enduring effects of prenatal and infancy home visiting by nurses on children: Follow-up of a randomised trial among children at age 12 years. *Archives of Pediatrics and Adolescent Medicine, 164*(5), 412–418. doi:10.1001/archpediatrics.2010.76.

Kilburn, M. R., & Karoly, L. A. (2008). *The economics of early childhood policy: What the dismal science has to say about investing in children*. Santa Monica, CA: The RAND Corporation.

Klevens, J., & Whitaker, D. J. (2007). Primary prevention of child physical abuse and neglect: gaps and promising directions. *Child Maltreatment, 12*(4), 364–377. doi:10.1177/1077559507305995.

Knox, V., Cowan, P. A., Cowan, C. P., & Bildner, E. (2011). Policies that strengthen fatherhood and family relationships: What do we know and what do we need to know? *The Annals of the American Academy of Political and Social Science, 635*(1), 216–239. doi:10.1177/0002716210394769.

Krug, E. G., Mercy, J. A., Dahlberg, L. L., & Zwi, A. B. (2002). The world report on violence and health. *The Lancet, 360*(9339), 1083–1088. doi:10.1016/S0140-6736(02)11133-0.

Langhinrichsen-Rohling, J., McCullars, A., & Misra, T. (2012). Motivations for men and women's intimate partner violence perpetration: A comprehensive review. *Partner Abuse, 3*(4), 429–468. doi:10.1891/1946-6560.3.4.429.

Lawrence, J. A. (2014). Managing dissonance: Implications for therapeutic practice with partner violence. *Partner Abuse, 5*(2), 119–151. doi:10.1891/1946-6560.5.2.119.

Leonard, K. E., & Schencak, M. (1996). Prospective prediction of husband marital aggression with newlywed couples. *Journal of Abnormal Psychology, 105*(3), 369–380. doi:10.1037/0021-843X.105.3.369.

Long, N. (2016). Future trends in parenting education. In J. J. Ponzetti (Ed.), *Evidence-based parenting education. A global perspective* (pp. 311–328). New York: Routledge.

Lundahl, B. W., Tollefson, D., Risser, H., & Lovejoy, M. C. (2008). A meta-analysis of father involvement in parent training. *Research in Social Work Practice, 18*(2), 97–106. doi:10.1177/1049731507309828.

Lyons-Ruth, K., & Block, D. (1996). The disturbed caregiving system: Relations among childhood trauma, maternal caregiving, and infant affect and attachment. *Infant Mental Health Journal, 17*(3), 257–275. doi:10.1002/(SICI)1097-0355(199623)17:3<257:AID-IMHJ5>3.0.CO;2-L.

MacMillan, H. L., Wathen, C. N., Barlow, J., Fergusson, D. M., Leventhal, J. M., & Taussig, H. N. (2009). Interventions to prevent child maltreatment and associated impairment. *The Lancet, 373*(9659), 250–266. doi:10.1016/S0140-6736(08)61708-0.

Main, M., Kaplan, N., & Cassidy, J. (1985). Security in infancy, childhood and adulthood: A move to the level of representations. *Monographs of the Society for Research in Child Development, 50*(1/2), 66–104. doi:10.2307/3333827.

Mansfield. (2009). Intervening early: Helping couples manage relationship issues when they first arise. In H. Benson, & S. Callan (Eds.), *What works in relationship education? Lessons from academics and service deliverers in the United States and Europe* (pp. 87–97). Retrieved from www.relationshipeducation.info.

Markman, H. J., Renick, M. J., Floyd, F. J., Stanley, S. M., & Clements, M. (1993). Preventing marital distress through communication and conflict management training: A 4-and 5-year follow-up. *Journal of Consulting and Clinical Psychology, 61*(1), 70–77. doi:10.1037/0022-006X.61.1.70.

Markowitz, S., & Grossman, M. (1998). Alcohol regulation and domestic violence towards children. *Contemporary Economic Policy, 16*(3), 309–320. doi:10.1111/j.1465-7287.1998.tb00521.x.

May, F. S., McLean, L. A., Anderson, A., Hudson, A., Cameron, C., & Matthews, J. (2013). Father participation with mothers in the signposts program: An initial investigation. *Journal of Intellectual and Developmental Disability, 38*(1), 39–47. doi:10.3109/13668250.2012.748184.

Melhuish, E., Belsky, J., Leyland, A. H., Barnes, J., & National Evaluation of Sure Start Research Team. (2008). Effects of fully-established sure start local programmes on 3-year-old children and their families living in England: A quasi-experimental observational study. *Lancet*, 372 (9650), 1641–1647. doi:10.1016/S0140-6736(08)61687-6.

Mikton, C., & Butchart, A. (2009). Child maltreatment prevention: A systematic review of reviews. *Bulletin of the World Health Organization, 87*(5), 353–361. doi:10.2471/BLT.08.057075.

Molinuevo, D. (2013). *Parenting support in Europe (Eurofound report ef1270).* Retrieved from http://www.eurofound.europa.eu/publications/report/2013/quality-of-life-social-policies/parenting-support-in-europe.

Murphy, K. A. (2013). Partner abuse prevention education: An integrative approach to programme development and evaluation. *Partner Abuse, 4*(2), 255–273. doi:10.1891/1946-6560.4.2.255.

Nicholls, T. L., Pritchard, M. M., Reeves, K. A., & Hilterman, E. (2013). Risk assessment in intimate partner violence: A systematic review of contemporary approaches. *Partner Abuse, 4* (1), 76–168. doi:10.1891/1946-6560.4.1.76.

Noack, T., Bernhardt, E., & Aarskaug Wiik, K. (2014). Cohabitation or marriage? Contemporary living arrangements in the west. In A. Abela & J. Walker (Eds.), *Contemporary issues in family studies: Global perspectives on partnerships, parenting and support in a changing world* (pp. 16–30). Chichister: Wiley-Blackwell.

Norwegian Ministry of Children, Equality and Social Inclusion. (2014–2017). *A good childhood lasts a lifetime. Action plan to combat violence and sexual abuse against children and youth (2014–2017)*. Norwegian Government Security and Service Organisation. Retrieved from https://www.endviolenceagainstchildren.org/assets/uploads/2016/05/Norway-A-Good-Childhood-lasts-a-lifetime-.pdf.

Olds, D. L., Henderson, C. R., Chamberlin, R., & Tatelbaum, R. (1986). Preventing child abuse and neglect: A randomized trial of nurse home visitation. *Pediatrics, 78*(1), 65–78.

Olds, D. L., Eckenrode, J., Henderson, C. R., Kitzman, H., Powers, J., Cole, R.,… & Luckey, D. (1997). Long-term effects of home visitation on maternal life course and child abuse and neglect: Fifteen-year follow-up of a randomized trial. *JAMA, 278*(8), 637–643. doi:10.1001/jama.1997.03550080047038.

Olds, D. L., Kitzman, H., Cole, R., Robinson, J., Sidora, K., Luckey, D. W., et al. (2004). Effects of nurse home-visiting on maternal life course and child development: Age 6 follow-up results of a randomized trial. *Pediatrics, 114*(6), 1550–1558. doi:10.1542/peds.2004-0962.

Perry, B. D. (1997). Incubated in terror: Neurodevelopmental factors in the "cycle of violence", pp. 123–149. In J. D. Osofsky (Ed.), *Children in a Violent Society* (pp. xx–xx). New York: Guilford Press.

Petch, J. F., Halford, W. K., Creedy, D. K., & Gamble, J. (2012). A randomized controlled trial of a couple relationship and coparenting program (Couple CARE for Parents) for high-and low-risk new parents. *Journal of Consulting and Clinical Psychology, 80*(4), 662–673. doi:10.1037/a0028781.

Ponzetti, J. J. (2016). Overview and history of parenting education. In J. J. Ponzetti (Ed.), *Evidence-based parenting education. A global perspective* (pp. 3–11). New York: Routledge.

Povich, D., Roberts, B., & Mather, M. (2015). *The working poor families project.* Retrieved from www.workingpoorfamilies.org.

Pruett, K. D., Pruett, M. K., Cowan, C. P., & Cowan, P. A. (2016). Supporting father involvement project: A value-added co-parenting program. In J. J. Ponzetti (Ed.), *Evidence-based parenting education. A global perspective* (pp. 176–191). New York: Routledge.

Prinz, R. J., Sanders, M. R., Shapiro, C. J., Whitaker, D. J., & Lutzker, J. R. (2009). Population-based prevention of child maltreatment: The US Triple P system population trial. *Prevention Science, 10*(1), 1–12. doi:10.1007/s11121-009-0123-3.

Reeves, C., & O'Leary-Kelly, A. M. (2007). The effects and costs of intimate partner violence for work organizations. *Journal of Interpersonal Violence, 22*(3), 327–344. doi:10.1177/0886260506295382.

Ridge, T. (2009). *Living with poverty: A review of the literature on children's and families' experiences of poverty,* Research Report No. 594. London: Department for Work and Pensions.

Rodrigo, M. J., Almeida, A., & Reichle, B. (2016). Evidence-based parent education programs: A European perspective. In J. J. Ponzetti (Ed.), *Evidence-based parenting education. A global perspective* (pp. 85–104). New York: Routledge.

Sammut Scerri, C. (2015). *Living with contradictions of love and violence: A grounded theory study of women's understanding of their childhood experiences of domestic violence.* Unpublished doctoral dissertation, University of Surrey, UK.

Siegel, J. P. (2013). Breaking the links in intergenerational violence: An emotional regulation perspective. *Family Process, (52)*2, 163–178. doi:10.1111/famp.12023.

Slaska, K. M., & Edwards, K. M. (2013). Disclosure of intimate partner violence to informal social support network members: A review of the literature. *Trauma, Violence & Abuse, 15*(1), 3–21. doi:10.1177/15248380/3496335.

Stanley, S. M., Amato, P. R., Johnson, C. A., & Markman, H. J. (2006). Premarital education, marital quality, and marital stability: Findings from a large, random household survey. *Journal of Family Psychology, 20*(1), 117–126. doi:10.1037/0893-3200.20.1.117.

Stanley, S. M., Pearson, M., & Kline, G. H. (2005). *The development of relationship education for low income individuals: Lessons from research and experience.* Paper presented at the meeting of the Association for Public Policy Analysis and Management, Washington, DC.

Steele, H., & Steele, M. (Eds.). (2008). *Clinical applications of the adult attachment interview*. New York: Guilford Press.

Stets, J. E. (1991). Cohabiting and marital aggression. The role of social isolation. *Journal of Marriage and Family, 53*(3), 669–680. doi:10.2307/352742.

Stith, M., Lechtenberg, M., & Cafferky, B. (2013). Implications for partner abuse state of knowledge. Findings for prevention, treatment and policy. *Partner Abuse*, 4(2), 241–254. doi:10.1891/1946-6560.4.2.241.

Taket, A., O'Doherty, L., Valpied, J., & Hegarty, K. (2014). What do Australian women experiencing intimate partner abuse want from family and friends? *Qualitative Health Research, 27*(7), 983–996. doi:10.1177/1049732314540054.

Topping, K. J., & Barron, I. G. (2009). School-based child sexual abuse prevention programs: A review of effectiveness. *Review of Educational Research, 79*(1), 431–463. doi:10.3102/0034654308325582.

UNICEF Innocenti Research Centre. (2012). Measuring child poverty: New league tables of child poverty in the world's rich countries (Innocenti Report Card 10). Florence: UNICEF Innocenti Research Centre. Retrieved from https://www.unicef-irc.org/publications/660/.

United Nations. (1990). *Convention on the Rights of the Child (UNCRC)*. Retrieved from http://www.ohchr.org/EN/ProfessionalInterest/Pages/CRC.aspx.

Van der Kolk, B. (2015). *The body keeps the score: Brain, mind, and body in the healing of trauma*. Great Britain: Penguin Books.

Van Wyk, J. A., Benson, M. L., Fox, G. L., & DeMaris, A. (2003). Detangling individual-partner- and community-level correlates of partner violence. *Crime and Delinquency*, 49(3), 412–438. doi:10.1177/0011128703049003004.

Webster-Stratton, C. (2016). The incredible years parent programs: Methods and principles that support program fidelity. In J. J. Ponzetti (Ed.), *Evidence-based parenting education: A global perspective* (pp. 142–160). New York: Routledge.

Webster-Stratton, C., & Mihalic, S. F. (2001). *The incredible years: Parent, teacher and child training series*. Center for the Study and Prevention of Violence, Institute of Behavioral Science, University of Colorado at Boulder.

Wilson, P., Rush, R., Hussey, S., Puckering, C., Sim, F., Allely, C. S., et al. (2012). How evidence-based is an "evidence-based parenting program"? A PRISMA systematic review and meta-analysis of Triple P. *BMC Medicine, 10,* 130. doi:10.1186/1741-7015-10-130.

Winokur, M., Holtan, A., & Valentine, D. (2009). Kinship care for the safety, permanency, and well-being of children removed from home for maltreatment. *Cochrane Database of Systematic Reviews, 21*(1), CD006546. doi:10.1002/14651858.CD006546.pub2.

World Health Organisation. (2013). *European report on preventing child maltreatment*. Copenhagen, Denmark: World Health Organisation. Retrieved from http://www.euro.who.int/en/publications/abstracts/european-report-on-preventing-child-maltreatment-2013.

World Health Organization. (2014). *Global status report on violence prevention 2014* (NLM classification: HV 6625). Luxembourg: World Health Organisation. Retrieved from http://www.who.int/violence_injury_prevention/violence/status_report/2014/en/.

World Health Organisation. (2016). *Violence against women: Intimate partner and sexual violence against women*. Retrieved from http://www.who.int/mediacentre/factsheets/fs239/en/.

Erratum to: Intervening After Violence

Clarissa Sammut Scerri, Arlene Vetere, Angela Abela and Jan Cooper

Erratum to: C. Sammut Scerri et al., *Intervening After Violence*, Focussed Issues in Family Therapy, DOI 10.1007/978-3-319-57789-0

The original version of the book was inadvertently published with incorrect author names order which has be corrected as "Clarissa Sammut Scerri, Arlene Vetere, Angela Abela and Jan Cooper" in Chapters 1–9 and also the missed out corrections have to be incorporated in Chapters 1, 2, 6, 8 and 9. The erratum book has been updated with the changes.

The updated online version of this book can be found at http://dx.doi.org/10.1007/978-3-319-57789-0

C. Sammut Scerri et al., *Intervening After Violence*,
Focused Issues in Family Therapy, DOI 10.1007/978-3-319-57789-0_10

Index

C. Sammut Scerri et al., *Intervening After Violence*, Focused Issues in Family Therapy, DOI 10.1007/978-3-319-57789-0

CPSIA information can be obtained
at www.ICGtesting.com
Printed in the USA
LVHW081440160822
726090LV00004B/52

9 783319 577883